Development, NGOs, and Civil Society

Selected essays from *Development in Practice*

Introduced by **Jenny Pearce**

A Development in Practice Reader

Series Editor: **Deborah Eade**

Oxfam GB

First published by Oxfam GB in 2000
Reprinted 2002

© Oxfam GB 2000

ISBN 0 85598 442 2

Available from:
Bournemouth English Book Centre, PO Box 1496, Parkstone, Dorset, BH12 3YD, UK
tel: +44 (0)1202 712933; fax: +44 (0)1202 712930; email: oxfam@bebc.co.uk

USA: Stylus Publishing LLC, PO Box 605, Herndon, VA 20172-0605, USA
tel: +1 (0)703 661 1581; fax: +1 (0)703 661 1547; email: styluspub@aol.com

For details of local agents and representatives in other countries, consult our website:
http://www.oxfam.org.uk/publications
or contact Oxfam Publishing, 274 Banbury Road, Oxford OX2 7DZ, UK
tel: +44 (0)1865 311 311; fax: +44 (0)1865 312 600; email: publish@oxfam.org.uk

Our website contains a fully searchable database of all our titles, and facilities for secure on-line ordering.

The views expressed in this book are those of the individual contributors, and not necessarily those of the editor or the publisher.

Published by Oxfam GB, 274 Banbury Road, Oxford OX2 7DZ, UK.

Printed by Information Press, Eynsham

Oxfam GB is a registered charity, no. 202 918, and is a member of Oxfam International.

Contents

Contributors

Christy Cannon Lorgen was awarded a D.Phil. from Nuffield College, Oxford, on the subject of NGO–state relations in Uganda. Her current work focuses on risk analysis for private-sector investment in Africa.

Peter Chamberlain worked for the Austrian Relief Committee in Pakistan (1989–93) and is now an independent consultant based in Australia.

Chris Collier is a Senior Policy Officer at the Humanistic Institute for Cooperation with Developing Countries (HIVOS) in The Hague. His main interest is in promoting human rights in developing countries, especially Africa.

Stephen Commins worked for many years in the NGO sector before becoming a Social Policy Specialist at the World Bank. He teaches International Studies at UCLA, and is an Editorial Adviser to *Development in Practice*.

Deborah Eade has worked in the NGO sector for 20 years and is Editor of *Development in Practice*.

Michael Edwards has worked for a number of international NGOs, including Oxfam GB and Save the Children Fund (UK). He recently left the World Bank NGO Liaison Office to become Director of the Governance and Civil Society, Peace and Social Justice Programme at the Ford Foundation in New York.

Jonathan Goodhand worked with international NGOs in Afghanistan, Sri Lanka, and Central Asia before taking up his current post as Central Asia Programme Manager at INTRAC.

David Hulme is Professor of Development Studies at the Institute of Development Policy and Management, University of Manchester. He has worked extensively in the fields of rural development, poverty reduction, NGOs and civil society, microfinance, and public-sector reform.

Gino Lofredo is an engineer, a journalist, and a writer of fiction. He has worked in development and relief programmes in Africa, Latin America, and the Caribbean, most recently in the emergency responses to Hurricane Mitch in Central America.

Amina Mama is Chair and Director of the African Gender Institute of the University of Cape Town in South Africa. Her paper in this volume was written while she was the Research Coordinator for ABANTU, of which she is now a Trustee.

Firoze Manji has worked in the international NGO sector for many years, both in Eastern and Southern Africa, and as Head of the Africa Section at Amnesty International in London. He is currently Associate Tutor in International Human Rights at the Department of Continuing Education at the University of Oxford, and is Director of Fahamu, an organisation producing computer and Internet-based training materials for NGOs.

Mick Moore is a Fellow of the Institute of Development Studies (IDS) at the University of Sussex, where he works on the political and institutional dimensions of development policy and practice.

Lilly Nicholls is a poverty-reduction economist in the Policy Branch of the Canadian International Development Agency (CIDA). Previously she worked for UNDP in New York and Central America. The paper in this *Reader* was based on the PhD. research she carried out at the London School of Economics.

Jenny Pearce is Professor of Politics and International Development at the School of Peace Studies at the University of Bradford. She was previously Director of the Latin America Bureau, and is a leading writer on Latin American issues. She has been a trustee of several British NGOs, and is an Editorial Adviser to *Development in Practice*.

Sheelagh Stewart co-founded the Musasa Project, which focuses on violence against women in Zimbabwe, and is now working as an adviser to the UK Department for International Development (DFID) in Malawi.

Alan Whaites is Director for International Policy and Advocacy with World Vision's Partnership Offices, and previously worked in Southeast Asia.

Sarah C. White teaches Sociology of Development at the University of Bath. She has written extensively on gender and development issues, with particular reference to Bangladesh.

Preface

Deborah Eade

Development, in the sense of a body of thinking and practice about why poverty exists and persists, and about how to eradicate it, has a relatively recent history. The development era is said to have been launched by President Truman in 1949, and indeed most of the best-known specialised UN agencies were established at around that time.[1] Development NGOs came into being even more recently, though many of today's familiar names — Save the Children Fund, CARE, Oxfam — began their lives as welfare or emergency relief agencies, and either 'converted' to development in the 1960s and 1970s, or at the very least discovered it. Thousands more were spawned as the development industry really took off. As it became better understood that the causes of poverty and vulnerability were structural, and not 'natural', so it became part of NGO lore that development was the best form of disaster prevention, and that a 'developmental' rather than a 'derring-do' response was more appropriate in emergencies. Of course, a great variety of approaches and activities were — and still are — bundled into the category of 'development', covering anything and everything from building latrines and sinking tubewells through to supporting union education programmes and human rights work. But, whether NGOs took a 'basic needs' or a 'structural change' approach, there was widespread consensus that getting rid of stubborn poverty would require something more than, and something quite different from, humanitarian relief. Civil society, by contrast, has a centuries-long history in Western political thought, dating back to the philosophers of Ancient Greece. It is very much alive and well today, although, as is increasingly obvious, it is a very imprecise term. Like some of its predecessors in the development lexicon — 'community', 'participation', 'bottom-up development' — it is more often invoked to convey a benign glow than to illuminate debate or practice.

Why is it that these three categories — development, civil society, and NGOs — should have come to be regarded not only as mutually reinforcing, but as overlapping or quasi-synonymous terms? To read some of the aid policy-related literature of the 1990s, and to judge by the recent funding patterns of the major donor agencies, one could be forgiven for thinking that civil society = NGOs, and that NGOs are an essential part of 'delivering' not only development aid, but development itself. In other words, that development depends on NGOs. How has such a myth been spun?

There are several different elements that may form part of an explanation. First, the neo-liberal project, as expressed through structural adjustment in the South, and as promoted in the North by its leading political ideologues (most notably Ronald Reagan and Margaret Thatcher), required a curbing of state spending, and a rolling back of social sector investment. In theory, an unfettered market would provide more efficient services and create the jobs that would generate the wealth needed to sustain them. As private voluntary agencies, NGOs could occupy this new niche quite comfortably, particularly, for instance, in participating in the social safety-net projects and social investment funds that were supposed to alleviate the immediate effects of structural adjustment. Hence, NGOs were encouraged to present themselves as appropriate channels for aid to the poorest, for those at risk of falling through the net — or for whom the net was simply never designed to protect. Many NGOs that had previously prided themselves on how little government money they accepted began to raise their self-imposed ceilings as the money flowed in.

Second, the break-up of the Soviet bloc, culminating in the collapse of the Berlin Wall in 1989, was associated with — and, by some observers, attributed to — the emergence of people's organisations through which opposition to the prevailing political system was powerfully articulated. These included church-based groups, unions, professional bodies, and also a nascent NGO sector. The idea of autonomous civil society organisations holding governments accountable, and at the same time pushing forward a democratisation agenda, was appealing to observers from different points in the political spectrum, pragmatists and romantics alike. The opening up of the centralised economies of Eastern Europe coincided very neatly with the advance of the neo-liberal agenda that was already underway both in North America and Western Europe, and also throughout much of the South.

Third, in Latin America there had been a long tradition of radical social organisation as a form of resistance to military dictatorships, particularly once the space for political dialogue was effectively closed off. NGOs had played a vital role in countries such as Brazil and Chile, often maintaining what little space might exist for debate, or holding on to an alternative vision of society. In Central America, the long-running civil wars that had engulfed much of the region throughout the 1980s were clearly reaching a military stalemate at the end of the decade. With US and EU attention turning to Eastern Europe, the funding plug was in the process of being pulled out, and external support began draining away. US backing for the *contra* in Nicaragua, and for the government and military in El Salvador, was becoming more difficult to justify to a domestic constituency in terms of 'stemming the tide of communism', and long-standing EU support for political solutions to the wars was beginning to wane. And the so-called collapse of socialism clearly had repercussions for the kind of future the left and centre-left movements in Central America could envisage. The heyday of *vanguardismo* had definitively passed. As the likelihood of some kind of peace process was taking shape, NGOs and alternative think-tanks began to turn to Antonio Gramsci — one of the most influential modern thinkers on civil society — rather than to Che Guevara in thinking through what their role might be in helping to build a new state, while also maintaining their own independent watchdog function and political protagonism. Similar kinds of debates later took place in South Africa, as NGOs and 'civics' had to re-define their role in the context of an ANC government coming to power — something that required some very rapid gear changes (see Pieterse 1997 for example).

That the rise of neo-liberalism should have coincided with profound transitional (but not by now revolutionary) processes that were rooted in their own societies and cultures may have been an accident of history. However, it was one that lent itself to the appropriation — hijacking, even — of these processes by the ideological wing of the Washington Consensus, with its focus on good governance and democratisation in the South and the East. It also led to donors and political commentators uncritically embracing anything calling itself 'civil society', NGOs included. There was a flourishing of neo-romantic notions of the self-provisioning and self-regulating community versus the intrusive and normative state. Even such sharp-tongued critics of 'casino capitalism' as David C. Korten (who had long stressed that genuine development must be 'people-centred'[2]) attributed almost messianic qualities to autonomous 'local communities'. These were to be the only hope of resistance against the onslaught of corporate capitalism. Civil society could do no wrong, and there was nothing it could not do. NGOs, for their part, sprang up like mushrooms, offering to be both the channel through which to strengthen civil society, and as civil society organisations in their own right. In some cases, they seemed to claim the divine right to represent or speak on behalf of civil society at large. It was conveniently overlooked that neo-Nazi as well as human rights organisations, that mafias as well as charities, union members as well as strike-breakers, animal-rights groups as well as the fox-hunting lobby all form part of civil society.

The Internet has opened up new opportunities for 'virtual communities' of like-minded people to share their ideas. Some civil society networks see the need for more effective states, for market regulation, for taxes on speculative financial transactions, and so on. Others view civil society as the sole guarantor of individual liberties, holding that socialism and the welfare state undermine the family, promote social disintegration, and generate dependency. These diverse groups are not harmoniously working towards the democratisation of public institutions or good governance, nor are they necessarily even tolerant of the others' right to exist. At best, they represent the interests of their members. Rather than seeing civil society and its multifarious organisational forms as a collective alternative to the state, then, it is clear that only an effective and open state can protect the rights of all citizens, where these might otherwise be trampled upon by others.

As a particular sub-species of civil society organisation, NGOs, as has often been said, are defined as a sector by what they are *not*, rather than by what they *are*.[3] They come in all shapes and sizes, and the agendas and actions of some are diametrically opposed to those adopted by others. Some proselytise as a condition of receiving project benefits; some focus on a theme or geographical area; some are specialist operational agencies, while others provide only funds and other support; some concentrate on high-profile international advocacy, others work quietly and unobtrusively at the grassroots. But, more often than not, development NGOs are in some way involved in transferring resources from societies which have plenty to those who have little. Hence, more often than not, NGOs depend on being able to mobilise those resources from their home constituency. It is this, more than any other single factor, which makes NGOs susceptible to following, or at least accommodating, the agendas and fashions set by their funders, be these official donor agencies, religious organisations, political foundations, or whatever.[4] In terms of narrow institutional survival, mobilising money takes precedence over mobilising people.

The tensions between the 'development industry' and civil society organisations are not necessarily negative ones. However, as Jenny Pearce argues in her introductory essay, the problem is that these tensions are often ignored or downplayed, and their changing nature is glossed over. The result is that NGOs may successfully adapt to a changing market in terms of ensuring a continued supply of funds, but at the expense of genuinely facilitating radical social change, or representing real alternatives to the dominant paradigm (see Fowler 2000 for a good discussion on these issues). Worse, NGOs (from South as well as North) can by their actions actually impede the healthy functioning of civil society organisations, as well as undermining the functions of the state. Pointing to the mix of scholar-activist-practitioners which characterises the journal *Development in Practice* from which the contributions to this *Reader* are drawn, she makes a powerful plea for NGOs to engage more energetically and more rigorously in theoretical debates on development, to be more humble in acknowledging the myriad other forms of social action, and to be courageous enough to recognise that unless they are prepared radically to change their ways of working, NGOs may well not be part of the answer to eradicating poverty and injustice in the twenty-first century.

Notes

1   The Bretton Woods Institutions had been founded in 1944, while the FAO was established in 1945, UNESCO and UNICEF in 1946, followed by WHO in 1948, and UNHCR in 1951. Yet UNDP, now one of the world's largest sources of grant funding for development co-operation, was not established until 1965. The oldest of the UN agencies is the ILO, which dates back to 1919. It remains unique among UN agencies for its tripartite structure, with representation by governments, business (employers), and unions (organised labour): in today's terms, state, market, and civil society.

2   David C. Korten heads the People-Centred Development Forum and is author of many books, including *The Post-Corporate World: life under capitalism* (1999), and, *When Corporations Rule the World* (1995).

3   It is interesting that the older term, 'voluntary agency', has largely fallen out of use in the international context. In the UK, for instance, the 'voluntary sector' is today generally taken to refer to local or national agencies, often sub-contracted by government. Even in the USA, where the term PVO (private voluntary organisation) was standard until a few years ago, 'NGO' has become far more common.

4   Even the UN is ultimately hostage to the domestic policies of its principal donor-debtor: by September 1998, the USA owed over half the US$2.5 billion unpaid dues, despite treaty obligations that are binding on member states. (Its 1998 arrears of US$197 million were

paid in November 1998 in order to retain its vote in the General Assembly.) The US Congress uses its massive negative leverage not only to insist on internal reforms within the UN (including major lay-offs), but actually to influence the policies of some of the specialised agencies. Committed funds were also withheld from UNFPA on the grounds that it allegedly supports coercive population-control policies in China (UN NGLS 1999: 21).

References

Fowler, A. (2000), *Civil Society, NGDOs and Social Development: changing the rules of the game*, Geneva 2000 Occasional Papers, Number 1, Geneva: UNRISD.

Pieterse, E. (1997), 'South African NGOs and the trials of transition', *Development in Practice* 7(2): 157–66.

UN NGLS (1999), *Go Between* 72, December 1998–January 1999, Geneva: NGLS.

Development, NGOs, and civil society: the debate and its future

Jenny Pearce

Introduction

In reviewing the contributions to this *Reader*, I was struck by three things. First, by the wealth of empirically informed conceptual analysis that they offer, succinctly addressing many of the key issues that emerged in the 1990s on the theme of development, NGOs, and civil society. Second, by the mix of scholar-activist-practitioner authors, for whom the issues discussed really *matter*, because if they were clarified the world might become a better place. But third, and despite the quality and relevance of the papers selected for this volume, by the difficulty of generating wider debate about their content.

This is certainly not the fault of the contributions: on the contrary, they cover the range of issues admirably. The problem is that they are appearing in a world in which the collapse of intellectual and political reference points has prompted an eclectic outpouring of ideas and views, without organised and coherent debate. As a result, good thinking and writing is lost; much is duplicated and reinvented; people talk but do not listen; people write and do not read; and *vice versa*. At the start of the new millennium, development debates — if they can be called that — are like concentric circles, orbiting each other but without touching. These circles appear to share a centre, in that the same language and concepts are used by all, from the World Bank to Southern NGOs and grassroots movements. The reluctance to clarify the distinct meanings invested in these concepts, however, reflects collective collusion in the myth that a consensus on development exists, or even that some clear conclusions have been reached about how to deal with global poverty. Take, for instance, a headline in the *International Herald Tribune* of 7 January 2000: 'Concept of Poverty Undergoes Radical Shift: Now a Solution Seems Possible'.

Not only is there very little consensus, but the real world of development NGOs and official donors is characterised by mistrust, and by fierce competition over resources and protagonism, all of which are very damaging to the anti-poverty cause. The inadequacy of responses to global poverty is only too apparent. UNDP's *1997 Human Development Report* gave a measured overview of progress and setbacks in addressing global poverty in the twentieth century, and a quantitative and qualitative picture of the scale of the problem still to be tackled (UNDP 1997, especially pp24–60). While there have been notable achievements, these have been neither continuous nor equally distributed. The economic restructuring of the 1980s and 1990s reflects what UNDP calls the 'ascents/descents' character of development processes. The suggestion is that economic liberalisation has widened existing inequalities, even when it encourages growth and accumulation for those already strong in the marketplace. Such strength may derive from legally acquired wealth, but also from coercive power and illegal dealings. Criminal mafias, of which there are now many in the South and in post-communist transition countries, have expanded with the relaxation of global financial and trade controls. Between 1987 and 1993, the number of people with an income of less than US$1 a day increased by almost 100 million to 1.3 billion people, one-third of the population of the 'developing world'. Yet, between 1989 and 1996, the number of billionaires increased from 157 to 447. The value of their combined assets exceeded the combined incomes of half of the poorest of the world's poor (UNDP 1997: 38 and 110). Since the early 1980s, more than 100 developing and transition countries have suffered cuts in living standards and failures of growth more prolonged than anything experienced by the industrialised countries during the Great Depression of the 1930s (UNDP 1997: 7).

If one looks at the global picture, rather than that of the 'developing world' in isolation, the problem of human poverty assumes much greater proportions than is suggested by statistics which show that one-third of the population in the South is income-poor and one-quarter is poor in terms of the UNDP's Human Development Index. More than 100 million people in the industrialised countries, for example, also live below the income-poverty line (UNDP 1997: 34). But human poverty is not just a question of the number of people living below an agreed minimum: a category of poor on the wrong side of the relatively recent exclusion/inclusion dichotomy.

Nor is it enough to consider that millions who are not in fact below the 'line' live on its borders in constant fear of crossing over, suffering not just the threat of actual indigence but conditions of daily exploitation.[1] Rather, the issue is whether the 'inclusion' side of the border is worth preserving, and whether what it claims to offer can really be made universally available. There are cogent thinkers in the South today who, along with their Northern intellectual allies, argue for an end to 'development' as an idea. Majid Rahnema suggests that 'development' could never offer a sustainable option to all the people on the planet, even if it were successfully delivered:

> The failures of development can no longer be attributed solely to the inability of the governments, institutions and people in charge of implementing it. In fact, if they had been successful in fulfilling all the promises they made to their peoples, and had there been enough money and resources to bring about the development of *all* the so-called underdeveloped countries of the world to the level of the 'most advanced', the resulting deadlocks and tensions would perhaps have taken an even more dramatic turn. For example, it has been estimated that a single edition of the *New York Times* eats up 150 acres of forest land. Other figures suggest that, were the rest of the world to consume paper, including recycled paper, at the same rate as the United States (with six per cent of the world's population), within two years not a single tree would be left on the planet. Moreover, considering that the number of private cars in the USA by far exceeds its population, an efficient development machine, capable of taking the levels of newspaper reading and car ownership in China and India up to those of the USA, would pose to those countries (and perhaps the rest of the world) problems of traffic, pollution and forest depletion on a disastrous scale. It is thus perhaps a blessing that the machine was actually *not* as efficient as its programmers wanted it to be!
> (in Rahmena and Bawtree 1997: 378–9)

Even if we do not accept the full implications of the post-development position, given that, like dependency theory, it offers a strong critique but little guidance to action and policy, it is surely time to question profoundly the dichotomised schema of a 'successful North' and 'unsuccessful South'. Such a schema discouraged people from asking what kind of world we wanted to build, and instead focused the debate on how the Others of the 'third world' could become more like Us in the 'first world'. Most of us thought that such a schema, first encapsulated by 'modernisation theory' in the 1950s, had been intellectually defeated by the 1960s and that it was effectively dead. However, it returned in new form and with new vigour in the 1980s and 1990s. Undoubtedly, its resuscitation was encouraged by Fukuyama-like musings on the 'End of History', as echoed by the millennium edition of *Newsweek*, which declared capitalism and democracy to be the effective victors of the second millennium. Yet, as 'Souths' proliferate in the North, and 'Norths' emerge in the South, we need to ask searching questions about 'development' as both an idea and an ideal, as well as about what NGOs might contribute to it.

My introductory essay aims first to identify what this collection of papers tells us about the current state of thinking about development, NGOs, and civil society, and to clarify the points of debate that have arisen over the last decade. Second, I shall argue that the age of a rhetorical consensus should be declared over. Instead, I would partly agree with Michael Edwards (1999) that we should shift definitively from the 'foreign aid' paradigm towards a new idea of international co-operation, based on broad alliances between the different actors and institutions involved in the struggle against global poverty and exploitation. Building global alliances, or 'constituencies for change', he argues, would enable human beings to co-determine their futures on the world stage. It is evident that only through mutual engagement can any real difference be made: debate needs to be encouraged, to explore what does and does not work. International co-operation cannot be based, however, on concealing the divergence of values, interests, political positions, and, ultimately, the power to pursue them within the present global order. Edwards calls for a form of co-operation that is democratic and rooted in dialogue; one not based on any universal model imposed from above, but on the politically feasible goal of a more humanised capitalism. The purpose of co-operation is, however, by no means uncontested: Edwards' goal itself is a source of contention, as is the goal of 'development'. His understanding of what is 'politically feasible' is questionable. Where dialogue should take place, and how to ensure the equality of participation that Edwards calls for, are extremely complex issues.[2]

Above all, however, this introductory essay will argue that the theoretical, normative, and political basis for a critique of the global order is still weak and/or absent among NGOs, and that rhetorical consensus is one result of this vacuum. This has implications for practice and action, and also for the generation of open debate in search of common ground and new forms of co-operation. From the contributions to this *Reader* comes the call for NGOs to examine and re-examine critically their role in the light of experiences during, and in particular after, the Cold War. For the past 15 years or so, NGOs have been courted by governments and multilateral institutions. The moment has come to count the cost of NGOs' responses, and to debate the criteria upon which choices about the future should be based. As they find themselves under greater scrutiny, it is surely time for some humbling self-analysis which includes the question *do NGOs have a future at all?*

The debate

An initial task for this essay is to draw out the major themes that arise from this *Reader* and assess what they tell us about the current debate on development, NGOs, and civil society. I identify four critical themes:

- NGOs and neo-liberalism;
- the roles and relationships of international (Northern) NGOs and Southern NGOs;
- NGOs and the state;
- theory, praxis, and NGOs.

NGOs and neo-liberalism

The first contribution to this *Reader*, that of Michael Edwards and David Hulme, reports on the first of three international conferences they organised during the 1990s (in 1992, 1994 and, together with Tina Wallace, in 1999) on NGOs and development. The 1992 conference reflected early tensions within the development NGO community as it found itself gaining unexpected respectability and potential funding from the world of official donors. Edwards and Hulme draw attention to the risks, as well as gains, implicit in the opportunity to 'scale up':

> Increasing interest and support for NGOs among official donor agencies may create a predisposition, or foster a shift, towards operational and organisational expansion. These incentives need to be treated cautiously, because decisions to expand with official finance may have various unwelcome consequences: for example, they may close off potential courses of action; or make NGOs feel more accountable to their official donors than to their intended beneficiaries; or imply support for policies of wholesale economic liberalisation.

By the mid-1990s, an untypically cynical tone creeps into the pages of *Development in Practice*. Gino Lofredo suggests that the appeals to caution articulated by Edwards and Hulme went unheeded. His satirical commentary on the growth of 'EN-GE-OH's among Southern professionals is a warning to those who too quickly and instrumentally adopted the official donor agenda. Development turned into just another 'business' in a neo-liberal era, ultimately dedicated to what he calls 'Sustainable (Self) Development'. By the end of the 1990s, Stephen Commins, writing this time about Northern NGOs, points to the negative outcome for those who chose to become 'the delivery agency for a global soup kitchen'. He suggests that the backlash has begun, and that NGOs are no longer seen as offering significant advantages either in community development or in complex emergencies. Instead, they are 'useful fig-leaves to cover government inaction or indifference to human suffering', both in complex emergencies and in economic restructuring.

To what extent have development NGOs succumbed to the pressures and incentives to pick up the social cost of neo-liberal restructuring, and thus enabled multilateral and governmental institutions to avoid breaking with their neo-liberal faith by re-creating welfare states? While the discourse of these institutions has become notably more socially aware and 'human'-oriented (and less 'anti-state' in an ideological sense), the underlying philosophy of market-led globalisation has not been questioned. Yet many progressive and well-intentioned NGOs of North and South (as well as the opportunistic ones) accepted funding from these institutions for carrying out community development, post-conflict reconstruction and, more ambitiously, democracy building, putting aside any residual doubts about neo-liberalism as such. Perhaps what has encouraged the beginnings of an anti-NGO shift is that, unsurprisingly, NGOs were unable to offer the solution to the social cost of economic restructuring. Criticisms of NGOs have focused on their technical deficiency, their lack of accountability, and their excessively politicised and critical character. This 'failure' has undermined their credibility among the technocrats within donor institutions, who demanded rapid and measurable outputs from investments in the NGO sector. And it weakened the influence of the pro-NGO social-development advocates within those institutions.[3]

If UNDP figures are correct, global poverty and inequality have grown in many parts of the world under the neo-liberal policy agenda and the processes of trade liberalisation, privatisation, and labour-market reform. The picture is not universally bleak, of course, and macro-economic performance did improve in some regions and countries. Consider, however, the case of India, whose levels of public spending were under threat in the late 1990s from a neo-liberal focus on reducing fiscal deficits and minimising the role of the state (UNDP 1997: 52). UNDP attributes India's relative achievements in poverty reduction between 1976 and 1990 to its public-spending levels. India has a reputed one million NGOs (Salamon and Anheier 1997), but it is unclear whether even this number can offer a sustainable substitute for state spending. This is not to say that some NGOs in India and elsewhere did not do good work. It must be recognised, though, that increasing numbers of NGOs, however dedicated and efficient, could never offer rapid solutions to a problem on the scale of global poverty, or even alleviate it sufficiently to ensure relative social stability.

More worrying is the evidence that NGOs have sacrificed some legitimacy in their own societies by their willingness to participate in implementing the social safety-net programmes that accompany donors' neo-liberal policies. Richard Holloway (1999) has made this point forcefully:

> While people inside the NGO world still think of themselves as occupying the moral high ground, the reality now is that few people in the South outside the NGO world think of NGOs like this. 'The word on the street in the South is that NGOs are charlatans racking up large salaries ... and many air-conditioned offices.'

An in-depth study of NGOs in Latin America, sponsored by ALOP/FICONG,[4] highlights the growing awareness of this problem in the South. For instance, the case study on Argentina concludes:

> In synthesis, the Promotion and Development NGOs are immersed in a social environment which shows interest in, and openness to, private institutions in the social field, but within a hegemonic ideological and practical model that does not prioritise social change nor see it as necessary. In other words, it is an environment (a 'market') which is basically interested in the more technical services of the Development NGOs (their services of financial intermediation or professional assistance) and not at all in their key social role of development promotion. This environment generates (via social recognition and financial opportunities) a strong tension in institutions, forcing them either to convert themselves into successful 'enterprises or social consultancies' or to maintain and strengthen their promotion role without the resources to carry it out. (Bombarolo and Pérez Coscio 1998: 45)

The pages of *Development in Practice* were not the only ones to carry warnings during the 1990s about the potential cost to NGOs of implementing official donor agendas.[5] The introduction to the edited volume that arose from the second international NGO conference, 'NGOs and Development: Performance and Accountability in the New World Order', put it bluntly:

> Our main conclusion is that NGOs must 'return to their roots' if they are to promote poverty reduction on a mass scale. With respect to this conclusion we posit a number of questions. Could it be that many [Southern] NGOs are so involved in service delivery that the local level associations they create empower NGO personnel and leaders but not the poor and disadvantaged? This can certainly be argued for some of the large NGOs in Bangladesh. Have [Northern] NGOs got so involved in lobbying donors directly that they have neglected their role in creating active citizenries that, through more diffuse political processes, can demand effective aid policies and other policy changes (for example, in trade, debt relief and foreign affairs) that will assist the poor in poor countries?
> (Hulme and Edwards 1997: 20)

As a participant in that 1994 conference, it was clear to me that NGOs of North and South, and the academics who worked with them, had already tacitly split. This split was not organised around an open debate on the dilemmas themselves, but around two broad approaches to them. One emphasised the technical changes that NGOs should take into account if they were to remain relevant to the economically restructured order in which they were working. A proliferation of papers (on institutional strengthening, capacity building, improving accountability, measuring effectiveness through log-frames and social development indicators) addressed some real and specific problems that development NGOs faced if they were to improve their interventions and prove their worth to donors. On the other hand, there was a minority who felt deeply uncomfortable with this new language and who stressed the need to get the politics right first, and to resist donor-driven agendas if these served only to bureaucratise and depoliticise NGOs. It was easy to dismiss the latter as the traditionalists of the left failing to keep up to date, or as utopians whose ideas bore little relation to the real world. Those who preferred the discourse of politics tended to weaken their position by not engaging with the fact that contributing real improvements to people's lives is what it is all about, and that improving the capacity to do this is not in itself the problem. Those who tried to bridge this divide found themselves viewed as marginal to the central issues. For example, despite decades of debate around gender and development (a social and political issue with considerable implications for development practice), it was still viewed as peripheral by those concerned with adapting to the New Policy Agenda, and ensuring the survival of NGOs within it (May 1995).

The possibility that improvements in efficiency and management should best be driven by political choices rather than *vice versa* was buried in the false dichotomy between political and technical agendas, an issue taken up later in this essay. This dichotomy, I argue, is one of the reasons why NGOs failed to develop their own critique of neo-liberalism, and why many ended up implementing a model with which they felt deeply uncomfortable.[6] Indeed, it might be said that 20 years of economic liberalisation have damaged the NGO sector, fragmenting it and fomenting competition in which, as the free-market model argues, only the most efficient survive. The rush to efficiency, as if it were a discrete and neutral outcome of technical decisions, appears to have been at the cost of the time-consuming and messy business of debating other values, such as how greater efficiency could be pursued without a cost to social-change objectives.

Although it was never homogeneous, the NGO sector has been transformed over the last two decades, in more than quantitative terms, to incorporate a multiplicity of agendas, functions, and values. In the meantime, neo-liberal restructuring has been implemented throughout the South. Thus, rather than starting the new millennium having proved the case for international development co-operation, NGOs are having to confront a crisis in foreign aid from which they themselves are beginning to suffer, even though they are as yet still relatively favoured within the declining aid budget. The end of the Cold War and the irresistible rise of neo-liberal philosophy have transformed the rationale for aid. The North now evades responsibility for poverty in the South, given that no geopolitical interests drive aid programmes, and given also that Southern governments, which are now unable to play off the superpowers, have a much weakened voice in international forums. The burden is placed (in part correctly) on the South's ability to put its own act in order — but only through competing in a global economy where the odds are already heavily stacked against it. Aid focuses increasingly on the emergencies, disasters, and conflicts which hit the headlines and Northern public opinion.[7]

The crisis in international co-operation, and the future role of NGOs within the economic reality of globalisation, was the context of the third NGO conference, 'NGOs in a Global Future', held in January 1999.

Reflecting the fragmentation of perspectives over the previous decade, this conference was probably the most eclectic of the three, 'a complex, wide-ranging conference where the diversity of experience and views was perhaps the hallmark' (Wallace 1999: 2). The fundamental challenge laid down by the organisers in their background paper did not receive the attention it deserved. They had called still more clearly for a shift away from the roles that had come to dominate the neo-liberal age of the late twentieth century — in other words, from development as delivery to development as leverage. NGOs were called to return to their role as promoters of social change and of non-market values of co-operation, non-violence, and respect for human rights and democratic processes, and to make these the 'bottom line' in decisions over economics and the environment, social policy, and politics (Edwards, Hulme, and Wallace 1999: 13). Rather than acting as 'unhappy agents of a foreign aid system in decline', the organisers urged NGOs to 'rethink their mandate, mission and strategies'(*ibid.*: 16). NGOs needed to look towards the gradual replacement of foreign aid with a broader agenda of international co-operation in which they reshaped their roles and sought alliances around common goals with other social and civic organisations. The conference discussions themselves, however, although attended by representatives from a wider spectrum of NGOs from North and South than the earlier two, failed to engage with these ideas, and no clear future directions emerged.

Nevertheless, the parameters of debate are now clearer. This is after years in which many NGOs of North and South have more or less reluctantly let themselves be led and/or influenced by official donor agendas and techno-efficiency determinism. Official donors have reached out to NGOs while also pushing the neo-liberal restructuring that many believe is part of the problem faced by the poor, not the solution. At the same time, in the course of the 1990s, donors have begun to question how representative and effective NGOs can claim to be — and not just international, Northern-based NGOs, but also those in the South. Many donors have begun, as part of this process, to rename their NGO Units as Civil Society Units. They have become interested in funding a broader range of associations in the South, moving away from a focus on middle-class intermediary groups, of which NGOs are an example. Such a shift begs many questions about the donors' assumptions, but for the purposes of this Introduction, it is yet another reason why NGOs of North and South are being forced to re-think their role and purpose, as well as their relationship with each other.

International (Northern) NGO and Southern NGO roles and relationships

The 1990s saw major changes in the relationships between international (Northern) NGOs and Southern NGOs, the nature of which is well illustrated in this *Reader*. A key problem to emerge in the 1992 conference was that of South–North NGO 'partnership', and as the decade wore on this idea of 'partnership' was increasingly seen to misrepresent the power of Northern NGOs as funders of Southern ones. As official donors also began to fund Southern NGOs directly, so the institutional identities of the latter grew less dependent on Northern NGOs. They began to set their own agendas and to develop research, policy, and advocacy capacities. In the late 1990s, Firoze Manji argued that British international NGOs (or BINGOs, as he calls them) had failed to accept this shift. Their arguments against the direct funding of Southern NGOs reflected their continuing paternalism, and they voiced criticisms that applied to themselves as much as to Southern NGOs (for example, their lack of accountability, their tendency to be driven by donors' agendas and to respond to the chance of funding rather than to need). In effect, they were responding to a basic fear for their own future.

The growth and increasing protagonism of Southern NGOs is a theme of the decade. But concerns also began to focus on the implications of the decline in the easy funding that had fed previous years of growth, and on questions of NGO legitimacy, rather than on the problems of expansion. In their 1998 contribution, Mick Moore and Sheelagh Stewart argue that development NGOs in poor countries need to re-establish public confidence in order to persuade donors to continue to channel funds through them. They identify four areas of concern:

- the failure of NGOs to develop accountability within their own countries rather than accountability to wealthy foreign organisations;

- the need for internal reform and mechanisms to 'institutionalise suspicion' within NGOs that are undergoing structural growth, and thus to regain trust and confidence in the eyes of the public, government, and donors;

- the need for NGOs to pre-empt the often intrusive and inappropriate formal, quantitative performance evaluation favoured by donors, by developing quality ratings of their own;

- and the need to overcome the tendency for small NGOs to compete with each other, by seeking economies of scale through collectively provided services within the NGO sector.

Collective self-regulation could, the authors argue, enable NGOs to confront their critics, which might lead to increased funding.

Debate about the future direction of Southern NGOs is urgently needed, given the challenges that they face at the beginning of the new millennium. It is difficult to foster such debate, precisely because the events of the 1990s served to fragment and divide the sector so much. Signs are emerging, however, that such a debate is beginning. In Latin America, the region I know best, the ALOP/FICONG volume alluded to earlier illustrates the efforts being made to confront today's dilemmas, and to enable NGOs to decide their own futures through a more transparent dialogue with the North. Shrinking aid budgets have not affected all regions and NGOs in the same way. The problem in Latin America, with its long history of NGOs, has been the tendency of the aid community to see the region as relatively rich or 'middle-income'. Having achieved its initial goal, funding has been withdrawn from many organisations that were initially supported as a means of bringing about democratisation. In addition, given the region's rich history of social organising, donors' interest in broader 'civil society' rather than 'NGO' funding has forced NGOs to justify their existence to grassroots organisations as well as to donors.

The problems that Mariano Valderrama emphasises (in Valderrama and Coscio 1998) are less those of restoring donors' confidence than that of finding ways for NGOs to re-connect with their original social-change objectives, while also managing to retain access to a diminishing source of funds. The future of development NGOs, he argues, is not only influenced by globalisation and liberal reforms. The funding crisis has drawn attention to the external dependence of NGOs, and it has provoked great uncertainty, but the problem cannot be reduced simply to one of fewer resources. Donors have shifted their funding to specific and short-term projects based on erratic criteria relating to topics and geographical priorities, with much greater conditionality attached, and without covering institutional overheads. NGOs have been encouraged to look for local resources and self-financing from, for instance, philanthropic businesses. The case studies that Valderrama draws on showed that this alternative is very limited. Engagement in self-financing activities (which usually involve selling services and implementing projects for the state, local governments, and official aid agencies) 'brings financial dividends, [but] often distracts development NGOs from the mission that gave birth and sense to them' (*ibid.*: 420). Valderrama concludes:

Development NGOs today confront a problem of identity and coherence. How do they intervene in the market and extend and diversify sources of financing without losing sight of the objectives which are their raison d'être, and which are clearly related to democracy and human development? Evidently, in this field there are no magic formulae and simple recipes.

Valderrama fears that the rational response of most NGOs is to solve their short-term funding problems by undertaking activities that cause them to lose their focus and that give them a mercantilist character. Valderrama does not see a solution for NGOs in increasing their size in pursuit of economies of scale, although he gives no clear alternatives. Echoing to some extent the suggestion of Moore and Stewart, he argues for more synergy among Southern development NGOs, and greater coordination with Northern NGOs. Coordination could also help to build a more favourable local environment for the NGO sector, for example by influencing the media and public opinion.

These issues already confront, or soon will, Southern NGOs in many other parts of the world, as funding that is channelled through NGOs comes under greater scrutiny. But, as the Latin American case shows, the funding crisis is precipitating a more profound self-questioning among NGOs about the direction in which external funding has taken them. Is a continued claim to social and political protagonism justified, when such funding has often distanced them from grassroots movements and processes? Could a shift towards more horizontal communication among Southern NGOs help to overcome the bilateral and vertical character of the donor–NGO relationship, something which has fostered such fragmentation and competition among NGOs? What kind of reception would Valderrama's plea meet among the Northern NGOs, many of whom are also going through a process of upheaval in order to adjust their role to external changes?

Firoze Manji points in this volume to the reluctance of many Northern NGOs to change paternalistic patterns of engagement with Southern counterparts and build new alliances based on 'solidarity not charity'. At the beginning of the new millennium, however, Northern as well as Southern NGOs are facing tough questions about their future identity and survival. Southern NGOs, particularly the larger ones and those willing to scale up further, may now have gained some relative independence from Northern NGOs, but not from the official donors who have financed this expansion. Northern NGOs that have continued to act as conduits for official aid[8] have had to face dilemmas in trying to preserve their own agenda. The ability to raise funds from the public undoubtedly helps, as does the greater diversity of funding sources to which Northern NGOs have access. The heterogeneity of size, ethos, and influence of NGOs within the North is at least as great as in the South, and responses to the changing context are equally mixed. For instance, the Transnational Institute (TNI) suggests that some of the largest private foreign aid agencies are already transnational 'businesses' (Sogge *et al.*1996).

In the vanguard of responses to change is undoubtedly Oxfam GB and the other members of Oxfam International. Their vision is to build a global network around a corporate Oxfam identity that can seriously challenge the hegemony in development policy of multilateral and bilateral institutions. However, the emphasis on decentralising the management of programmes to the South (but with constant vertical and horizontal communication among them), together with a shift away from the 'project' mentality that has dominated the world of development aid, has necessitated a costly organisational restructuring. For some, the shift will create a global institution, with trunk and branches in the North but roots in the South, through which will flow the evidence and information needed to shape and legitimise Oxfam's advocacy role on the international stage. For others, it is another hegemonising project which is in contrast to the strategy of broader alliance-building and co-operation, both vertical and horizontal, argued for by Michael Edwards, or the international solidarity model of Firoze Manji.

Another vision was articulated by Michael Taylor, the former Director of Christian Aid (Taylor 1997), who argued for a serious shift to internationalism by Northern NGOs, not just attempts to address international issues from Northern strongholds. Thus, no international NGO would have a core identity in a Northern country, but would be one part of an organisation, each of whose parts, wherever located (whether North or South), would build up a strong and competent capacity of its own and combine with the others to speak to the international organisation together. His model is the Jubilee 2000 debt campaign, with its national coalitions in Northern and Southern countries that meet together to agree a common international platform. And last, but by no means least, it is important to mention the conclusions of David Sogge and Kees Biekart, who believe that private aid agencies may well not have a future at all:

> Must today's private aid agencies, like the poor who justify their
> existence, always be with us? And must they go on getting and

spending in the ways described, and questioned, in the preceding pages? … The answer to both questions is: Not Necessarily. The agencies have no Manifest Destiny. Their righteous calling confers no special immunities and privileges, such as a 'right' to intervene. They are not captive to some immutable economic laws of motion, however much commerce grips them in its hammerlock. (Sogge et al. 1996: 198)

There are undoubtedly many other models and propositions. But at the core of this debate is not just relationships between NGOs of North and South, but whether or not the non-government organisation *as such* is still useful or relevant to an agenda for change in either part of the world. The emergence of the donors' broader agenda of 'civil-society strengthening' and democracy building in the course of the 1990s, for example, should provoke not only a concern for their own financial future among Northern and Southern NGOs, but also a serious debate on the implications of this agenda for grassroots movements and NGOs' own relationship with them. To what extent is the shift in emphasis towards advocacy, lobbying, and education, while enhancing disaster-relief and emergency capacity, a sufficient rationale for Northern NGOs to exist? Have Southern NGOs proved themselves more effective than states in the development process? And, if not, what kind of state, as well as what kind of NGOs, should we be thinking about?

NGOs and the state

Goodhand and Chamberlain offer a significant entry-point to a theme that recurs throughout this *Reader*. They discuss here a complex political emergency (something which has become only too common in parts of the South) where the state is chronically weak, and yet the means of waging war are sophisticated and available. In their case study of Afghanistan, NGOs — themselves mostly external creations and staffed by members of the country's very small educated elite — 'are occupying the space left by the collapse of the state, and so wield great influence in the absence of effective government institutions'. Goodhand and Chamberlain conclude that such NGOs are 'not a panacea for the intractable problems of development in Afghanistan', although they clearly have a role, given the erosion of state and civil-society structures in the country. However, there is a danger that, as NGOs try to negotiate spaces with the different strongmen who control these structures, they in fact end up severely compromised.

Complex political emergencies are extreme expressions of the wider issue of the role of NGOs in countries where the state is weak. Two case studies in this *Reader* focus on how NGOs can avoid further weakening the very idea of public goods and service delivery, to which many development NGOs remain committed. Christy Cannon discusses the complexities of this in Africa, where a functioning public sector has never existed. Her study of NGOs in the health sector in Uganda suggests that NGOs could attempt to enhance the capacity of government at the District level, where NGO leaders and government medical personnel can get to know each other better, and the latter can help to influence and lobby national government. Christopher Collier's case study from Zambia follows a similar theme, suggesting that NGOs should help poor people to make claims from government and not to expect less from it because NGOs are providing the goods and services. Such a role, however, requires the active participation of NGOs in decisions about public resources, not a simple service-delivery role that by-passes the state, as many donors have favoured.

In the above illustrations, the idea that national states have a role to play in the provision of public goods is not questioned: how to strengthen the state and make it sensitive to the needs of the poor is the critical issue. The nature of the debate on the relationship between states, markets, and civil society had evidently advanced qualitatively by the end of the 1990s, with the state making a come-back of some kind. This is illustrated particularly well in this volume by Alan Whaites. It is wrong, he suggests, to see development as nurturing a strong civil society, while ignoring the weakness of an ineffective state. He argues that redressing such imbalances should be the aim of development, on the understanding that an effective government structure is just as essential to development as a strong civil society. Weak states can become hostage to the most powerful groups in a society, creating a real obstacle to development. This links to the arguments presented earlier in this essay about the impact of neo-liberalism on the way in which the role of NGOs in development is conceptualised. International NGOs, argues Whaites, in effect contributed to the strengthening of civil societies at the expense of the state when they took advantage of the shrinkage of government services that was brought about by structural adjustment programmes.

Alan Whaites makes the important suggestion that the theoretical framework that development practitioners derive from liberal philosophers of civil society, such as de Tocqueville, cannot be applied unreflectively to situations in the contemporary South. Here, the problem is weak rather than strong states, and the weakness of civil society has arguably been exaggerated.

There is some evidence to support this argument. But the issue is perhaps less the strength or weakness of the state than its capacity to develop the ability to distance itself from dominant groups. There is a long history of Marxist theorising on the capitalist state to this effect. It is perhaps time to recall the famous but long-forgotten debate of the 1970s between Ralph Miliband and Nicos Poulantzas. Is the capitalist state the instrument of the particular ruling-class groups that occupy positions within its machine of government, or is the state able to look after the interests of capitalism because it is structurally set up to do so? In the latter scenario, the state has an ability to retain its distance from the direct influence of the ruling class. Adrian Leftwich's collection of essays on development and democracy concludes that, where this situation obtains, late capitalist development has been more effective (Leftwich 1995).[9]

In conclusion, it is not enough to reverse the paradigm that came to the fore in the early 1990s, so that from strengthening civil society we shift to strengthening the state or simply to building a greater equilibrium between the two. Another series of questions is needed if NGOs are to take up the challenge, outlined earlier, of re-appropriating their own agenda of social change in the face of donor imperatives and those of the economic liberalisation policies that have driven globalisation over the last two decades. Such questions include:

- In whose interests should the state act?
- What kind of relationship do we want to build between the state and 'civil society'?
- How does the operation of the market, and capitalism in general, affect our vision?
- And ultimately, what kind of world do we want to live in?

In other words, prior to, or at least alongside, the policy issues raised by Whaites lies a series of theoretical, normative, and political questions. The failure to address these questions in the name of the supremacy of practice and/or of technical determinism, I shall argue, lies behind the loss of direction and fragmentation of NGOs in the 1990s.

Theory, praxis, and NGOs

Many NGO workers are committed to the idea of making a practical contribution to building a better world. As such, they contrast their action-oriented approach to that of academics who reflect, analyse, and criticise from their ivory tower. In the field of NGO studies, there has been a *rapprochement* between the two, and the pages of *Development in Practice* reflect this to some extent. However, the remaining essays in this *Reader* seek to go beyond this collaborative potential on policy and practice, and ask what might be the potential for collaboration in the realm of development theory, normative reflection, and politics.

A key argument of this introduction centres on the failure of NGOs to develop new tools for theoretical analysis and normative critique, following the collapse of different socialist models of development that had previously guided their actions. The result has been a problem-solving approach to development, defended on the grounds that too much abstract theoretical debate prevents practical achievements. Michael Edwards has argued:

> The challenge for the future is not an intellectual one. More research is always needed, but we already know the principles of project success: engage with local realities, take your time, experiment and learn, reduce vulnerability and risk, and always work on social and material development together. The real issue is why so many agencies cut corners on these principles, and the answer to that question lies in … the short-termism, control orientation and standardisation that have infected development work for a generation or more. In this world view, projects are a mechanism to deliver foreign aid, not short-term building blocks of long-term change. (Edwards 1999: 86)

Much of what is described here is familiar to anyone with recent experience of the NGO world, but I would argue that there *is* a serious intellectual challenge, and that sorting it out is as important as getting the praxis and attitudes right. It might not be an empirical research problem as such, but it is about where NGOs ultimately decide to locate themselves in the global system. This raises not abstract, theoretical questions but core issues, such as: *what and who is your work for?* Among other outcomes, the failure to ask such questions has led to the false, linguistic consensus of the 1990s and, to be somewhat harsh, to an intellectually lazy reliance on a handful of concepts and words as a substitute for thought.[10] This has weakened and confused practice and, I would argue, contributed to the present crisis of legitimacy within the NGO sector. Several articles in this collection, as well as my own experiences from Latin America, lead me to such a conclusion.

Two articles appeared in 1996, and are reproduced here, which made a valiant attempt to call NGO attention to the practical implications of different ways of using concepts. Sarah White makes a fundamental point about the concept of 'participation'. The word must be seen as political because it has no *intrinsic* connection with a radical project, since it can just as easily entrench and reproduce existing power relations. We can invest meanings in such concepts through learning from praxis and being guided by theoretical clarity and ethical principles. But if we treat them as unproblematic, neutral, or technical terms, they can become words whose meaning is defined by whoever chooses to do so, and for whatever purpose. The concepts are then depoliticised and in effect rendered useless for shaping praxis. White demonstrates this by deconstructing some different ways in which participation as a concept can be used, and how that influences processes on the ground in Zambia and the Philippines. She suggests that there are always questions to be asked when 'participation' is invoked, 'about who is involved, how, and on whose terms'; and the interests of those represented in the concept must be analysed. Finally, she underlines that if participation is to mean anything, it will challenge existing power relations and it will bring about conflict: 'the absence of conflict in many supposedly "participatory" programmes is something that should raise our suspicions'.

The second article is on the concept of civil society and development, a 'conceptual marriage' that, with my colleague Jude Howell, I have spent some time exploring (Howell and Pearce, forthcoming). Alan Whaites seeks to show how lack of conceptual clarity confuses practice. In particular, he focuses on two visions of 'civil society'. On the one hand, there is the liberal, Tocquevillean approach which contrasts civil and traditional society, identifying the former with groups who have detached themselves from primordial loyalties of blood and kin and cut across such boundaries to form coalitions around small issues. On the other hand is the view of Jean-François Bayart, which has a more universal vision of civil society (more appropriate, Bayart would argue, to the African context), and which includes primordial associations.[11] Whaites calls for greater attention to be paid to the way in which civil associations emerge out of community groups along lines that de Tocqueville articulated. He is implicitly cautious of the notion of reinforcing primordial attachments in the name of civil society. This contributes to what ought to be a major debate among development practitioners in terms of choosing whom to work with in the South, and why. But, without the intellectual work on the concept of 'civil society', the debate is effectively avoided. I would add that there is another view of 'civil society' (particularly critical in countries with traditions of left-wing organisations and mobilisation) which appropriates the term to help describe the Gramscian, counter-hegemonic struggles against the market as well as the state. This challenges NGOs to select who they are going to support according to certain criteria, something that requires serious conceptual and strategic discussion.

There is no 'correct' view of civil society, but there is an essential point to make about the way the concept is used. The use of the term as a normative concept (i.e. what we would *like* civil society to be, or what we think it *ought* to be) is often confused with an empirical description (i.e. what it *is*) (Pearce 1997). The constant slippage between the two in the development literature and in the practice of multilateral agencies, governments, and NGOs has contributed to a technical and depoliticising approach to the strengthening of civil society which has had political implications. It has, for instance, mostly privileged the vision of Western donor agencies and turned 'civil society' into a project rather than a process.[12] In other words, by assuming that there is no debate around what we would like 'civil society' to be, and assuming that it is an unproblematic and empirically observable given, whose purpose is unquestionably to build democracy and foster development, the vision of powerful and well-resourced donors predominates. Failure to clarify their own position means that many NGOs end up simply implementing that vision on the donors' behalf. If doing so coincides with their own objectives, there is no problem — but if it is an unintended outcome of lack of reflection, there is indeed a problem.

Two articles published in *Development in Practice* at the turn of the millennium draw our attention to other aspects of the discussion about theory, praxis, and NGOs. Lilly Nicholls discusses the conceptual weaknesses of efforts to generate new, more human-centred ideas of development. The critical question she raises is whether the ideas of Sustainable Human Development (SHD) and People-Centred Development (PCD) are sharp enough to inform praxis:

> SHD/PCD ideas may be appealing, but the key question is whether the paradigm is conceptually sound and can be implemented in the world's poorest countries (Uganda, in this case) where it is most needed. And if so, whether multilateral agencies such as UNDP, and indeed much smaller and less bureaucratic international NGOs such as ActionAid are capable of translating its more ambitious components into practice.

Nicholls' conclusion is very negative. SHD/PCD ideas are based on such complex and abstract principles that the gap between the theory and a realistic development strategy and action plan cannot be overcome. In addition, the ideological ambiguity and internal contradictions of the ideas themselves limit their translation into an effective development strategy. The argument that theory matters to practice centres on the need for conceptual tools that guide the implementation of policy, not for abstract principles that sound good but have no relation to action.

Finally, and to show that out of *Development in Practice* comes more than just critique, is the paper by Amina Mama. She demonstrates that doing research that builds theory and knowledge not from abstract principles but from the 'ground' up may be a more fruitful way forward than the attempt to take such principles to the 'ground' and merely apply them. Mama's research team (composed of African women researchers in the ABANTU for Development network, working under the difficult conditions of military rule in Nigeria) investigated how a gender perspective could be incorporated into a regional programme to strengthen civil society. The researchers used a participatory method, starting from local, actually existing, understandings of 'policy' within NGO communities. The research 'uncovered levels of gender activism that might not have been discernible' without the participatory method, and insights into 'locally diverse relationships between state and civil society', opening up possibilities for praxis that might not have been possible otherwise.

In conclusion, this section makes a plea for NGOs to reconsider the way they view the relationship between theory and praxis. In the first place, it calls for recognition that theory underpins everyone's understanding of the social and political world; it is not extraneous to it, and we are all part of its construction and potential deconstruction.[13] Theory, and the policies which derive from it, have political effects and implications that should not be ignored. The more explicit the theoretical assumptions that inform our understanding, the more responsible we are in our commitment to the people whose lives we claim to improve. The problem-solving approach to development, on the other hand, leads to a technocratic, solution/output focus (as opposed to a learning/process focus) that views people as clients, beneficiaries, and recipients rather than as active participants in agendas for change.

These issues echo debates taking place within my own area of Peace Studies which, like development, is fundamentally concerned with an agenda for change. Two colleagues have argued against the danger of producing 'technically exploitable knowledge' rather than knowledge to enhance capacity for 'enlightened action' (Featherstone and Parkin in Broadhead 1997). The construction of the latter kind of knowledge is the responsibility of practitioners as well as theorists. Among other potential tools, those of critical social theory provide some important starting points. These have begun to inform peace researchers and are, I would argue, of relevance also to the field of development. They ask us to recognise, for instance, that knowledge is historically constructed and that we are agents in, not outsiders to, that process. It suggests we must ask what, and whom, the knowledge is for, and how can we develop a practical and theoretical knowledge that is transformative and non-exploitative. It assumes that nothing is immutable, given that everything has been constructed by someone and for some purpose: it only asks us to clarify the purpose for which we would reconstruct what presently exists.

The debate ... and its future

This introduction has identified four critical areas for reflection and debate that have come out of papers published in *Development in Practice* over almost a decade, as well as from other sources.

1 Neo-liberalism and globalisation driven by the values of neo-liberalism have seriously harmed the anti-poverty and anti-exploitation struggle in the world today. The benefits to the few have not compensated for the increased poverty, inequality, and uncertainty which very many have experienced. The idea of NGOs as value-driven facilitators of change has been adversely affected by the decision of many to implement the welfare, social-net programmes of institutions that are committed to economic liberalisation and concerned to reduce its social cost. At the same time, fragmentation and competition has grown among NGOs and encouraged further division within a historically heterogeneous community. The millennium begins with the challenge to NGOs to reflect critically on this reality. As the more ideological form of neo-liberalism which dominated the 1980s and early 1990s is replaced by concerns to build a more regulated global capitalism, NGOs must decide where they want to stand in relationship to it. Otherwise, they will drift into implementing the donor-defined agendas of the new age, as many of them did in the past decade or more.

2 The roles of Southern and Northern NGOs, and their relationship to each other, are having to evolve in response to the new world order and

policy agenda of the 1990s and beyond. This has been widely recognised, and different models are gradually emerging. But, if the differences are to be respected while co-operation rather than competition is fostered, a more open and transparent debate and self-reflection needs to take place among NGOs of the South as well as between them and NGOs in the North. It is likely that NGOs, like the relatively privileged social groups who mostly staff them, will be polarised around the social and political tensions of the broader world. Some may choose to institutionalise themselves as service-deliverers, others to engage in the growing number of spaces for dialogue on global governance issues. Others may accept that they are ultimately facilitators, not agents, of social change (Pearce 1993), and re-connect with grassroots activists. This does not render irrelevant the search for common ground in order to build more effective alliances. But it should be recognised that the survival of the very idea of 'NGO' and the NGO sector, at least in its present form, can no longer be assumed.

3 NGOs cannot and should not replace the state in promoting 'development'. There have been many discussions on what should be the relationship between the two, and how NGOs can make the state more accountable and sensitive to the needs of the poor. There has been less debate on what the role of the state is, and what we would like it to be. Is it worth fighting for in some form, given the apparent anti-state logic of capitalist globalisation? Or should local and regional sites be the new focus of attention, as the World Bank's 1999/2000 Report suggests? Greater care in how the concept of 'civil society' is used is important if it is to be given a role in rethinking the state. Used as an empirical description of voluntary associations and social groups, it necessarily reflects the social differences embedded in any society. These may not 'determine' the character of the state, but they do shape it in critical ways. They are in turn shaped by the dynamics of the market, as well as power relationships of all kinds. As such, 'civil society', used in this empirical sense, can also have an impact on re-shaping the state; and therein lies room for action and change. This is contingent on the particular objectives each group might have, and is by no means inevitably progressive.

4 In order to clarify what action and change they want to bring about, NGOs, as one set of associations within an empirical 'civil society', need to develop their theoretical, normative, and political critique of the global order and the discourses of 'development' that have hitherto

dominated the post-war epoch. They should not assume that practice is sufficient, and that people who try to conceptualise processes are necessarily diverting energy from the 'real' problems. Not only is practice always a reflection of implicit theoretical assumptions, it can rarely be 'improved' by technical solutions alone, which themselves mask political and normative choices. For NGOs, this should be one major lesson of the last decade or more. The purpose of greater clarity around their critique should be to improve practice and promote debate, and to seek common ground with others engaged in the same enterprise.

I will conclude by reflecting a little more on the impact of current shifts in thinking about the global order on the choices open to NGOs at the beginning of the new millennium, and the potential impact on their future. The paradigmatic shift towards building new forms of global governance and a role for 'civil society', however understood, has been established. There is now a more explicit acknowledgement that some form of regulation in the global economy is necessary. Today, the World Bank puts out a message of co-operation: another clear step away from the ideological neo-liberalism of the 1980s. Its 1997 Report accepted that the state and civil society, as well as the market, have a role in its tripartite model for country-based development. And now the Bank argues:

> The message of this report is that new institutional responses are needed in a globalising and localising world. Globalisation requires national governments to seek agreements with partners — other national governments, international organisations, non-government organisations (NGOs) and multinational corporations — through supranational institutions. (World Bank 2000: 3)

As spaces for global co-operation and participation 'from above' proliferate, NGOs face a new set of choices, a situation which makes the plea for debate and clarification of the foundations of their critique more urgent. The benefits of co-operation and resistance to co-option depend on first knowing why, and for whom, you choose to engage in dialogues in supranational spaces dominated by more powerful institutions and corporations. We must also understand the limits of dialogue. Willingness to struggle for what you believe to be right must surely remain a tool of the powerless and their allies, part of their necessarily diverse 'repertoire of contention' (Tarrow 1998: 20). Clarity on what you believe to be right, and why, is essential.

NGOs are not political parties, nor are they grassroots social movements. Their identity crisis lies in the fact that they are in between, and they have won a part in the drama to some extent because of the crisis in the former and the often temporary, unstable nature of the latter. In the development field, the neo-liberal antagonism towards the state also played a key role, of course. If NGOs are institutionally reified outside this context as part, for instance, of an emerging 'Third Sector',[14] we can easily forget that they are merely organisational spaces which reflect the *choices* open to the better-educated and socially aware 'middle' social sectors of North and South, i.e. those with relative privileges *vis à vis* the rest of their societies in class, ethnic, and/or gender terms.

For development NGOs (i.e. those concerned with global poverty and exploitation), the choices for how to engage with or challenge global capitalism at the beginning of the new millennium are becoming clearer. There is the option of continuing to work within the evolving neo-liberal approach to globalisation, administering welfare to those whom market forces cannot reach. Alternatively, globalisation can be recognised as an inevitable process, but NGOs can take advantage of new supranational spaces to argue for new forms of regulation in markets and international regimes in favour of the poor. Multinational corporations are also opening up spaces for dialogue with their NGO critics around the theme of corporate ethics. Or NGOs can actively side with the anti-globalisation movements, in all their diversity, as they emerged in Seattle during the 1999 World Trade Organisation (WTO) negotiations. As Seattle showed, anti-globalisation may or may not mean anti-capitalism, but it does mean anti-neo-liberalism, even in its moderated form. On the other hand, NGOs can take the financial consequences of an option which prioritises grassroots support work, building on the Gramscian idea, for example, of the 'organic intellectual'. This would reflect an understanding that global change depends on how the relative and absolute poor, the millions of the world's working and workless population with no material stake in the perpetuation of the existing order, choose to act.

These do not exhaust all the options for NGOs, nor are these options all mutually exclusive. There is room for plural choices of action and tactical alliances. But what *is* dangerous is to enter any of these without clarity of purpose, and without thinking through the implications from the perspective of a theoretical, normative, and political critique of the existing global order.

The events in Seattle await a full evaluation, but they are highly significant in relation to the subject of this *Reader*. All NGOs, including development NGOs, won unprecedented acknowledgement of their power and influence in the wake of those events. *The Economist* (1999) nervously asked: 'Will NGOs democratise, or merely disrupt, global governance?'. *The Economist* tends to lump all critical groups into one basket, and thus claimed 'the battle of Seattle is only the latest and most visible in a string of recent NGO victories'. The reality is very different, of course. Seattle actually reflected the differences that exist among lobbyists, organised labour, campaigners, and protesters worldwide, of which the NGO is only one variant. One observer noted, 'even in the run-up to WTO week in Seattle, the genteel element — foundation careerists, NGO bureaucrats, policy wonks [sic] — were all raising cautionary fingers, saying that the one thing to be feared in Seattle this week was active protest' (St Clair 1999: 88). There will be many debates, as there should be, about whether it was direct action, dignified restraint, or the arrogance, ignorance, and bad planning of Northern governments (particularly the US) that made the difference in Seattle. Whatever the conclusion, it cannot be denied that creative street-protest played its role. The real question is how the momentum will be maintained, as corporate capital and governments prepare a new trade agreement. This is precisely the kind of situation that forces development NGOs, for whom any such agreement is a major issue, to clarify where they stand, as well as to recognise the limitations of their role, and show humility with respect to the many other forms of social and collective action.

Given the diverse and in many respects contradictory set of possibilities, we ought perhaps to abandon the search for *the* role of NGOs in development, or *the* role of 'civil society', and even such a thing as an uncontested goal of 'development'. We could concentrate much more on discussing the choices for action and the principles and implicit theoretical assumptions that guide them. We could learn from practice, discussion, and critical thought, rather than referring to ideology or check-lists. This would allow us to assess the real impact of external interventions in situations of poverty and exploitation, and help us to decide where and how to act in the global order. Making assumptions explicit is one way of identifying differences, clarifying choices, and ultimately fostering debate and co-operation among people who are committed in some way to building a better world.

Acknowledgement

I would like to thank Janet Bujra, Donna Pankhurst, and Deborah Eade for reading and commenting on this paper.

Notes

1   If the poverty line is put at US$2 a day, for instance, the figure of those below it is 2.8 billion, almost 50 per cent of the world's six billion people. I am grateful to my colleague, Janet Bujra, for reminding me that the emphasis on global poverty *per se* can conceal the social relationships of exploitation which remain critical to any understanding of poverty and impoverishment.

2   There is an important debate in the field of discourse ethics on this very point, from which Edwards' interest in a dialogic form of engagement derives. The Mexico-based philosopher, Enrique Dussel (1998), for example, challenges the propositions of Jurgen Habermas, with their origins in the 'North'. He argues that the discourse principle must first be realised in the 'community of victims', the majority of whom are in the 'South', as part of the process of recovering the right/ability to speak. I am grateful to Ute Buehler for drawing my attention to this literature.

3   For instance, preliminary findings of the Operations Evaluation Department (OED) of the World Bank on the contribution of NGOs to development effectiveness in Bank-supported projects found that 'NGO partnerships do not always lead to successful outcomes. While NGOs in all their various forms are numerous, the number with proven development capabilities and a willingness to work closely with governments on a meaningful scale — essential in most Bank-supported projects — remains small. This and other factors has led to skepticism among some borrowers and Bank staff about the role of NGOs in Bank operations. For some borrowers, NGOs are viewed more as critics than as potential partners. For some Bank staff, NGOs are seen as adding demands on their time without corresponding benefits' (World Bank NGO Unit Social Development 1998: 13).

4   ALOP is the Latin American Association of Promotion Organisations (Asociación Latinoamericana de Organizaciones de Promoción). FICONG is the Institutional Strengthening and Training Programme for NGOs in Latin America and the Caribbean (Programa de Fortalecimiento Institucional y Capacitación de ONGs de América Latina y el Caribe).

5   International NGOs, many of whom received money from their governments, increasingly adopted the language of efficiency and competence in order to earn their funds, and then demanded it of their partners in the South. See Tina Wallace (1997) on the impact of the 'log-frame'.

6   In the article reprinted in this *Reader*, Edwards and Hulme had observed even in 1992 that 'while NGOs have succeeded in influencing official donors and governments on individual projects and even on some programme themes (such as environment in the case of the World Bank), they have failed to bring about more fundamental changes in attitudes and ideology, on which real progress ultimately depends'.

7   There has been a 20 per cent drop in real terms in Official Development Assistance flows from the OECD Development Assistance Committee countries, from US$60.8 billion in 1992 to US$48.3 billion in 1997. The average proportion of GNP given to overseas aid declined to 0.22 per cent in 1997, less than one-third of the 0.7 per cent target (Rasheed 1999: 25).

8 Edwards, Hulme, and Wallace (1999: 8) suggest that this is because donors still value reliable delivery and financial mechanisms of accountability, for which Northern NGOs are considered to be a safer option than Southern counterparts. In addition, few Southern NGOs have the capacity to deliver large-scale humanitarian relief.

9 This conclusion certainly came out of my own contribution to that volume ('Democracy and development in a divided country: the case of Chile'), which attempted to explain the relationship between the changing nature of the state in Chile, the Pinochet dictatorship, and the 'success' of the macro-economic model of the 1980s and 1990s. The variable of the state and its relative distance from powerful socio-economic interests was a more critical issue than democracy or dictatorship *per se*.

10 To be fair, Marxism often served in the past to provide a common 'language' through which to avoid critical thinking and debate.

11 This debate is replicated in much of the literature. Gellner (1994) articulates the liberal view, while an anthropological critique is found in Hann and Dunn (1996). Wachira Maina raises the policy implications for this distinction in his case study chapter, 'Kenya: the state, donors and the politics of democratisation', in Van Rooy (1999: 134–167); and Mahmood Mamdani (1996) makes it a very central theme.

12 This is the topic of Jude Howell and Jenny Pearce, 'Civil society: technical solution or agent of social change?', forthcoming in a volume of papers delivered at the 1999 Birmingham conference, edited by Michael Edwards, David Hulme, and Tina Wallace.

13 These reflections derive from an unpublished paper that I presented with Sarah Perrigo to the Political Studies Association conference in Nottingham, March 1999, entitled 'From the Margins to the Cutting Edge: challenges facing peace studies in the next millennium'. I am grateful to Sarah for her contribution to our discussion on political theory and peace studies which informs these reflections.

14 An important contemporary discussion not addressed in this Introduction concerns those who see NGOs as part of a voluntary and non-profit sector of increasing political and economic significance. Lester Salamon (1997) and others associated with the journal *Voluntas*, and the Center for Civil Society Studies at Johns Hopkins University, are putting forward a particular construction of the role of non-state organisations that is gaining considerable influence in the academic and policy world.

References

Bombarolo, F. and L. P. Coscio (1998), 'Cambio y fortalecimiento institucioal de las ONGDs en América Latina: el caso de la Argentina', in Valderrama L. M. and L. P. Coscio (1998).

Dussel, E. (1998), *Etica de la Liberación en la Edad de la Globalización y de la Exclusión*, Madrid: Editorial Trotta.

Edwards, M. (1999), *Future Positive: international co-operation in the twenty-first century*, London: Earthscan.

Edwards, M., D. Hulme and T. Wallace (1999), 'NGOs in a Global Future: marrying local delivery to worldwide leverage', background paper (mimeo) to 'NGOs in a Global Future' conference', 10–13 January, University of Birmingham.

Featherston, B. and A. Parkin, in Lee-Anne Broadhead (ed) (1997), *Issues in*

Peace Research, 1997–98, Bradford: Department of Peace Studies, pp. 19–58.

Gellner, E. (1994), *Conditions of Liberty: civil society and its rivals*, London: Hamish Hamilton.

Hann, C. and E. Dunn (eds) (1996), *Civil Society: challenging western models*, London: Routledge.

Holloway, R. (1999), 'Freeing the Citizen's Sector from Global Paradigms. And Trying To Get a Grip on the Moral High Ground', paper presented at 'NGOs in a Global Future' conference, 10–13 January, University of Birmingham.

Howell, J. and J. Pearce (forthcoming), *Civil Society and Development: a critical appraisal*, Boulder CO: Lynne Rienner.

Hulme, D. and M. Edwards (eds) (1997), *NGOs, States and Donors: too close for comfort?*, Basingstoke: Macmillan.

Mamdani, M. (1996), *Citizen and Subject: contemporary Africa and the legacy of Late Colonialism*, Princeton NJ: Princeton University Press.

May, N. (1995), 'Performance and accountability in the New World Order', *Development in Practice* 5(1): 71–73.

Pearce, J. (1993), 'NGOs and social change, facilitators or agents', *Development in Practice* 3(3): 222–7.

Pearce, J. (1997), 'Civil society, the market and democracy in Latin America', *Democratisation* 4(2): 57–83.

Rahnema, M. (1997), 'Towards post-development: searching for signposts, a new language and new paradigms', in M. Rahnema and V. Bawtree (eds), *The Post-Development Reader*, London: Zed Books.

Rasheed, S. (1999), 'Poorest nations and development co-operation: in search of an elusive ethic', *Development* 47(3): 25–30.

Salamon, L. and H. Anheier (1997), *The Nonprofit Sector in the Developing World*, Manchester: Manchester University Press.

Sogge, D. (ed) (1996) *Compassion and Calculation: the business of private foreign aid*, London: Pluto Press and Transnational Institute.

St Clair, J. (1999), 'Seattle diary: it's a gas, gas, gas', *New Left Review*, November/December 1999: 81–96.

Tarrow, S. (1998), *Power in Movement, Social Movements and Contentious Politics*, Cambridge: Cambridge University Press.

Taylor, M. (1997), 'Past Their Sell-By Date? NGOs and their future in development', Seventh Bradford Development Lecture, delivered at the University of Bradford, 11 November 1997.

The Economist, 11–17 December 1999.

UNDP, *Human Development Report 1997*, Oxford: Oxford University Press.

Valderrama L., M. and L. P. Coscio (eds) (1998), *Cambio y Fortalecimiento Institucional de las Organizaciones No Gubernamentales en América Latina*, Buenos Aires: Ediciones FICONG-ALOP.

Van Rooy, A. (ed) (1999), *Civil Society and the Aid Industry*, London: Earthscan.

Wallace, T. (1999), 'NGOs in a Global Future', final conference report (mimeo), Birmingham: School of Public Policy, University of Birmingham.

Wallace, T. (1997), 'New development agendas: changes in UK NGO policies and procedures', *Review of African Political Economy* 24 (71): 33–55.

World Bank (2000), *Entering the Twenty-first Century: world development report 1999/2000*, Washington DC: World Bank.

World Bank NGO Unit Social Development (1998), *The Bank's Relations with NGOs: issues and directions*, Paper No. 28, Washington DC: World Bank.

Scaling up NGO impact on development: learning from experience

Michael Edwards and David Hulme

There are 4,000 non-government organisations (NGOs) engaged in development work in OECD countries alone, and a further ten to twenty thousand in the South. But despite the increasing size and sophistication of the NGO sector, the impact of its activity is often transitory and localised. NGOs often find it difficult to interact effectively with social, economic, and political forces at the national and international levels, with the result that grassroots development efforts can be easily undermined. Faced by this, NGOs are asking themselves searching questions about their future role and effectiveness, and are experimenting with a range of strategies to increase, or 'scale up', the impact of their development work.

With this issue in mind, Save the Children Fund (UK) and the Institute for Development Policy and Management at the University of Manchester convened a workshop in January 1992, to explore the lessons learned so far by the development community in relation to 'scaling up'. Over 80 delegates from around the world, from a range of NGOs, governments, official donor agencies, and academic institutions, attended the event. The issues raised through a number of case study papers (listed at the end of this article), examining four main types of strategy for achieving greater impact, were discussed by delegates in small groups. The strategies were deliberately chosen to encourage the consideration of 'scaling up' in terms much wider than simply increasing the size of NGOs or of NGO-funded development projects. Although larger operational programmes may be one way to increase impact, there are many others. This was confirmed by workshop delegates, who preferred to use the phrase 'increasing impact' to describe the processes under review, rather than 'scaling up', which seemed to imply organisational or programme growth.

The strategies considered at the Manchester workshop were:

- working with and within government structures to influence policy and systems;
- operational expansion;
- national and international lobbying and advocacy;
- strengthening organisations of the poor (including networking and federations).

Other strategies included legal reform, training, alliance-building among NGOs, and what Robert Chambers called 'self-spreading and self-improving': the dissemination of ideas, approaches, and methods of work through interactions among people at distinct levels and in different areas.

Clearly, these strategies are not mutually exclusive, and there is a good deal of overlap between them. Discussion focused as much on the linkages and compromises between the different approaches as on the strategies in isolation. There was, however, general agreement that we should differentiate between strategies which entail the NGO increasing its own size and expanding its operations and those where impact is achieved through some form of transfer to, or catalytic effect on, other organisations. Generally, these two approaches entail different costs and benefits, and it may prove difficult to combine both within a single NGO.

Delegates were at pains to point out that different types of NGO — international donors, intermediaries, networks and federations, and grassroots movements of various kinds — all play different roles in the development process. Therefore, they face diverse choices and alternatives and will adopt different strategies in seeking to increase their impact on development. Added to this was the observation (made with particular force in Somthavil Klinmahorm's paper on Special Education in Bangkok) that 'scaling up' is often a spontaneous process, rather than a result of a pre-planned strategy.

Underlying all these observations is the crucial importance of context in determining which strategy is chosen, and how effective it is in practice. This, allied to the other complicating factors listed above, made generalisation over time and space very difficult. Indeed, there was no attempt in the workshop to arrive at hard-and-fast conclusions, or to identify universal solutions to problems. Instead, delegates considered it was much more important to share ideas and experiences from a rich diversity of backgrounds and contexts than to reach an artificial consensus. What follows is, therefore, a preliminary attempt to sketch out broad themes, to identify particular experiences that seemed significant, and to highlight key issues for further debate.

Increasing impact via co-operation with government

Relationships between governments and NGOs have often been characterised by antagonism, yet there are sound reasons for NGOs to enter into a creative dialogue with the institutions which determine official development policy and deliver basic development services. The state remains the ultimate arbiter and determinant of the wider political changes on which development depends, and it controls the economic and political frameworks within which people and their organisations have to operate.

A number of workshop delegates presented case studies describing their attempts to improve government policy and practice in directions which will ultimately enable poor people to gain more control over their lives in areas such as health, education, and food security. All agreed that this had to be a long-term partnership, since the pace of reform is always slow and subject to continual reverses. Beverley Jones (Christian Aid) and Gebro Wolde (Ministry of Agriculture) highlighted the problems faced in Ethiopia by attempts to introduce a participatory approach to agricultural planning. Recent political changes in Ethiopia may hasten this process, but thus far it has been extremely difficult to generate genuine involvement and 'ownership' by farmers at the grassroots. Similar points were made by Delanyo Dovlo (in relation to health work in Ghana), Jamie Mackie (in a review of the work of Voluntary Service Overseas within government structures in Africa), and Somthavil Klinmahorm (discussing SCF's influence over the special education policy of the Bangkok Metropolitan Administration). In part, these difficulties reflect the inevitable problems of working in poorly-resourced government structures, where salaries and motivation are low, staff turnover is very high, and bureaucratic systems are rigid. There can also be considerable differences in ethos and styles of work between NGOs and governments, a problem cited in the cases of Ethiopia and Mozambique. A number of papers concluded that, despite these constraints, the chances of achieving impact on policy and practice were enhanced when NGOs agreed to work within government structures from the outset. This increased the sustainability of the intervention, and enabled the NGO concerned to understand and deal with the constraints faced by the official system.

A further point of agreement was that personalities and relationships between individuals are a vital element in successful partnerships between governments and NGOs. But, even when these relationships do exist, this is no guarantee of lasting impact. As Klinmahorm's paper demonstrated, it is partly because individuals move on, and partly because there is often a major barrier between the 'pilot project' stage of co-operation (which is heavily dependent on the NGO and one or two like-minded government officials) and the acceptance and diffusion of new approaches throughout the government hierarchy. The key to 'scaling up' successfully via working with government lies in breaking down this barrier; and this requires a deliberate change in strategy on the part of the NGO in question to enlist real commitment at all levels of the system, but particularly at the top. VSO has had some success in doing this by using what Mackie called 'the planned multiplication of micro-level inputs' — the slow and careful evolution of different forms of support which are small in themselves, but ultimately significant in their aggregate effect on policy and practice. Such approaches appear most likely to have impact in smaller countries, where NGOs may have better access to crucial decision-makers.

Overall, the workshop recognised the crucial importance of making government bureaucracies more responsive to grassroots needs, while cautioning against an uncritical acceptance of the ability of NGOs to influence government policy, especially where there are vastly more powerful forces (such as the World Bank) at work. The decision to work *with* but not *for* government must rest on the extent to which the structures under consideration may be reformed, the relationship between government and its citizens, and the level at which influence can be exerted most effectively. International NGOs must take into account the strength of the national NGO sector, and be careful not to undermine its initiatives, before deciding to work with government. NGOs must also calculate the potential opportunity costs involved, and the 'trade-offs' which may exist in relation to other strategies. For example, NGOs may find it difficult to operate simultaneously as a conduit for government and as an agent of social mobilisation; or to work both within government and as an advocate for fundamental change in social and political structures. There are also dangers in NGOs identifying themselves too closely with governments which may subsequently be overthrown or voted out of office. National and international NGOs may well be discriminated against by a new government because of their previous affiliation, however progressive the declared official intentions of the administration. Nevertheless, even under the most authoritarian governments, there are often opportunities for specific policy change within limited fields. One example cited concerned the Ministry of Health in Chile under the Pinochet regime, which developed a highly progressive policy on breast-milk substitutes, with help and advice from local and international NGOs. Overall, there is no intrinsic reason to discount working with government as a strategy for increasing impact, and every reason to explore and experiment with this approach to clarify and reinforce those conditions which lead to success.

The direct approach: 'scaling up' by operational expansion

For many NGOs, the obvious strategy for increasing their impact on development is by expanding projects or programmes which have been judged to be successful. Over the 1980s this approach has been pursued in the South (where it has led to the evolution of a set of big NGOs — so-called BINGOs — in Asia), and in the North (where many NGOs have significantly expanded their operational budgets and staffing, as well as increasing the number of countries in which they work).

- There was no consensus at the workshop about the relative desirability of this strategy, and a large number of delegates argued the 'anti-growth' case. Their concerns about the consequences of NGO operational expansion were several:

- A belief that the comparative advantage of NGOs — the quality of their relationships with beneficiaries, their capacity to experiment, and their capacity to be flexible in relation to local contexts — is lost when they expand.

- The danger that internal organisational objectives, such as job security, increasing employment opportunities, and overtaking competitor NGOs, displace development objectives.

- The likelihood that NGOs' large-scale service-delivery operations will be cited by multilateral assistance agencies such as World Bank, IMF, USAID, as evidence to support the ideological case for the reduction of the scale of public-service delivery systems: this creates worries about the potentially negative impact of such a strategy on the poor majority who do not directly benefit from NGO operations.

Others recognised these concerns, but remained convinced that an expansionist strategy was justified when there was evidence that existing operations were alleviating poverty, and that resources could be acquired to permit a programme to benefit more people.

Presentations fell into two categories: case studies, and analyses of the management issues associated with the growth of NGOs. In the first, Howes and Sattar reviewed the expansion of the Bangladesh Rural Advancement Committee (BRAC), which has become one of Asia's largest NGOs, with a staff of more than 4,500 and an annual turnover of around £10 million. Usefully, they described BRAC's approaches to 'scaling up' under the headings of *additive mechanisms* and *multiplicative mechanisms*. Under the former, they described moves to expand into new geographical areas, and efforts to integrate new activities into existing programmes, or to incorporate complementary project activities (such as the establishment of a crop storage project to facilitate the marketing of products for a successful agricultural programme). Under the latter heading, they described BRAC's policy of encouraging the creation of new developmental organisations, and then withdrawing — an approach which would not entail BRAC's expansion in terms of staff and budgets. In the 1980s, BRAC tended to emphasise the former approach, but more recently it has switched to multiplicative mechanisms.

The distinction between these two strategies raised much interest, and merits further examination. Discussion of multiplicative strategies took place mainly in the session on supporting community-level initiatives (see below). These were highly recommended by delegates, but the focus on the grassroots did mean that little attention was paid to 'multiplying' at other levels. Robert Chambers made this point in his paper on 'self-spreading and self-improving' approaches. He illustrated the potential importance of NGOs that have the capacity to recruit and develop committed individuals who subsequently establish new and (it is hoped) high-quality NGOs. Some agencies explicitly adopt 'seed bed' strategies for nurturing future NGO leaders (for example, Tilonia in India and the Ford Foundation in some regions). Others contribute unintentionally when their staff leave and pursue their own initiatives: for example, the individual responsible for re-awakening Sri Lanka's dormant thrift and credit movement depended heavily on skills and knowledge he had acquired while working for the large national NGO, Sarvodaya Shramadana.

Only limited information was available on the results achieved by expansionist strategies. Howes and Sattar reported that BRAC had achieved 'a large measure of success', and Kiriwandeniya provided data on the developmental achievements of Sri Lanka's Federation of Thrift and Credit Co-operatives as it expanded in the 1980s. These positive experiences need to be tempered, however, with other evidence of expansion leading to reduced impact. Korten (1990: 126) has charted the evolution of the

International Planned Parenthood Foundation (IPPF) from a pioneering, crusading role on a forbidden topic to 'an expensive and lethargic international bureaucracy'. In a similar vein, Dichter (1989: 3), who experimented with geographical project replication for Technoserve for many years, has concluded that 'replication is not what it is cracked up to be'.

Rip Hodson (formerly of Action Aid and currently at the London School of Economics) examined the performance issue, and argued that the disappointing results of some attempts to expand NGO operational activities was 'more likely to be due to management problems than to strategy failure'. From this perspective, the main question is not whether to abandon expansionist approaches. Rather, it is how to manage growth so that organisational structures, systems, and culture do not undermine operational performance. Billis and Mackeith also examined the management dimension, and provided a preview of their current research into the management challenges facing development NGOs based in the UK. Interviews with directors and senior managers of these organisations had revealed a range of problems, a number of which were consistently raised. Most significantly, these included:

- Tensions about decision-making: should it be hierarchical or democratic?
- Tensions between headquarters and field staff.
- Tensions about the ways in which fund-raising staff and operational staff perceive their missions.
- Tensions among staff about the relative merits of growth and no-growth strategies.

There are no standard resolutions for these problems, but Billis and Mackeith pointed to a substantial body of knowledge and experience about the ways in which UK NGOs, tackling domestic problems, have coped with rapid expansion in the 1980s. They suggested that these experiences could have broader relevance than has been appreciated.

The experiences of agencies pursuing expansionist strategies clearly vary, but all cases indicated that such an approach should be adopted only after considerable thought and planning. NGOs taking this approach must plan for the stresses of organisational restructuring and cultural change. They must determine how financially dependent they will become on official aid, and consider the consequences of this for their own accountability. They must face up to the possibility that future options for enhancing impact will be lost (an issue that is further elaborated in the conclusion to this article).

'Scaling up' via lobbying and advocacy

Many of the causes of under-development lie in the political and economic structures of an unequal world: in unfair terms of trade, low commodity prices, and oppressive burdens of debt; in the uneven distribution of land and other resources among different social groups; and in the restrictions and regulations which prevent poor people from making better use of the opportunities they have. It is impossible to address these issues fully through 'development projects'. Action is also needed to lobby for change at the national and international levels. NGOs who choose this route to achieve greater impact must decide between constructive dialogue with the institutions they are trying to lobby (the incrementalist or reformist approach), and 'shouting from the sidelines' (the abolitionist approach). At root, this choice rests on the degree to which the NGO judges that its 'target' is able to be reformed over time.

John Clark (formerly of Oxfam UK and Ireland,[1] but now employed by the World Bank) argued that contemporary global trends provided a unique opportunity for NGOs to influence the future course of development policy among bilateral and multilateral donors. The break-up of Eastern Europe, the higher profile given to NGOs in neo-liberal thinking on 'governance and democracy', increasing interest in environmentalism, and the expanding scale of the NGO sector all combine to provide new and wider opportunities for NGO lobbying on a more significant level. Whether NGOs are able to take advantage of these, Clark argued, depends on the degree to which they are able to develop new skills and manage the move to an age of information rather than project activities. It also depends on new partnerships with grassroots movements which can provide the experience and evidence on which lobbying must be based. In this transition, it may well be that relationships between Northern and Southern NGOs are transformed into a more genuine partnership, as NGOs in the North concentrate much more on international advocacy in support of Southern efforts.

This theme was echoed by Nigel Cross of SOS Sahel, who emphasised the need for new techniques and methodologies (such as oral history) in ensuring that grassroots views were not misrepresented in advocacy work. Ahmed Sa'di, of the Galilee Society for Health Services and Research, argued eloquently for the right of poor people to generate and use their own knowledge and research to advocate their own rights.

Similar themes were raised by Tony Hall (London School of Economics) in his paper on NGOs and the Itaparica hydro-electric scheme financed by the World Bank in Brazil. The success of NGO efforts in this case was based on a combination of pressures on the Brazilian authorities; 'from below' (the popular movements at grassroots level, which resisted the scheme), 'from above' (the international NGOs which lobbied the World Bank), and from the Bank itself. The key question becomes how to strengthen complementarities between local and international action in different political and economic contexts. What new skills will be required of NGOs in this task, what new forms of information, and what new partnerships or alliances?

In the case of the Voluntary Health Association of India (VHAI), Alok Mukhopadhay argued that success in lobbying for changes in the health policy of central government is strongly rooted in action, organisation, and information at the grassroots. If this were not the case, there would be a real danger that advocacy might become merely rhetorical. The sheer size of the network represented by VHAI is a powerful factor in encouraging the Indian Government to respond to pressure. Conversely, the example of SOS Sahel shows the impact that a small NGO can have by concentration on a particular 'niche' activity (in this case, social forestry development in the Sahel), and by lobbying for change based on this fairly narrow but immediate experience. As in other approaches to scaling up, context is all important in determining the effectiveness of lobbying by NGOs. The success of VHAI is possible only in a relatively open democracy and with the kind of free press that exists in India. To give another example, John Parry-Williams demonstrated how SCF UK was able to assist the Ugandan authorities in developing a better legal framework to protect children's rights because this issue enjoyed high-level political support at the time.

On a more critical note, Chris Dolan's assessment of the future of lobbying by NGOs in the UK concluded that a major collaborative effort on the scale required to achieve greater impact on macro-level issues was unlikely to take shape. British NGOs, Dolan argued, lack the shared vision and ideology to make such an alliance a reality, and are prevented from coming together by increasing competition for funds. He also identified weak linkages *within* NGOs (between programme work and advocacy) as a barrier to effective lobbying, particularly important given the perceived need for lobbying to grow out of practical experience. Whether NGOs generate this experience directly or via their 'partners' is another matter, but this linkage was seen as essential if NGOs' advocacy is to gain credibility in the eyes of official donors. In the case of British NGOs, it is indispensable under the conditions imposed on such activities by UK charity law. Pleas were made, therefore, for Northern NGOs to be much clearer about the issues on which lobbying by individual agencies was likely to be effective and issues where collective action was essential, and to come together around these in a much more forceful way.

Legitimising NGO advocacy in the eyes of donors and governments was seen as an essential task for the 1990s, particularly in view of the increasing tendency for donors to view NGOs as implementers of projects and providers of services, rather than as participants in a dialogue on policy. Indeed, there were calls for NGOs to play a more active role in training the staff of bilateral and multilateral agencies. Perhaps surprisingly, however, examples were cited in which participation by NGOs in 'safety-net' programmes (designed to compensate for the harmful effects of structural adjustment) had actually strengthened their ability to lobby multilateral donor agencies on behalf of the poor. The best example of this seemed to be the Economic and Social Fund financed by the World Bank in Bolivia. Although in this particular case participation in welfare projects enhanced people's capacity to lobby for improvements in the delivery of services, the same might not be true in other countries. Again, context is crucial.

It is not just official donor agencies which need to be convinced of the value of NGO lobbying, but also the members of the general public who support NGOs in the North. A number of papers highlighted the importance of development education in the North in generating more public support for new NGO roles, and specifically for NGOs' advocacy work.

In conclusion, while NGOs have succeeded in influencing official donors and governments on individual projects, and even on some programme themes (such as the environment in the case of the World Bank), they have failed to bring about more fundamental changes in attitudes and ideology, on which real progress ultimately depends. There is some evidence that there are certain 'softer' issues (such as health, education, and child welfare) which are easier to lobby on than others (such as land reform and economic policy). All lobbying (at least by charities in the UK) must be carefully formulated, and this means that the NGO agenda for advocacy must demonstrably grow out of grassroots experience if it is to claim to 'speak for the poor'.

Indeed, it was this theme — the need to link grassroots action and experience with lobbying and advocacy at the national and international levels — which emerged most strongly in the workshops.

Supporting community-level initiative: mobilisation, networking, and federation

A number of papers focused on strategies to increase impact by fostering the growth of self-governing grassroots organisations (GROs) and people's or popular organisations (POs), and encouraging them to link up through networks and federations. This approach was strongly supported because of its perceived capacity to permit a scaling up of impact without weakening the organisation's claim to legitimacy, or compromising its accountability to its membership.

In such a strategy, the major task of NGOs is to serve as an intermediary to accelerate the pace of the creation of GROs, provide them with assistance as they expand, and foster links between them. A rapid expansion in the numbers and capacities of such groups was seen as permitting not merely an increase in their development 'projects', but a much greater impact on state policies and on local, regional, and national political processes. Among delegates, however, opinions differed over whether the broader benefits of the proliferation of GROs would come from their contribution to political pluralism, or whether a more aggressive orientation, directly confronting oppressive social forces, was required.

The papers in this session took on a Latin flavour with two papers on the Philippines (Latin Asia), one on Central and South America, and another on Peru. The recent experience of the Philippines was of great interest, as the last decade has seen an extraordinary growth in the number of locally registered NGOs (around 18,000) and the establishment of numerous networks and federations. Karina Constantino-David described the problems arising from this explosion of voluntary organisations, and examined the experience of the Caucus of Development NGO Networks (CODE-NGO) in its attempts to create a forum through which NGOs could collaborate without compromising their individual philosophies and activities. The rapid growth of the voluntary sector in the country has been associated with the registration of large numbers of 'mutant' organisations that falsely claim to be non-government or non-profit-making. By Constantino-David's estimates, only about 2,000 organisations can be regarded as genuine development NGOs. Over the 1980s, these interacted in various ways, and by 1988 three-quarters of them had affiliated with one of the country's ten national NGO networks. At that time, discussions were opened to see if these networks, and their constituent NGOs, could find a framework for joint action and collaboration. Many of the NGOs concerned expected this to be feasible, given the extraordinary heterogeneity of the constituency. A gradual approach — focusing on consensus-building exercises, developing trust, extending personal relationships, and preparing a 'covenant' for NGOs — permitted the establishment of CODE-NGO. Clearly, it is too early to comment in detail on the performance of the Caucus. But the initial achievements — including the creation of a self-regulatory mechanism, a women's bank, collaborative policy advocacy, and collaborative personnel development activities — augur well for the contribution of this 'super-network'. The vision it has is to develop a people's movement in the Philippines to challenge the present narrow base of political power.

The work of the Philippine Rural Reconstruction Movement (PRRM) was examined by Horacio 'Boy' Morales. At present, this involves intensive social mobilisation at village level in five districts, forming associations and co-operatives that combine into a People's Council which will prepare a District Development Plan. Ultimately, PRRM intends to extend this model across the nation, fostering a transfer of power from the present nexus (between the state, big business, and the church) to People's Councils. In the early stages of the process, PRRM has already become aware that this will entail vast expansion in its own staff and financial resources. Clearly this has considerable significance for operations, in terms both of sustainability and the compromises that might occur if the Movement seeks large-scale external support.

Diana Mitlin and David Satterthwaite summarised an extensive study conducted by the International Institute for the Environment and Development (IIED) on the provision of shelter and urban services in Latin America. This had found that it was essential to rely more on community-based organisations, as both the state and private business lacked the capacity to provide such services effectively. Although such groups sometimes formed spontaneously, there was sometimes a need for intermediary NGOs to stimulate their formation, provide them with support, and help them to form partnerships with central and local government agencies and financial institutions. A major finding of the IIED study was that the NGOs that performed best, in terms of expanding housing and service provision, concentrated on pulling in the financial and technical resources of other agencies for use by community-based organisations, rather than on stepping up their own provision of direct services.

Linkages were also seen as being of great importance in Elsa Dawson's paper on the SCF-supported Villa El Salvador Health Project in Peru. This case study highlighted the synergy or mutual enhancement between building community capacity and lobbying on policy. The credibility gained and information generated by involvement at the local level strengthened the lobbying activities of the Peruvian NGO (INCIDES), which in turn increased the likelihood of policy reforms that would support community-based health initiatives. Judith Randel's paper on Action Aid activities in Uganda also illustrated the potential for community-based initiatives to be used as an entry point for developing a policy dialogue with the World Bank.

ACORD's twenty years of experience in local institutional development in Africa were analysed in detail by Chris Roche. He described the collapse of ACORD's early attempts to create structures for poverty alleviation by close collaboration with government agencies at district and regional levels, and attributed this to a lack of consideration of the organisation of beneficiaries at the grassroots. This was replaced by a direct operational approach in the early 1980s. In turn, this has been supplanted by a strategy of social mobilisation at village level, and establishing alliances and federations between grassroots organisations. The initial results are promising, and are consistent with contemporary attempts to help to strengthen democratic practices in Africa. However, by its nature the strategy is slow to show results, and it is highly dependent on context. Roche illustrated the way a change of regime in one country had led to policy reforms that made ACORD's new approach more difficult to implement.

In summary, the workshop reconfirmed the importance to NGO activities of local capacity building. In addition, it emphasised the need of NGOs to assist grassroots organisations to make links through networks and federations that strengthen them (in terms of advocacy, leverage over resources, or access to technical expertise) without their having to sacrifice autonomy to the state, to donors, or to intermediary NGOs.

Conclusion: some lessons and key issues

Not surprisingly, the extensive workshop proceedings indicate there are no straightforward answers to the question of how to enhance the impact of NGOs on development. There are strong arguments for the adoption of any, or all, of the strategies that we have identified. But each faces significant obstacles that must be overcome if it is to be effective; and the efficacy of all of them can be challenged by critical counter-arguments. It is simply not feasible to assume that there can be an 'optimal' strategy that can be given unequivocal endorsement. Proposals about the selection of 'scaling up' strategies need to be based on a contingency theory that recognises the differing capacities of individual NGOs and the significance of context-specific factors. This does not, however, imply that all strategies are equally valid: NGOs have considerable room for manoeuvre in their choices, and in each specific context there will be more and less effective mixes of strategies for attaining development goals.

Southern and Northern NGOs need to think more imaginatively about the forms of 'partnership', the styles and structures of management, and the types of information that will underpin the new roles they must adopt if they are to take a position on the centre stage. Clearer conceptual frameworks must be developed for the analysis of relationships between Northern and Southern NGOs, and with grassroots or community organisations; the types of federations and networks to which they might ally; the gains and losses incurred by adopting different strategy mixes. Greater priority must be given to documenting strategies, and monitoring and evaluating outcomes, if experience is to contribute effectively to the selection of future strategy. For Northern NGOs, a major challenge is to work out how they can contribute to institutional development in the South.

A summary of the tentative lessons that can be drawn from experience, and a listing of the key issues that must be considered when a choice is being made, is presented below. Such a framework and listing is by no means comprehensive, and requires elaboration. For example, it does not include what Robert Chambers calls 'self-spreading and self-improving' approaches. These are approaches whereby techniques developed by NGOs, such as participatory rural appraisal, are spontaneously diffused, or where new NGOs are created by staff with previously gained experience in established NGOs. This is significant, because it draws attention to the processes by which the next generation of fledgling and experimental NGOs evolves. It points to the possibility of an NGO enhancing the overall impact on development by assisting its best young staff to set up new agencies!

Scaling up via co-operation with governments

Lessons

- NGOs must work within the constraints of government systems that are for many reasons resistant to change.
- Personal relationships with key staff are crucial.

- The problems of employing expatriate staff, such as unsustainability and problems of handover, must be thought through.
- High mobility of government staff reduces the impact of advice and training: tackle this issue if feasible.
- Allow government to take the credit for success.
- Plan for very long time horizons.
- Recognise that the influence of larger donors on policy reform outweighs that of NGOs: select a complementary strategy to lobby donors as appropriate.

Key issues

- Can governments be reformed? If so, which types should one focus on?
- How should Northern NGOs relate to Southern governments?
- How should NGOs cope with the practical difficulties of working within government systems?

Scaling up via operational expansion

Lessons

- NGOs adopting this approach must anticipate dramatic strains as organisational culture and structures change.
- Sustainability should be planned from the start, especially in terms of finance, workforce, and legal considerations.
- Extensive pursuit of the preferences of donors for service delivery is likely to convert NGOs from agencies with a distinctive vocation and ethos into public-service contractors.
- This strategy may place limits on other approaches: for example, the tone of advocacy work and the scale of social mobilisation may be compromised.

Key issues

- Does operational expansion automatically reinforce existing power structures?
- Do the needs of donors define a narrow role for NGOs in terms of strategies and activities?
- Does expansion reduce accountability to those on whose behalf the NGO works, including its supporters?
- Can NGOs expand operations without becoming bureaucracies?

- Does operational expansion by NGOs displace the state and strengthen policies of liberalisation and unfettered markets?
- Are there any services that *only* NGOs can provide, so that operational expansion is the only option?

Scaling up via lobbying and advocacy

Lessons

- To date, NGOs' influence has been confined largely to projects rather than to fundamental attitudes and ideology.
- Donors are keen to see NGOs as project implementers, rather than participants in a policy dialogue.
- NGOs' knowledge of donors is partial, and this limits their impact.
- A basis in practical experience is important for NGOs to generate information and enhance their credibility.
- British charity law significantly determines the work of UK NGOs with charitable status in the sphere of lobbying and advocacy.

Key issues

- How to carry out successful advocacy while remaining within British charity law?
- How to balance programme work with advocacy and lobbying, and link the two more closely?
- Which issues and targets are most important for advocacy and lobbying?
- Should NGOs seek to focus their advocacy work on symptoms or causes, programme design, or underlying ideology?
- How can Northern and Southern NGOs combine to influence donors more effectively?

Scaling up via supporting local initiatives

Lessons

- The opportunity for effective involvement in work at the local level is very dependent on the attitude of the state. Where such approval is denied, NGOs must carefully analyse their options for being either 'apolitical' or partisan.

- Official aid agencies are unwilling to support serious initiatives to mobilise and empower disadvantaged groups.
- Many NGOs are happy to obfuscate the extent to which their social mobilisation programmes are intended to empower or deliver services. At times this may be a tactical device, but commonly it is based upon an unwillingness to make this key decision.

Key issues

- Should strategies of social mobilisation be the major role for Southern and Northern NGOs in the future?
- What steps can be taken to ensure that grassroots organisations are controlled by their members, and do not merely follow the dictates of their sponsoring NGO?
- Are regional or continental patterns of social mobilisation very different? If so, what might Africa or Asia learn from Latin America, and *vice versa*?
- Should networks of local organisations remain politically unaffiliated, or should they openly align with political parties?
- What are the implications for empowerment work when 'parent' NGOs become heavily involved in mounting service-delivery activities financed by international donors?
- How can cadres of professional social mobilisers be developed without a reduction in the quality of relationships with intended beneficiary groups?

Three particular points should be noted in relation to the findings and issues identified above.

1 All 'scaling up' strategies have implications for the links (to community-based or grassroots organisations, the 'poor', volunteers or private contributors) through which NGOs base their claim to legitimacy, i.e. their right to intervene in the development process. The degree to which a strategy compromises the logic by which legitimacy is claimed needs to be carefully considered, and can provide a useful means of testing whether organisational self-interest is subordinating the fundamental aims when a choice is being made.

2 Related to the above is the recognition that increasing interest and support for NGOs among official donor agencies may create a predisposition, or foster a shift, towards operational and organisational expansion. These incentives need to be treated cautiously, because decisions to expand with official finance may have various unwelcome

consequences: for example, they may close off potential courses of action; or make NGOs feel more accountable to their official donors than to their intended beneficiaries; or imply support for policies of wholesale economic liberalisation.

3 The interactions between different strategies need to be carefully considered. Several case studies demonstrated that strengthening local initiatives and lobbying for policy change may be mutually reinforcing. Agencies should ensure that they are taking full advantage of such potential synergy. More research is needed to explore such relationships and the conditions which encourage their development.

4 Clearly, 'scaling up' the impact of NGOs on development is not synonymous with expanding the staff and budgets of the NGOs themselves. The choices facing NGOs are complex, since all options seem certain to generate internal organisational problems, and all require careful political analysis to gain an insight into who gains and who loses when a particular option, or set of options, is selected. Either by design or by default, all NGOs will have to make these strategic choices in the coming years. The quality of the decisions taken will be a major determinant of whether or not they manage to make a difference on a scale commensurate with the issues they were set up to address.

Note

1 Since this article was first published, Oxfam UK and Ireland has become two organisations: Oxfam GB, and Oxfam Ireland.

List of workshop papers

(These papers represent the views of the individuals who presented them, and without prior agreement should not be attributed to the organisations to which they are affiliated.)

Billis, D. and J. Mackeith, 'Scaling Up NGOs: the management dimension', London School of Economics, University of London.

Chambers, R., 'Self-Spreading and Self-Improving: a strategy for scaling up?', Institute of Development Studies, University of Sussex.

Clark, J., 'Policy Influence, Lobbying and Advocacy: lessons of experience from global advocacy work', International Economic Relations, World Bank.

Constantino-David, K., 'The Caucus of Development NGO Networks: the Philippine experience in scaling up NGO impact', College of Social Work and Community Development, University of the Philippines.

Cross, N., 'Small is Neat: the influence of niche NGOs on development policy and practice', SOS Sahel.

Dawson, E., 'The Villa El Salvador Health Project, Peru', Institute of Development Studies, University of Sussex.

Dolan, C., 'Will British NGOs Scale Up Their Advocacy and Lobbying in the 1990s?', Wits Rural Facility.

Dovlo, D., 'Government-NGO Partnership in Sustaining Health Care Services in Ghana', Save the Children Fund, Ghana.

Edwards, M. and D. Hulme, Theme Paper: 'Scaling Up NGO Impact, Learning from Experience', Save The Children Fund.

Hall, T., 'Itaparica: NGOs and the politics of empowerment', London School of Economics, University of London.

Hodson, R., 'Small, Medium or Large: the rocky road to NGO growth', London School of Economics, University of London.

Howes, M. and M. G. Sattar, 'Bigger and Better? an assessment of BRAC's scaling up strategies, 1972–1991', Institute of Development Studies, University of Sussex.

Jones, B., 'The FFHC Agricultural Programme in Southern Ethiopia', Christian Aid.

Kiriwandeniya, P. A., 'Walking the Tightrope: expanding the Federation of Thrift and Credit Co-operative Societies in Sri Lanka', SANASA, Sri Lanka.

Klinmahorm, S. and K. Ireland, 'NGO-Government Collaboration in Special Education in Bangkok', Save The Children Fund, Thailand.

Mackie, J., 'Multiplying Micro-Level Inputs to Government Structures', Voluntary Service Overseas.

Marsden, D., 'A Case Study of the Aga Khan Rural Support Programme in Northern Pakistan', Centre for Development Studies, University College of Swansea.

Marshaal, J., 'Where There Is No Government: the role of NGOs', University of Palestinian Medical Relief Committees.

Mitlin, D. and D. Satterthwaite, 'Supporting Community-Level Initiatives', International Institute for Environment and Development.

Morales, H., 'NGO Networks in the Philippines', Philippine Rural Reconstruction Movement.

Mukhopadhyay, A., 'Networking and Lobbying in the Health Sector in India', Voluntary Health Association of India.

Parry-Williams, J., 'Scaling Up Impact via Legal Reform in Uganda', Save The Children Fund (UK), Uganda.

Pratt, B., 'Institutional Development: training and management in NGOs', INTRAC, Oxford.

Premchander, S., 'Scaling Up NGO Impact Through Income Generation Programmes', Action Aid.

Randel, J., 'Scaling Up and Community Capacity: some experiences of Action Aid Uganda', Action Aid.

Robinson, M., 'NGOs and Rural Poverty-Alleviation: results of an empirical investigation and its implication for scaling up', Overseas Development Institute.

Roche, C., 'From Scaled-Up, Through Scaling-Down, to Scaling-Up Again: lessons from ACORD's experience in Africa', ACORD.

Sa'di, A. H., 'The Role of Research in NGOs', Galilee Society for Health Services and Research.

Wolde, G., 'NGO Trends in the Agricultural Sector in Ethiopia', Ministry of Agriculture, Ethiopia.

Other references

Dichter, T. W. (1989), 'NGOs and the replication trap', *Findings 1989*, Technoserve.

Korten, D. (1990), Getting to the 21st Century: voluntary action and the global agenda, West Hartford, Connecticut: Kumarian Press.

This article was first published in *Development in Practice* Volume 2, Number 2, 1992.

Help yourself by helping The Poor

Gino Lofredo

How to get rich in the 90s

You still don't have your own EN-GE-OH? You haven't got a non-profit foundation, complete with legal status? Not even a private consulting firm? Then, my friend, you're really out of it. Any professional who hasn't got one of these late twentieth century accessories is lost — clearly someone with no imagination, no sense of opportunity, no strategic vision, out of time and out of place. You might as well forget about your career, and go and sell lottery tickets or become a street busker.

Let me explain. Twenty years ago a newly qualified graduate in the humanities or social sciences had various employment options. He or she could climb up the ministerial ladder, or use their contacts with the students' movement to wangle a university post. Or they could start at the bottom, doing market research for some transnational toothpaste company. If Daddy had the cash, they might start up a business, selling spaghetti, for example. If they liked action films, they could go into the military — or possibly develop a theory of revolutionary armed struggle. If all else failed, they could go and wash plates in Los Angeles or New York.

Today things are different. The state is in collapse and out of fashion. Forward-looking businesses don't want trendy left-wing sociologists, but people who know how to sell things and who can speak English. Setting up a company means playing roulette with the family fortune. The military are unemployed. The guerrillas are dead and buried. To do the washing-up in Los Angeles you need a PhD from some European university.

But, make no mistake, EN-GE-OHs are the business of the 1990s. If you wasted your time studying philosophy, social sciences, history, international relations, literature, pedagogy, political economy, anthropology, journalism, ecology — and anything else that won't earn you a living selling fried chicken — a good EN-GE-OH is your best option. Let me explain.

Fairy tales

To understand what an EN-GE-OH is, you need to understand The Project. It's rather like a fairy tale. Take Cinderella. You know she has problems: her mother dies, then her father, then she's adopted by a wicked stepmother and so gets stuck with two ugly step-sisters. Cinderella has many nice, simple friends, such as little birds and mice. She wants to go to the prince's ball, but she can't. The Fairy Godmother come and fixes things for her. Cinderella goes to the ball. The prince falls in love. More problems come up, but in the end they are married. The birds sing and the mice dance, and everyone's happy. Projects are a bit like that.

Terrible problems afflict good, kind, and simple folk who have harmless beliefs and picturesque customs. Other kindly souls befriend these folk, who've been marginalised by capitalism, and want to help them — but they don't have the means. A representative from an international agency arrives, sees what's needed, uses a special magic spell to get hold of the cash, and everyone lives happily ever after. That is how the story goes.

EN-GE-OHs are a bit like the birds and mice in the fairy tale. They want to help poor people and support the Fairy Godmother as she goes about her noble business. You get the picture. Projects are Fairy Tales. Cinderella is The Poor, or The Beneficiary. The Fairy Godmother is the International Agency representative. The Little Mice are EN-GE-OHs. The Magic Coach is the Funding. And marriage with the Prince is Sustainable Development. The only difference is that in the real world, it's the birds and the mice who marry the prince, and the EN-GO-OHs who ensure their own Sustainable (Self) Development. It all depends on understanding the subtle charm of Projects, and their intimate relationship with EN-GE-OHs.

First step: setting up an EN-GE-OH

First you need to get your legal status sorted out. This is invaluable, especially if someone who's resentful of your relationship with the Fairy Godmother (whom they'd been courting) decides to denounce you to the press, or the police, because of some impropriety committed on the difficult road to Sustainable (Self) Development — such as leading poor

Cinderella up the garden path. To get legal status, you usually need a general secretary, a treasurer, some trustees, and a well-connected contact who'll help you get it through the Ministry. But a word of advice: don't involve other like-minded professionals, if you want to stay at the top.

Second step: the sales pitch

The sales pitch is the aphrodisiac that drives the Fairy Godmothers wild. Here, you have to be up to date and well prepared. For instance, it would be fatal to start talking about Integrated Rural Development, when everyone knows that today we talk about Sustainable Natural Resource Management. You'd be ruled out if you talked about Mother-Child Education when the fashion now is for Peasant Women's Participation. It would be like raving about Michael Jackson to an opera buff. You have to be flexible. An EN-GE-OH Director needs to be familiar with all the existing or potential fads of the Fairy Godmothers. If one of these decides to take up an interest in protecting a threatened species of tropical monkey in Ray-Ban sunglasses, you need to be able to show that from childhood the fate of these endangered animals has been your burning concern.

Third step: public relations

Once you've mastered all the standard jargon — Activities, Conceptual Frameworks, Experience and Background, Aims and Objectives, Human Resources — you're ready for the next step: Public Relations.

Your first aim as the up-and-coming Director of an unknown EN-GE-OH is to get on to the Fairy Godmother circuit. It's one of the hardest features of the New Order of Civil Society. You'll have to hunt down the Fairy Godmothers at all the cocktail parties to open or close seminars, congresses, and international meetings on the following key topics:

- Critical Poverty
- Protecting the Environment
- Protecting Children and other Threatened Species
- Educational Reform
- New Information Order, New Economics Order, and any other New Order that crops up
- Defence of Indigenous Cultures
- Informal Economy and Micro-Enterprise
- Popular Education and Adult Literacy Campaigns
- Information Technology and Development of the Rural Community
- Anything to do with the 'Challenge of the Twenty-First Century'.

You also need to go to the receptions given at the major embassies: Germany, Belgium, Netherlands, USA, Sweden, Italy, and France, as well as those given by UNESCO, UNICEF, FAO, WHO, UNDP, the World Bank, etc.

Basic tips: You need to be on form for these social-cum-professional occasions. It's not just a question of having a few drinks and smiling inanely in a corner. Take a nap before the event, so that you're at your best. Dress well. Always take a load of business cards and a dozen leaflets about your institution. Eat and drink the least amount possible. Learn how to spot a Fairy Godmother at a glance. They are usually fair-haired, tall, and slightly informally dressed. They are also generally surrounded by locals, who are either listening to every word, in a kind of beatific trance, or energetically reciting one of their prepared speeches, with passionate intensity. Alternatively, they might be looking askance as one of the other supplicants is speaking.

You can learn a lot by watching. The important thing is to get a sense of when it's right to make an intervention. What you're aiming for is the incisive remark that cuts the ground from the others' feet, so that the Fairy Godmother will show an interest in you.

There are various risks here. Some are obvious: alcoholism, divorce, partial or total alienation. Others are more serious. Something to be avoided at all costs is to make any ironic or cynical reference to the holy development crusades in which the Fairy Godmothers and their agencies are engaged. Jokes, however well meant, are only for old hands. Don't even risk seeming flippant, until you've got a couple of projects under your belt. And don't be discouraged if it all takes a long time. That's part of the training.

Fourth step: the funding request

Once you've got the Fairy Godmother's ear, you need to lead her gradually to the point where you can present a Funding Request. This is what separates the winners from the losers. And you want to be a winner. So you need to show the Fairy Godmother how well you get on with Cinderella, and that she in turn respects and supports you. To do this, you'll need to expose the Fairy Godmother to the rarefied atmosphere of what is called 'The Field'.

Field Visits: 'Field' is a word much used in the North, where it has a kind of tantric significance. For the Fairy Godmothers, a successful 'field visit' is almost a guarantee of project approval, a one-way ticket to Sustainable (Self) Development. When you feel the Fairy Godmother is ready for a 'field visit', you need to prepare Cinderella and her little friends, and train up a couple of Poor Beneficiary groups. It doesn't matter who they are, or how you get hold of them. The important thing is that they are there when you arrive with the honoured guest from the omnipotent North. No detail should be overlooked. Cinderella and the rest need to look the part, preferably dressed in local costumes. A good tip is to make sure they know a couple of the folk songs that political exiles have made popular in the North. You need lots of emotional colour and human interest. Perhaps you could even throw in a birth, baptism, or burial, just to add to the excitement.

Essentially, you're organising a piece of theatre for the Fairy Godmother, who is prepared to pay to see this played out in the day-to-day life of ordinary people in 'The Field'. So, make sure your actors know what's at stake. If they fail to convince the Fairy Godmother, you won't be able to afford the AppleMac or the Land Cruiser — essential for your image as defender of Sustainable Development. Should the locals start to be uneasy, or demand something in return for their part in the play, tell them you'll build a school, or an access road. Whatever. In any case, they're used to broken promises, and after a drink or two they'll have forgotten everything. The important thing is for the Fairy Godmother to witness your good relations with Cinderella and her friends.

Writing up Proposals: You need to write up the proposal, devise a plan of action, and invent a budget. Some EN-GE-OH Directors work round the clock on these, making sure that everything holds together. But why make problems for yourself? Just hire a couple of unemployed specialists for the smallest fee you can get away with. Tell them that if the project works, they'll be taken on full-time on international salaries. They might fall for it and do the work for free. Two words of warning. First, never let the consultants know which agency you're negotiating with, to put them off the track. Second, get the consultants to draw up a budget for only half what you intend to request. You alone should manage the budget details.

Budgets: There are two vital elements that shouldn't be left to informal agreements with the Fairy Godmother: your salary and the overhead. There are others too: international training, travel expenses and *per diems*, teaching materials, consultancy fees (to pay back the odd favour here and there at your discretion), and infrastructure. The better you take care of these details, the more rapid will be your rise to Sustainable (Self) Development.

Conclusion: development is a business

Like any other business, the development impresario needs to keep an eye on the competition. As this becomes more intense, you need to spend about half your time running down the opposition. This isn't the world of 'gentlemen's agreements', but of people like yourself who've learned how to help themselves by helping The Poor. Business is a harsh teacher.

But in the end, the ones you need to be most concerned about are the ones who are, in fact, genuine, and who therefore jeopardise everyone's career by putting their rhetoric into practice.

Postscript

Much has changed since I wrote the Cinderella story in the late 1980s, and yet the game is still on; probably more subtle, and probably on a larger scale. Yet, the amount of aid money that goes not to the poor but to the NGO managers has become trivial compared with the colossal sums that are syphoned off the well-intentioned programmes that are promoted by the big multilateral institutions, the billions in loans, and the megaproject budgets; and let us not forget, in this age of private and market-driven utopias, the sums syphoned off the private banking sector and private contractors in developing countries. For example, one single banker at the Banco del Progreso in Ecuador managed to 'disappear' (sic) at short notice, in an offshore labyrinth, some US$1,000 million belonging to 700,000 small depositors. Some independent estimates show that about 15 per cent of the sales in the privatisation of state enterprises in Latin America went to build private fortunes for about 10,000 individuals; that is to say about US$10,000 million in commissions. So, when we trash the NGOs — as so many of them deserve — we should also remember we are discussing the crumbs on the floor while the real banquet is happening elsewhere.

This paper was reprinted from the journal Chasqui, and was published in Development in Practice *Volume 5, Number 4, 1995.*

NGOs: ladles in the global soup kitchen?

Stephen Commins

This paper is a reflection on four questions as they relate to Northern or international NGOs (in this paper, 'NGOs' refers to Northern NGOs unless otherwise indicated):

1 If NGOs are to have a role in a globalised world, will it be primarily as the delivery service for global welfare — ladles in the soup kitchen — or will they find alternative identities?

2 Are NGOs equipped to represent or deliver alternative development models?

3 If funding 'success' often covers weaknesses in NGOs, what are the changes that need to be made in order to deepen and broaden impact?

4 How can NGOs establish their independence and autonomy from governments? Are there ways for them to be both representative (or locally rooted) *and* global? How can NGOs best combine an ambitious vision with a genuine humility?

Owing to the rapid changes in the international political economy, and to the deeply embedded political and social factors in each complex emergency, NGOs are in danger of becoming increasingly marginal in terms of the importance of their work. To put it in stark terms, they are becoming the delivery agency for a global soup kitchen, handing out meagre comfort amidst harsh economic changes and complex political emergencies, in a world that is characterised by global economic integration and the social exclusion of low-income communities, as well as continuing and widespread levels of civil strife. In effect, NGOs are handing out bits of comfort, doling out cups of soup, to the victims of massive economic changes and to the survivors of brutal civil wars. While NGOs have claimed the right to a moral as well as programmatic voice in international affairs, their organisational legitimacy and operational impact are in fact being weakened.

For the past two decades, NGOs have occupied a privileged position in the industrialised countries, both in the public eye and with bilateral donors. NGOs have presented themselves as having a significant impact in shaping donor policies and humanitarian responses. Particularly during the latter part of the 1980s and the early 1990s, NGOs were seen as the most effective and efficient entities for delivering international relief and development programmes. That perception is now changing, which raises questions about the future of the NGO sector.

The various strands of what is described as globalisation are helping NGOs into roles that will minimise their long-term impact. The major institutions shaping the world economy — transnational corporations, capital and currency markets, the governments of the largest developed countries, and the international institutions that are promoting a market-centred agenda (World Bank, IMF, and WTO) — have had an explicit confidence that global integration will promote greater economic benefits worldwide. Yet the World Bank's new report on poverty makes it clear that macro-economic growth by itself does not necessarily reduce poverty and inequity. Further, the economic and social crisis that began in East Asia in mid-1997 has highlighted the instabilities and uncertainties of global markets. NGOs, as organisations that emerged in a bipolar world of North–South and East–West, have not adjusted to the new global landscape. Both in humanitarian emergencies and economic restructuring, NGOs are in danger of becoming useful fig-leaves to cover government inaction or indifference to human suffering.

Increased scrutiny and questioning of future roles is difficult for many NGO staff, who are comfortable in the high moral ground often occupied by these agencies. But there is an increasing body of well-researched literature on the future of NGOs in general, the operational quality of NGO work in development, and the uncertainties facing NGOs and other humanitarian agencies in complex emergencies. A growing number of critical assessments suggest that the operational impact of NGOs in community development was less than claimed. Further, the rise of complex emergencies that are characterised by warlords and banditry has shattered the image of neutral humanitarianism that cloaked the work of NGOs in such places as Ethiopia and Cambodia in the past. Finally, the globalisation of economic relations, the struggle for developing effective national economic policies, and the increase in the clout of NGOs in the 'South' have all presented new challenges in the traditional work of Northern NGOs. They are faced with potential marginalisation as global institutions are reshaped by financial markets, new corporate investment patterns, and the impact of information and communication technologies. By and large, most NGOs in the 'North' have responded with, at best, incremental changes to their practices, without changing core assumptions.

This last point does not mean that NGOs should not have their own programmes of work; nor should NGOs aim only to have an impact on global institutions. Indeed, the 'scaling-up' from programme experience to achieve large programme impact or to affect policy making are among the most important 'value added' aspects of NGO work. Scaling-up can be directed towards local, regional, or national policy issues, as well as global institutions. Linking programme experience and policy making is, however, far less common than most NGOs would care to admit and requires more internal coordination than presently exists. In a world where it is regularly argued by the large global actors and conventional commentators that we are in era of 'TINA' ('there is no alternative to the present drive of global capital'), NGOs can either accept the role of passing out the soup, or they can seek to be something quite different, however difficult that is to achieve.

The future of Northern or international NGOs is now linked to their ability to examine their purpose and goals in a rapidly changing world. A critical examination would offer an opportunity for NGOs to reconsider and reconceptualise their present roles and the future options, not merely in terms of their programmes but in a way that is more fundamentally embedded within their rationale for existence. NGOs need to assess both the existing programme and policy impacts of their work, and potential future options for NGOs that seek to affect global development and humanitarian relief. This requires briefly assessing several levels of NGO work, from local programmes, to relations with national governments, to the complex set of relations that exist with multilateral agencies. Future explorations should be designed to begin with an overview of NGO work at different levels, and then to look at the future of NGOs, given the changing realities of the global economy.

An equally significant question is whether NGOs are increasingly falling short in their responses to complex humanitarian emergencies — the internal wars (Rwanda, Bosnia, Liberia, Sudan) that lead to large-scale disasters that are caused by human agency and usually connected to social and political breakdowns. It is apparent that the humanitarian context for NGO operations has changed considerably in the past decade. The spread of complex humanitarian emergencies has taken an increasing proportion of international assistance, reducing funds available for long-term development. NGOs may well argue that they are not the masters of violent political settings nor of the political aims of donor governments, yet in practice most NGOs have tended to ignore the tough questions of relief and development politics, rather than seeking to determine where they fit and how to maintain a voice and presence of integrity.

The growth and vocal presence of Southern NGOs likewise present a significant challenge to the role and purpose of Northern NGOs in the future. Northern NGOs need to explore critical questions in the area of their organisational legitimacy, their relations of accountability, and the actual impact of their programmes. While Southern NGOs have begun to question the intermediary or lead role taken by Northern NGOs, governments in the South are also taking a harder line on NGO operations and priorities. In the past few years, several governments in Africa have tightened up regulations on NGO registration, NGO programmes, and even whether certain NGOs are welcome to work in the country. Each country has specific circumstances behind the government's actions, but the overall trend is unmistakable. NGOs are viewed more sceptically in terms of whether they can deliver what they promise and whether they are usurping the role of the government in shaping development programmes and priorities. When combined with the increased criticism from Southern NGOs, the overall direction is for reduced room for manoeuvre and greater demands for transparency, quality of programmes, and accountability to institutions of the South rather than donors in the North.

NGOs are in danger of holding on to a world that is passing away. The language in many NGO documents, and the design of many of their programmes, reflect the concerns of yesterday, not the challenges of the coming years. If NGOs are to refuse to accept a role only as welfare providers, they need to undertake more radical and deeply rooted changes than have yet emerged within most organisations. NGOs have a unique depth of experience in both development and complex emergency settings that could feed into new models of good practice and innovation, as well as policy making. If NGOs were able to work in new partnerships among themselves (which is still too rare in terms of depth and continuity), with sympathetic research groups (not extractive academics), and allies among donors, they could have an impact both on their own internal operations and on wider policy making decisions.

The challenge for each NGO is to locate itself as one of a number of NGOs struggling to determine a future role in international development and humanitarian trends, and also within wider global changes. NGOs need to place their work and overall effectiveness within a wider framework of political, economic, and social changes ('globalisation'), so that the assessment is realistic in terms of options for the NGO sector in the future. The major global institutions and most powerful bilateral donors at times appear to want NGOs to be the ladles, to serve as the front line for global welfare. There are very few coherent ideals or visions about a global future other than in the Washington Consensus of market liberalisation, with the costs of economic integration temporary and less than the global gains. Indeed, out of the East Asia crisis, as many questions are coming from parts of the World Bank or UN agencies as from NGOs. Given the external context, NGOs can either limit their role to providing succour amidst the pain and marginalisation around them, or they can seek to build from their programme experiences to alternative policy frameworks, ones that are modest, non-utopian, and yet willing to challenge a global future that appears to exclude more than it includes.

This paper was first published in Development in Practice *Volume 9, Number 5, in 1999.*

Collaboration with the South: agents of aid or solidarity?

Firoze Manji

In line with other donor countries, the United Kingdom has been channelling a significant proportion of its development aid through non-government organisations (NGOs). As part of a review of the effectiveness of this form of aid, several studies have been commissioned by the British Overseas Development Administration (ODA).[1] The latest study focused on exploring British development NGOs' attitudes to increasing the proportion of aid channelled by the ODA directly to Southern NGOs (Bebbington and Riddell 1995). Based on a questionnaire survey, this study provides a fascinating insight into the British NGO (BINGO) psyche. It suggests that, despite years of exposure to and interactions with the Third World, there remains a considerable deficit of respect and trust for their counterparts in the South.

According to the survey, most (80 per cent) of BINGOs are opposed to aid being channelled directly to Southern NGOs, for a number of reasons. They allege that Southern NGOs

- lack the experience to undertake rigorous monitoring and evaluation of projects;
- lack experience of how to manage projects in accordance with donors' requirements;
- with direct funding, would shift their accountability away from their own constituencies towards donor agencies;
- would become more directly influenced by donor agencies in setting their agenda, and hence more 'donor-driven';
- would eventually revolve more around the availability of money than the meeting of needs;

- would end up filling a void created by a retrenching state;
- would be susceptible to manipulation by donor agencies, and more susceptible to political influence.

In addition, they argue, there would be a loss of the 'neutrality' provided by BINGOs; and it would be cheaper to fund projects in the South via BINGOs.

What is striking about this list of reasons against direct funding of Southern NGOs is that, were logic to prevail, most Northern NGOs would not qualify to receive funds from ODA either. Are these characteristics really the exclusive property of Southern NGOs? To what extent are they shared by their Northern counterparts? Let us look at the reasons individually, and then as a whole.

In my experience, very few NGOs — either in the North or the South — can, with all honesty, always claim to demonstrate their extensive experience of monitoring, management, and proper evaluation of projects. Most agencies will admit that virtually all NGO projects fail to demonstrate adequate monitoring and evaluation. Poor management has been the bane of many projects, something that has become increasingly recognised if attendance rates at project-management training courses are anything to go by. Most experienced development NGOs would probably agree that monitoring and evaluation could be improved, and even the long-established BINGOs are frequently criticised for not managing their projects in accordance with the donors' requirements.

What about accountability? Most BINGOs are non-membership organisations. As such, they are rarely accountable to anyone other than a self-appointed Board. In most cases, even those who contribute regularly to the organisation have no rights to determine its policy or to elect its Trustees. In almost every case, their constituency — if one understands that to mean either those who directly benefit from the projects, or the Southern NGOs — has no rights to determine a BINGO's policy or practice. So how accountable are BINGOs? Certainly, they are required to be accountable 'upwards' to their donors, an accountability for which there are both structural mechanisms and rights embodied in the grant documents (if not in law). But such mechanisms are seldom accorded to their Southern partners (or their beneficiaries). Would it not, therefore, be fair to say that, for the majority of BINGOs, accountability has long ago shifted away from their constituencies towards the donor agencies? Have BINGOs perhaps not been interested in establishing structural mechanisms that could increase, over time, the degree to which they could become accountable to their Southern counterparts?

How many BINGOs have, for example, representatives of their Southern counterpart organisations on their Board of Trustees? That this is more the exception than the rule speaks volumes about their concern for ensuring their own 'downward' accountability.

Can BINGOs really claim to be immune from the influence of donor agencies? Are they not guilty not only of being driven by these but also, in turn, of setting and influencing the agenda of their Southern counterparts — with whom, let us be clear, they have a donor-recipient relationship? Looking at the kinds of projects and programmes in which BINGOs have been involved over the last three decades, it is clear that the focus of their attention shifts with the trends and fancies of the donor agencies. Project proposals and reports, for example, mimic the latest jargon ('modernism', 'environment', 'sustainable development', 'civil society' and so on) on which ODA has decided to focus. When donor agencies hold the money, is it surprising that NGOs are prone to being driven by their agenda?

Do BINGOs always respond to need, rather than to the source of potential funding? Looking at the proportion of ODA's funds which have moved from the poorest parts of the world towards, for example, Eastern Europe and the former Soviet Union, a shift equally reflected in the funding profiles of many NGOs, many observers might feel that need tends to be a neglected parameter for determining priorities. Wherein lies the justification for the claim that British development NGOs are any more likely than Southern NGOs to respond to needs rather than chasing after money?

As for filling the void of a retrenching state, one needs only look at the British indigenous NGO scene over the last decade. As successive governments have clawed back social expenditure, numerous charities have ardently rushed to fill the vacuum. Is there any evidence that Southern NGOs are any more prone to this phenomenon than their British counterparts?

Claims that British NGOs are somehow more 'neutral' than Southern ones are hard to take seriously, and suggest a depth of paternalism that is surprising at this end of the twentieth century. Like their missionary precursors one hundred years ago, British NGOs have for years played, and continue to play, a less than neutral role with respect to the interests of British foreign policy, of which overseas development assistance is not an insignificant part. BINGOs have their own biases and prejudices, as this survey so clearly demonstrates. Just because these prejudices are so widely held does not mean they should be taken to represent a form of neutrality. The tragedy may be, if BINGOs tend to be neutral, it is frequently in relation to the less than benign role of British imperial policies.

The arguments advanced by British NGOs against direct funding hide a more profound discomfort. I believe this may be an expression of the primordial fear among some BINGOs that if donor agencies start funding Southern organisations directly, their own future is at risk: it is the *cri du coeur* of the dinosaur facing potential extinction. It is tempting to draw the conclusion that the *raison d'être* for development may no longer be to build sustainable development and institutions in the South, but rather to keep the home team going. Direct funding of Southern NGOs does, of course, represent a direct threat to the survival of Northern NGOs in their present form. What is required, surely, is a discussion about what the new role of Northern NGOs should be in an era where Southern NGOs are fully able — at least to the same degree as BINGOs — to manage funds provided directly to them by donors.

Are there not also good reasons to question the commitment, capacity, and willingness of British NGOs to 'build capacity' in the South? The results of this survey suggest that, after more than 50 years of 'development', British NGOs feel that they have signally failed to build viable, independent, sustainable Southern institutions, institutions capable of managing donor agencies' attempts to manipulate them, able to run programmes effectively and carry out rigorous monitoring and evaluation. If this is so, what exactly has been the purpose of their activities over the last few decades? Are we to assume that pronouncing a commitment to 'sustainable development' and institutional capacity building is just public relations for the benefit of the 'punter' whose contributions are being sought?

This raises a serious issue: is it feasible for an organisation to be effective in institutional capacity building if, at the same time, its relationship with its Southern counterpart is mediated through money? From the perspective of most Southern NGOs, there may be, in effect, little difference between dealing with ODA and dealing with a Northern NGO, since in both cases the relationship is one of donor-recipient. No matter how sympathetic the donor may be, the fact that the Northern NGO is the one with the money means that the Southern NGO must be the one with the begging bowl. No matter how good the personal relationship between the Northern NGO and the Southern NGO, the latter must accept the humiliation of being the receiver of charity. Perforce, there is a relationship of unequals. And inequality never built capacity: it nurtures dependence; it establishes the material basis for dancing to the tune of the donor.

My purpose here is not to argue the case for or against direct funding of Southern NGOs by ODA. But I am deeply uneasy about the underlying motives of BINGOs that lead them to oppose such funding. What is perhaps more disturbing is the lack of critical assessment of ODA's policies, especially in assessing the extent to which BINGOs are themselves being used by the British State in the same way that they fear Southern NGOs might be used if the money were channelled to them directly. Five hundred years of British good will in Africa and elsewhere in the Third World has been characterised by pillage, slavery, genocide, colonisation, and more recently a development paradigm that results in more wealth flowing from the South to the North than the other way around (aid budgets notwithstanding). And this is to say nothing of the support and arms provided to despots and dictators. By now, one would have thought a healthy scepticism about British foreign policy and development aid would be the norm. Perhaps BINGOs should be looking at how they themselves might be being used and manipulated by donor funds, just as they so perspicaciously highlight the risks faced by Southern NGOs.

What is needed today is a greater reflection by Northern NGOs on the nature of their relationship with their Southern counterparts. If we are seriously committed to the struggle to eliminate poverty and injustice and their causes, then we need to assess the degree to which the nature of that relationship may be hampering rather than enhancing our common goals. We need to examine how to build alliances with Southern NGOs that are based on solidarity, not charity. We need to look at whether we are being used, albeit unconsciously, by aid agencies to achieve ends that subvert rather than promote those values we hold dear. We need to question whether the overall effect of British aid has indeed led to improving the conditions of the poor in the South, and, if not, after all these years of trying, to ask why. We need to explore ways in which we can be as accountable to our Southern partners as we expect them to be to us. And we need to break away from the tradition of paternalism which has been so lucidly revealed in the recent study. To do otherwise is to risk becoming the agents of aid.

Note

1 Since this article was first published, ODA has been superseded by DFID, Department for International Development.

Reference

Bebbington, A. and R. Riddell (1995), *Donors, Civil Society and Southern NGOs: new agendas, old problems*, London: IIED/ODA.

This paper was first published in Development in Practice *Volume 7, Number 2, 1997.*

Corporate governance for NGOs?

Mick Moore and Sheelagh Stewart

Problems

In terms of the volume of official funding, the development NGO sector has been enjoying a boom since the early 1980s. Stimulated by concerns about the excesses of 'statism' and attracted by notions of 'strengthening civil society', bilateral and multilateral aid donors switched significant fractions of their budgets from national governments to NGOs.[1] Many countries saw an explosive growth in the number and variety of development NGOs. Endowed as it is with a high proportion of reflective and self-critical thinkers, the NGO community was not content simply to bask in the sunshine. There has been a ferment of concern, first about possible malign effects of this growth on the ethics, values, and organisational competence of NGOs, and, increasingly, about how to adapt to a less luxuriant future with a decline in the rate of funding increases.

The problems have been diagnosed in many different ways, and a wide variety of solutions propounded. It is, however, striking that there appears to have been very little discussion of an option that would be considered standard for a sector of private business whose products or procedures had come under serious critical public criticism and scrutiny: the introduction of collective self-regulation in order to re-establish public confidence in the sector. We argue that such collective self-regulation could make a significant contribution to solving four generic problems faced by development NGOs in poor countries, NGOs that depend to a significant extent on foreign funding. These are labelled the 'accountability', 'structural growth', 'evaluation', and 'economies of scale' problems respectively. We first summarise these problems and then explain how collective self-regulation could help remedy them.

1 The Accountability Problem

This has both a 'real' and a 'perceived' dimension. The 'real' problem is quite clear and is articulated repeatedly by friends and critics of NGOs alike:

> Who are these people accountable to? They set themselves up as specialists and experts on problems that they define themselves, live entirely on foreign money, and can do what they want provided they keep their funders happy. They claim to speak on behalf of the poor, the disadvantaged, women, the disabled, AIDS victims or whatever, but how do we know that they are in any way representing or serving their clients?

These concerns are not entirely misplaced. It is clear that some NGOs are not accountable even in the most narrow sense of the term, i.e. they are not in practice sanctioned if they fail to use their budgets for the purposes that their financiers intend. And most of that money is *public*: not necessarily 'public' in the sense that it comes from a government, but in the sense that it is given by a public somewhere and/or, more importantly, it is explicitly intended to have impacts over issues that in contemporary democracies are regarded as being the legitimate business of the state. Further, insofar as money is given to NGOs for the purposes of advocacy or to 'strengthen civil society', it is intended to change the way in which public business is done. Every widely accepted concept of good governance requires some kind of public accountability of organisations that (a) use public money and/or (b) are intended to influence public business. The widespread perception of weak or absent accountability becomes a problem for NGOs — and their funders — in many countries. Many national governments with an authoritarian streak view NGOs as a threat. They use the non-accountability of NGOs — or accountability to no-one except wealthy foreign organisations — as an excuse to harass and control them.

2 The Structural Growth Problem

Once they are successful, small businesses world-wide commonly face the problems of replacing one-person-management (or family-management) with a more institutionalised structure. The founder is used to having total control and doing things his or her way. It is difficult to persuade her/him to create independent management or expert roles, or to respect the authority and autonomy of independent managers and experts once they are in place. The founder wants to continue to hire and fire staff as s/he feels like it, or to be the only person with full access to the accounts. It is at this point — when individual or family management ceases to match up to needs — that many small businesses fail to realise their potential, or simply fail. There are close parallels with NGOs, which are often founded and run by individuals or small groups who are dedicated to the organisation and the cause it represents. Perhaps they see their own dedication and commitment as the reason for success, and feel they are entitled to reap the fruits of success, even if these fruits only come in the form of such intangibles as recognition, respect, and status. Like small business people, the founders of NGOs may not want to share managerial authority and status with newcomers at the point where the organisation has the potential to take off into rapid growth. But take-off is likely to come even more suddenly to NGOs than to small businesses, and the consequent crises and conflict — between founders and their values, and 'new professionals' and their values respectively — tend to be even more severe and, sometimes, devastating.

Sheelagh Stewart's research into NGO funding in Nepal and Zimbabwe shows that NGOs often achieve 'funding success' (e.g. large volumes of donor financial support) very quickly. Once they are 'discovered' and funded by one donor, the word about their existence quickly gets around small, in-country donor funding communities. Donors are keen to find good NGOs to fund. Partly because they lack criteria to judge NGOs (see below), donors tend to adopt what is for them individually a rational rule of thumb: do what other donors are doing. The result can be similar, on a much smaller scale, to the early 1980s when most international banks decided that Third World governments were the best available borrowers for all that money sitting in the oil exporters' accounts. The result was over-lending and the Third World debt crisis. In Nepal and Zimbabwe, Stewart examined in detail the external funding history of 30 local NGOs in the period 1989–96. These were all urban-based organisations involved in advocacy issues. It is clear in retrospect that these organisations grew much faster over the research period than many other local NGOs.[2] Within a mere eight months of receiving their first significant tranche of external funding, their budgets had on average increased fivefold, and the number of staff employed had grown fourfold, as had the number of organisations from which they received funding. At the baseline point, they each received support from, on average, 1.7 donors. At the end of the period, each was funded by an average of seven donors. Their experiences of rapid organisational growth were extreme, but illustrate in a graphic fashion a set of processes that have beset development NGOs world-wide.[3]

Very rapid rates of funding growth pose difficulties to all organisations, but especially to development NGOs. Their styles, ethos, and values are often severely challenged by the formality and the bureaucratic discipline that is imposed by the volume and variety of external funding from public organisations. Suddenly, it is the donors' needs, the regular reports, the accounting and honouring the 'contract' with the funder, that have priority. Internal power and status may shift to the staff members, often new 'professional' recruits who can understand donors' needs and can interact effectively with them. This is not the place to tell in detail how such tensions affect NGOs. Let us simply note that half the NGOs in Stewart's sample had undergone a severe internal crisis, typically between 18 months and three years after the receipt of the first major grant. The main point is that development NGOs face the same types of organisational growth problems as small business, but often in a very concentrated form.

The founders of NGOs often do not want to adopt the more formal ('bureaucratic') structures that are implied by rapid growth in funding and in the diversity of donor sources. Why should they accept the 'institutionalised suspicion' that the new professionals represent: strict external auditing; recruitment of personnel by open competition; submission of frequent, detailed reports to funders; formal minutes of meetings; and elaborate measurement and reporting of the 'impacts' and 'outcomes' of their activities? Founders may suspect that all this is an excuse to place power, authority, and perhaps even illicit resources, in the hands of the incoming professionals managers, accountants, and impact evaluation specialists. Their suspicions may be true. But that is a matter of individual cases. The fact is that 'institutionalised suspicion' is essential to the proper functioning of any large scale organisation and especially to one that, like all development NGOs, has a significant public dimension.

There is plenty of scope to debate the precise arrangements for institutionalised suspicion (and we return to this below), but arrangements of this kind must be in place. Without them, organisations lose the confidence of those stakeholders who do not exert direct, personal control over the organisation. NGOs need institutionalised suspicion as much as any other public organisation. Indeed, the whole of the NGO community has an interest in the establishment of effective arrangements for such suspicion within all organisations in the sector. It is a matter of the reputation and trustworthiness of the sector as a whole. Allegations that some NGOs are unaccountable or untrustworthy will reflect on the sector as a whole in the eyes of the public, government, and donors. Donors will find it far easier to justify the continuing shift of development funds to NGOs if NGOs in general meet the standards of institutionalised suspicion that are normal in other types of organisations.

3 The Evaluation Problem

This is most immediately a problem for donors, but failure to resolve it eventually reflects back on NGOs, so it should be perceived as their problem. This, simply stated, is: 'How do we know whether NGOs are being effective and making good use of their money?' The consequent debate is wide-ranging and not at all specific to NGOs. Demands for formal, quantitative performance evaluation of organisations receiving public funding are becoming the world-wide norm. Performance evaluation is relatively easy in 'post-office'-type organisations where (a) activities are routine, (b) objectives are few and clear, (c) there is no great distinction between immediate 'outputs', medium-term 'effects', and long-term 'impacts', and, (d) outputs, effects, or impacts can be measured relatively cheaply and reliably without the measurement process itself distorting the objectives of the organisation or the goals of the staff. Few public organisations are like post-offices. Many, including many development NGOs, are very different: their activities are experimental rather than routine; their goals are often intangible (such as changing the consciousness of clients or the opinions of policy-makers); they may be operating in the face of official obstruction and hostility; and it may be difficult to find other organisations with which their performances can usefully be compared in any quantitative sense.

In such circumstances, people (donors) who wish and need to evaluate organisational performance have to do the best they can. They have three broad sets of options, and will tend to choose a variety rather than any one approach. The first is directly to measure performance where this appears feasible and is not likely to lead to too much distortion. The second is to obtain feedback from clients and other stakeholders about how well they perceive the organisation to be doing. The third is to see how far the organisation matches up to norms for organisations of its type in terms of its structure and processes: is the auditing process as rigorous as one would expect? Are the assets and liabilities reported to the extent one would expect? Are the procedures for recruiting and renewing staff contracts adequate in the circumstances? The more an organisation meets (or exceeds) norms about structure and process, the less its evaluators (donors) need concern themselves with other types of evaluation. Being seen to be a well-structured and well-run organisation may be a valid alternative to direct quantitative performance evaluation, if that evaluation is problematic and intrusive.

4 The Economies of Scale Problem

Most NGOs are very small. They lack easy and cheap access to the specialist knowledge they require. For example, they may be aware that 'staff development' is important, but have little idea about how to do it. They end up sending their staff for English language and computer training and asking donors to fund someone to go on such overseas training seminars as come to their attention. They may be struggling with the different reporting requirements of different donors, and have no access to someone fluent in written English who knows what Oxfam America requires, and how this differs from the demands of the Swedish International Development Co-operation Agency. Or, they may succumb to a very tempting funding offer from a hitherto unknown source without being able to check out the donor. Only later do they discover that part of the price they pay is providing support to Christian evangelism. Informal communication and various types of national NGO resource centres help to deal with these issues, but not very effectively. One major problem is that the NGO sector is internally competitive, in the worst sense of the term (see below). This militates against co-operation to overcome economies of scale problems.

Solutions

There is no silver bullet that in one shot will solve these four problems of accountability, structural growth, evaluation, and economies of scale. There is, however, a relatively standard set of organisational technologies that take us a good way with each of them: the introduction and enforcement, by NGOs collectively, of national norms of corporate governance for NGOs. Because NGOs in many countries are, with good reason, nervous of anything that even hints of more regulation and control by government, it is appropriate to talk first of who should be setting norms before discussing what the norms might look like, and how they might improve things.

NGOs could (we mean should) form voluntary national professional associations, like associations of engineers, accountants, or insurance companies, aimed at promoting the sector, partly through self-policing of standards. 'Policing' is, however, too strong a term. We are talking of 'norms' rather than 'rules'. One would not want nor expect these norms to be applied rigidly. This would be contrary to the flexibility and adaptability that should be as central to the practice of NGOs as it is to their values. Norms might take the following general form: an NGO that has been in existence for three years or more and has an annual budget exceeding X should be expected (a) to publish an annual report within Y months of the end of each financial year, (b) to disclose in that report all payments made, in cash and in kind, to all staff, directors, consultants, etc., by staff category, and (c) to have a written policy on staff development, and report annually on policy compliance. Particular provisions might not be appropriate to particular cases; there would be no expectation of universal compliance, but an implied expectation that NGOs would wish to explain their non-compliance.

This is no place to lay out a blueprint about the substantive content of these norms, for at least two reasons. First, norms should be evolved 'in country' if they are to be appropriate to local circumstances and take on moral force. Second, norms have to be country-specific because they are additional to existing national legislation under which NGOs are generally registered, and to which they are certainly subject. Each national legal framework is different. The only element we would wish to see blueprinted is diversity: the existence of a range of sets of norms applicable to different categories of NGOs. To explain why and how this should be so, it is useful to take the analogy of business or company legislation. And the analogy is far less stretched than it might first appear to those who believe NGOs to be very distinct types of organisation, a world apart from commerce or government. The private sector, too, is very diverse: from the one-person street-trader to the large and highly bureaucratised transnational corporation with an annual turnover that is a multiple of the GNPs of many individual countries. This vast diversity and flexibility exists under the law because the law allows for many categories of enterprise, each with different reporting and taxation obligations, and with different public responsibilities. In the typical Anglophone model, economic enterprises can be treated as: individual self-employment; partnerships; private companies; public companies; or public companies quoted on the stockmarket. Their obligations in relation to employment law (e.g. in relation to redundancy payments or the requirement that they employ disabled persons) will typically vary according to the number of employees or some other indicator of size. National codes of practice for the corporate governance of NGOs should embody the same principle: a range of statuses, with corresponding obligations, determined by the size of the organisation, its age, or other factors that appeared relevant. Similarly, the issues covered by self-regulation norms would vary according to status. The typical list is likely to include several of the following issues:

- timeliness of issuing of annual reports;
- issues to be included in the annual report (or elsewhere publicly available), such as degree of disclosure of assets and liabilities, of salaries and all other benefits paid to staff, directors, board members, and consultants;
- employment, recruitment, and staff development policies and practices;
- sources of finance;
- arrangements for internal or external scrutiny of financial transactions, employment practices, organisational policies, etc.;
- arrangements for the evaluation of organisational performance.

One would expect that, for larger and more established NGOs, self-regulation norms would tend to mandate a relatively clear division of power and responsibility between the internal management and a supervisory board representing a mixture of internal and external stakeholders — along the lines of a large public company. Indeed, encouraging movement toward such arrangements within larger NGOs is one of the most important single reasons for introducing self-regulation. Not only should these bring greater transparency, but they should also provide the opportunity to introduce greater accountability, by reserving places on boards for, for example, (a) elected members, in the case of those NGOs that are also membership organisations, (b) (elected) representatives of client groups, and (c) other members of the 'NGO community' — chosen perhaps from a list of eligible board members maintained by the 'professional' NGO association. Such 'professional' board members would play the same role as the reputed independent businesspeople who sit as directors on the boards of large companies: voices representing broad shareholder or public interests.

Independent supervisory boards — and the institutionalised tension between board and management that they imply — may not be appropriate for small NGOs leading a precarious or unstable life. In this context, other, lighter methods of regulation are appropriate. If the professional NGO association does its job and only gives and renews membership to those NGOs that observe the self-regulation norms appropriate to them, the regulation function becomes quasi-automatic. Membership of the Ruritanian NGO Association itself becomes a certificate of professional quality.

What are the advantages of such a self-regulation system? They parallel the four generic problems of NGOs set out above:

1 By providing clear standards and practices of accountability and transparency, they take much of the sting out of the charge of non-accountability, and much of the force out of the argument that government must step in to regulate NGOs because one else is doing the job.

2 They ease the problem of introducing 'institutionalised suspicion' mechanisms into NGOs that have out-grown their founders' management and leadership capacities. There is now an objective argument for doing the right thing: 'unless we do it, we shall lose our membership of and recognition by the NGO Association.'

3 They provide donors with some kind of quality rating that can be traded off against more expensive, detailed, intrusive individual inspections or output evaluations. If donors know that membership of the Ruritanian NGO Association is really 'earned' and not a rubber stamp, they will be that much more willing to fund members without attaching tight strings. If membership of reputable NGO Associations becomes the norm, then the reputation (and financial health) of the NGO sector as a whole can only improve.

4 They require the creation of collective organisations for self-regulation that will have an incentive to provide the collective services that their members cannot efficiently provide for themselves. NGO Associations need to fund themselves, and will tend to want to expand their activities. Provided they are not funded by donors — which would be a great mistake — they will do what business associations do: supplement membership fees by finding services they can sell to their members. Business and professional associations sell their members information and research, insurance, arbitration, specialised technical advice, meeting facilities, and dozens of other services. NGO Associations could provide: staff training, shared management consultancy services, insurance, or information on potential funding

sources. The best NGO Associations should be able to give their members reliable advice on the demands, quirks, needs, pitfalls, and opportunities they face with particular funders.

The beauty of self-policing through voluntary association is that it needs no central initiative or control, but can be done in decentralised fashion. Let six NGOs working on AIDS issues establish the Ruritanian Association of AIDS NGOs and initiate a self-policing system. If it seems to be effective, donors will like it and have a bias in favour of directing their funds to Association members. More NGOs are likely to want to join. Alternatively — and especially if they feel that the founder members of the Association want to preserve founders' privileges — other NGOs may elect to establish a rival association. Fine. That is also what private business does. There may be a little competition, a little uncertainty, and a little experimentation. But that is fully within the spirit of NGO-ism. The associations that are doing a good job and are not acting to exclude new members will tend to win out in the end. But the possibility of competition from other actual or potential associations will help to keep those that are in business honest and decent. Large parts of the private business sector regulate themselves in these ways, to the long term advantage of their members and society at large. It is a little anomalous that private enterprise, viewed by many people as the cockpit of competition, should co-operate so widely while NGOs, characteristically the advocates of a more co-operative pattern of social organisation, should often appear to compete so much among themselves and to co-operate so little. The reason is not that NGO staff are psychological hawks masquerading as doves. It is that the NGO sector has grown so fast in developing countries that the appropriate sector-wide institutions have yet to emerge, and their funders have yet to provide encouragement.

The sector is, however, changing. There are signs in some countries that donors are coming together formally to share information about the NGOs they are funding. This is a rational thing for them to do, especially in large countries where they face serious problems in obtaining information about local NGOs. National NGOs need not complain: insofar as it helps to improve transparency and honesty in the NGO sector as a whole, we should all be in favour of such processes. Just as the existence of centralised national trade unions movements have historically stimulated the formation of national employers' associations, and *vice versa*, the collective organisation of NGO donors is likely to stimulate the national organisation of local NGOs. The NGOs have a great deal to gain from this, including more information on their donors and more bargaining capacity. Their gains are likely to be larger if they get organised first.

Acknowledgement

The authors gratefully acknowledge the financial support of the Economic and Social Committee for Overseas Research (ESCOR) of the Department for International Development. The Department is in no way responsible for any of the views expressed here. A copy of the research report may be obtained from the authors ('Final Report Number 5968. The Impact of External Funding on the Capacity of Local Non-Government Organisations'). We are most grateful to Deborah Eade and to Judith Tendler for very helpful comments on an earlier draft of this paper.

Notes

1 'The Gift Relationship', *The Economist*, 18–24 March 1994; Farrington J. and D. Lewis, *Non-government Organisations and the State in South Asia: rethinking roles in sustainable agricultural development*, London, Routledge, 1994; and Fowler, A. 'Distant Obligations: speculations on NGO funding and the global market', *Review of African Political Economy*, 55, 119.

2 This was not part of the research design: the organisations were chosen because they were urban-based and involved in advocacy, not because their budgets had grown so fast.

3 Oxfam has a rule of thumb that an annual budget increase of more than 25 per cent in real terms is 'likely to lead to severe organisational difficulties' (Deborah Eade, private communication, 3 July 1997, citing Deborah Eade and Suzanne Williams, *The Oxfam Handbook of Development and Relief*, Oxford: Oxfam, p. 439).

References

Farrington, J. and D. Lewis (1994), Non-government Organisations and the State in South Asia; rethinking roles in sustainable agricultural development, London: Routledge.

Fowler, A. (1992), 'Distant obligations: speculations on NGO funding and the global market', *Review of African Political Economy*, 55. pp. 9–29.

This paper was first published in Development in Practice *Volume 8, Number 3, 1998*

'Dancing with the prince': NGOs' survival strategies in the Afghan conflict

Jonathan Goodhand with Peter Chamberlain

Introduction

In the era of democratisation and good governance, NGOs have become the donors' 'favoured child', with access to growing resources and influence (Edwards and Hulme 1995). They are viewed both as 'market actors', which are more efficient and cost-effective than governments, and as the agents of democratisation, an integral part of a thriving civil society (Korten 1990; Clark 1991). Official donors show their support for the economic and political roles of NGOs in what has been called the 'New Policy Agenda' by channelling money through them (Edwards and Hulme, op. cit.). As one USAID official put it: 'We get a double bang for our buck that way' (Larmer 1994). Underpinning this consensus is the presumption that political democracy and socio-economic development are mutually reinforcing. The state, market, and civil society — which, following Korten (1990), we shall refer to as *prince, merchant* and *citizen* — are related in a series of virtuous circles. A basic tenet of 'NGO lore' is that NGOs promote and strengthen civil society, and thus subject the prince and merchant to greater public accountability. There is, however, an element of triumphalism in the discourse about the New World Order, and the belief that NGOs are 'part of the warp and weft of democracy' (Larmer, op. cit.). Such words ring hollow in a world characterised by instability, fragmentation, and deepening poverty. Far from 'democratising development', NGOs are often the providers of palliatives to competing factions in conflict (Slim 1994). Rather than promoting accountability, NGOs are perhaps 'dancing to the tune of the prince', whether the prince is a government, an insurgency movement, or a local war lord.

We should scrutinise and challenge the assumptions underpinning the mythology about NGOs; and donors should base their actions on a realistic assessment of NGOs' capabilities, rather than on the suppositions of 'NGO lore'.

Background to the Afghan conflict

The end of the Cold War has not meant the end of history, as Fukayama suggested (Rupesinghe 1994). Far from being a 'New World Order', today's world is characterised by a dangerous disorder in which political instability is endemic.[1]

The Afghan war is a potent example of contemporary conflicts, often described as 'complex political emergencies' (CPEs), which are characterised by combinations of multiple causes, such as civil and ethnic conflicts, famine, displacement, disputed sovereignty, and a breakdown of national government. The Afghan conflict resulted from a complex mix of factors, caused by years of bad development, Cold War politics, militarisation, and tribal and ethnic schisms. It thus highlights many critical issues: the breakdown of the nation-state, ethnicity, fundamentalism, nationalism, displacement, sovereignty, and the role of humanitarian agencies.

CPEs are not temporary crises after which society returns to normal: they have long-term, structural characteristics and result from the failures of development. By the mid-1970s, Afghanistan had become a schizophrenic society, comprising an urban elite whose idea of a strong, unified state was at odds with the tribal and ethnic loyalties of the predominantly rural population. From these contradictions arose the socialist and the Islamist movements. Both were based on the 'myth of revolution', and it was the clash between these ideologies which became the catalyst for the conflict.

The 'Lebanonisation' of Afghanistan

The Afghan conflict was characterised by the implosion of the nation-state, the development of predatory political movements and war economies, and the erosion of structures within civil society. Macrae and Zwi (1992) describe the deliberate targeting of production and distribution, as well as restriction of movement and disruption of markets, in the context of Africa. In Afghanistan, rural subsistence economies were deliberately destroyed by Soviet forces during the 1980s, and terror was used to cow the population, one-third of whom were displaced to Iran and Pakistan.

The withdrawal of Soviet troops in 1988 did not signal an end to the conflict. A process of 'Lebanonisation' (Roy 1989) followed, in which the contradictions within the resistance movement re-surfaced. The conflict mutated from a counter-insurgency war with an ostensibly ideological basis into one characterised by war-lordism and banditry. The overall picture is one of fluidity and turbulence; alliances are constantly shifting, and violent conflict is interspersed with fragile peace. Competing 'princes' have a vested interest in the continuation of disorder; where their fortunes are based on coercion and, increasingly, on the opium trade, they have little to gain from an emergent state. Conflict has come to represent the norm, not a diversion from it. Few donors are willing to resume bilateral aid to Afghanistan when dialogue with a strong central government remains impossible. Afghanistan has become the classic 'weak state' (Duffield 1994), suffering from systematic instability, and with declining strategic importance on the world stage.

Prince, merchant, and citizen: new roles in Afghanistan

Korten's model of functional complementarities between prince, merchant, and citizen does not resonate in the Afghan context. New divisions in Afghan society are based on political allegiance and wealth. CPEs are often characterised by the emergence of parallel economies beyond the control of the state. The new 'princes' in Afghanistan are the commanders and mullahs. For example, the economy of Jalalabad is now largely based on smuggling, opium production, and banditry, and it is the commanders with influence in the regional council who control and encourage such an economy.

> As one enters Jalalabad, a long line of repainted vehicles for sale at the side of the road, mostly stolen in Peshawar, provide a stern reminder of the type of forces really in control of the area. (Cutts 1993: 14)

Civil society is intensely segmented, and people's loyalties are directed towards family, clan, and lineage rather than community. Kinship loyalties have always been stronger than obligations towards the state. Dupree (1989: 249) describes the 'mud curtain' which villagers erect to protect themselves against the incursions of the state: 'Once the modernisation teams leave, the villagers patch up the breaks in their mud curtain and revert to their old, group-reinforcing patterns.'

With the fragmentation of the resistance has followed a process of re-tribalisation; political allegiances have waned at the expense of a renewed ethnic awareness. The Tajiks, Hazaras, and Uzbeks, for example, have all found a new ethnic assertiveness as a result of the war. It is difficult to view such a chronically anarchic and divided society other than in Hobbesian terms. Villages have undergone the same process of fragmentation, with war sweeping away many of the traditional structures, and leaving an institutional vacuum that has been filled by the military commanders.[2] There are few stable foundations from which to reconstruct.

The conflict has produced a combustible cocktail in which both the traditional and state constraints have been eroded, while the technological means to conduct war have increased. NGOs are occupying the space left by the collapse of the state, and so wield great influence in the absence of effective government institutions.

The humanitarian response

The humanitarian response to the Afghan conflict reflects trends in global aid allocation. While development budgets are stagnating, there has been a marked increase in relief aid and, since the 1980s, an enhanced role for NGOs. During the Cold War, when the UN was constrained by considerations of national sovereignty, NGOs attempted to supply humanitarian aid in contested areas (Duffield, op. cit.). NGOs are 'rushing in where soldiers and bureaucrats fear to tread' (Larmer, op. cit.), a phenomenon perpetuated by the sub-contracting of NGOs in areas where multilateral and bilateral agencies are unable or unwilling to get involved, such as controversial cross-border programmes.

With the 1979 Soviet occupation of Afghanistan, virtually all Western development programmes came to an end.[3] NGOs intervened through non-mandated cross-border programmes. Until 1988, NGOs were the principal means by which humanitarian relief and rehabilitation was provided to areas held by the Mujahideen. Initially, intervention was on a limited scale, involving fewer than 15 NGOs and between US$5 and US$10 million per year. By 1991, however, there were some 100 NGOs involved in such operations. In 1989, total expenditure from the US government alone was US$112 million (Nicholds and Borton 1994).

The 1988 Geneva Accords included an agreement that the international community, under UN auspices, should undertake a substantial programme of relief and rehabilitation inside Afghanistan.

The UN Secretary-General appointed a Coordinator for Humanitarian and Economic Assistance Programmes Relating to Afghanistan (UNOCA) to assist in mobilising and coordinating resources. UNOCA (and many international donors) favoured strengthening the capacity of Afghan organisations to manage their own affairs, and 'Afghanisation' or 'de-foreignisation' entered the lexicon of Peshawar-based agencies.

UNOCA and other UN agencies thus encouraged the formation of Afghan NGOs (ANGOs), which were then sub-contracted for specific activities. The process is illustrated in the area of mine-clearance where, since the capacity of existing NGOs was limited, three were set up to cover different areas of Afghanistan (Nicholds and Borton 1994).

By 1994, there were over 200 registered ANGOs (Barakat *et al.* 1994), often scathingly referred to as 'UN NGOs', reflecting a view that they were merely a fabrication of the donors. However, ANGOs have become major players in cross-border relief and rehabilitation work. In 1991, approximately 21 per cent of UNDP's US$2 million budget was channelled via ANGOs, through 66 projects or contracts (Carter 1991).

Typology of Afghan NGOs

The term 'Afghan NGOs' covers a range of organisations, many of which bear only a tenuous relationship to the family of NGOs. Carter (op. cit.), for example, argues that 'Afghan Implementing Agency' would be more accurate. Rahim (1991, cited in Nicholds and Borton, op. cit.) distinguishes four types:

1 Independent NGOs formed by non-affiliated professionals.
2 NGOs backed by local *shuras* (groups of elders) and commanders.
3 NGOs established by political parties, either individually or in coalition.
4 NGOs established by international organisations (UN or international NGOs).

A fifth category, 'briefcase NGOs', might be added to describe organisations that exist only in name, spawned in response to the easy availability of external funding. In reality, most ANGOs are hybrids: all, for example, have to develop links with parties, commanders, and local administrations, whether they are a UN 'spin-off' or a professional 'consultancy firm'. Most have developed from the top down, and they are now having to work backwards to find a community base of support (Carter, op. cit.).

Afghan NGOs: response to the conflict

Inevitably, such diversity has drawn varied assessments of ANGOs' roles and performance. Some claim that ANGOs could become the agents of transformation and reconstitute Afghan civil society from the bottom up. Critics argue that behind most ANGOs stands a foreign initiator and, therefore, a foreign definition of response to Afghan need. Pragmatists see a limited role for ANGOs, essentially as contracting mechanisms for the delivery of relief assistance.

CPEs have accelerated changes in the thinking and practice of humanitarian agencies, giving rise to the need for revised notions of change and causality (Roche 1994). Relief and development are not discrete processes which unfold separately; the imperatives are similar in terms of addressing vulnerabilities and building capacities to enable communities to cope with change and survive future shocks (Anderson and Woodrow 1989).

Some would argue that ANGOs may transcend the prevailing relief paradigm, and promote new forms of public action that build local capacities and foster peace. Rather than 'dancing with the prince', they constitute a countervailing force to the often arbitrary power of the prince.

Critics of the ANGO phenomenon argue that they were an opportunist response to a donor-led demand. Humanitarian agencies often respond to protracted crisis by '[replacing] well thought out, bottom-up participatory approaches, reintroducing the kind of top-down centrally driven crash programmes long ago discarded by the more thoughtful and experienced agencies' (ACORD 1993: 3). Baitenmann (1990) contends that most NGOs working cross-border were the conscious agents of political interests. In-field co-operation with combatants meant that NGOs made direct payments into the war economy. Cash-for-work projects, for example, were often re-directed to fund commanders' military activities. While NGOs may invoke the concept of neutral humanitarianism, 'dancing to the tune of the prince' has for them become an essential survival strategy.

A more pragmatic interpretation of ANGOs' role is that they are engaged in a holding operation. As Johnston and Clark (1982) note, 'when power confronts persuasion head-on, power wins' (p.13). By being non-confrontational, ANGOs may create some room for manoeuvre for themselves and for 'pro-citizen' groups within civil society. They may also have a role in protecting and nurturing future leaders, as they have in Latin America (Garilao 1987).

Positive change in such an environment can occur only through a process of 'transformation through stealth' (Fowler 1993). ANGOs have a 'Janus-headed role' (Edwards and Hulme, op. cit.), in which they claim to be apolitical, but have a core agenda of supporting democratisation and peace.

The relationship between ANGOs and the prince

The humanitarian response to CPEs is characterised by divergence between the rhetoric of neutrality and the reality of aid that is increasingly politicised. In Afghanistan, this response has become part of the political economy of violence. Cross-border operations were part of a political and ideological Cold War battle against the Soviets. Cross-border NGOs strengthened the base of the insurgency, their very presence legitimising the rebels (Baitenmann, op. cit.). It may be asked whether NGOs were indeed strengthening civil society, or rather attempting to shape it in ways that external actors considered desirable. Today, Afghanistan has lost its strategic value and is what Duffield (op. cit.) describes as one of the 'weak states' on the margins of the global economy. Most of the Western players have made, or are making, a strategic withdrawal. A drip-feed of humanitarian assistance continues as a feature of the West's 'accommodation with violence' (Duffield, op. cit.), and the creation of ANGOs may have facilitated this withdrawal (Marsden 1991).

Dancing with commanders and parties

ANGOs have two options in cross-border work: to co-operate with civilian authorities like *shuras*, or to develop ties with commanders. Initially, the latter was the only practicable option, since commanders constituted the real power-holders in any locality. In return for 'protection', commanders insisted on a share of donors' *largesse*. NGOs had a real impact on the local balance of power by supporting some commanders in preference to others. They may have contributed to local conflicts and diminished social cohesion. Cash-for-food distributions in the early 1980s are an extreme example, where poorly monitored programmes are suspected of having provided Mujahideen commanders with funds for their military activities. Some donors were prepared to accept 'wastage levels' of up to *40 per cent* for their programmes in Afghanistan (Nicholds and Borton, op. cit.).

Channelling aid through commanders and parties has created precedents which NGOs find difficult to break. As military assistance declined, so humanitarian aid assumed importance as a source of patronage for commanders. Many NGOs have become an extension of the patron-client relationship between commanders and communities, and villagers clearly associate particular commanders with certain NGOs (Goodhand 1992). The dilemma is that projects will not survive if they threaten the established power-holders; but unless they maintain a distance, they become part of the patronage system. Survival depends on understanding the local configurations of power, and success depends on the ability to draw on this authority without being co-opted by it. There is a fine line between survival as a means to an end, and survival as an end in itself.

The strategies adopted by ANGOs to remain operational in a turbulent environment are various. Some of them are considered below.

The human factor: The importance of creating space is illustrated in an ANGO director's comment that he spent 80 per cent of his time on political issues, 15 per cent on tribal matters, and only 5 per cent on the projects (Goodhand, op. cit.). ANGO managers have to be pragmatists, and they recognise that the support of commanders and parties is a prerequisite for survival. They must also have the Mujahideen credentials, party connections, and family background to build the necessary support and alliances, both inside and outside Afghanistan. Some ANGO managers may well emerge as future leaders of Afghan society. Working for an ANGO may, in retrospect, prove to be a more astute career path than that followed by the political party careerists.

Selective collaboration: ANGOs are playing a new game by old rules: an intricate balancing act of exploiting the 'economy of affection' of parties and commanders without being colonised by them. However, there is a danger of 'meeting villainy halfway'. The key to creating space is selective collaboration, rather than identifying with any one leader. It is a case of building strategic alliances with political and religious leaders, without losing one's room for manoeuvre.

Diversification: Some ANGOs have employed staff from various political backgrounds to guard against being partisan, and to maintain their range of options and contacts. Diversification is an essential strategy for survival; it is about trying to cover all your bases and to cope with uncertainty.

'Pointing the finger': When under pressure, field staff are often able to deflect it by pointing the finger towards a distant authority outside the network of patronage — whether it is the head office, an expatriate adviser, or the donor. Donors and international staff can be valuable in absorbing such pressures on local NGOs, provided that there is a level of understanding and trust between the two parties.

Keeping a low profile: Keeping a low profile is about not making enemies. It may mean submerging one's identity and occasionally allowing the prince to take credit. A dual role is needed: the de-politicised public operation which emphasises humanitarianism, and the private operation which retains a core agenda of empowerment (Edwards and Hulme, op. cit.). Providing some bags of wheat to a commander, or employing some of his Mujahids, may be a necessary price for long-term gains.

Pragmatism and values: a Faustian pact?

When does the struggle for survival become an end in itself? At what stage does strategic co-operation become co-option? Many ANGOs have fallen into a kind of Faustian pact, in which 'eternal life' is brought at the price of their 'pro-citizen' soul. But all interventions represent an interaction between pragmatism and moral values, and the weighting given to each will vary with every decision. Management becomes the 'science of muddling through'. Responding to commanders' demands involves a constant balancing of ends against means. Coherence comes through having a strong sense of values and a guiding philosophy. 'Dancing with the prince' may be a means to an ultimate end of peace and reconstruction.

The relationship between ANGOs and the citizen

UNOCA encouraged the development of ANGOs in the belief that they constituted the most effective mechanisms for delivering aid. Their understanding of the cultural and political dynamics of Afghan society, and their network of local contacts, enable them to get to the parts that international NGOs cannot reach. ANGOs have extended the reach of aid programmes to remote communities.

It has been argued that ANGOs are not only more effective, but also more cost-efficient. A UNDP evaluation found that they had significantly lower costs than organisations employing many expatriates (in Carter, op. cit.). Also, owing to the high turnover among expatriates, there was considerably more continuity within Afghan organisations than in international NGOs. Finally, ANGOs have provided on-the-job training, especially at the senior management level, which expatriate-run NGOs cannot provide. Many Afghans are now developing skills in managing organisations and dealing with donors that will be essential in a future government (Carter, op. cit.).

Working behind the 'mud curtain'

ANGOs' principal advantage is that they were formed for Afghans by Afghans. As such, they have the political instincts and cultural awareness to act with sensitivity and caution in the complex web of Afghan society. Many Afghans have voiced a fear that external agencies undermine Afghan cultural values. ANGOs, however, can work quietly and carefully behind the 'mud curtain', and may thus also be producing an important resource: a cadre of 'organic intellectuals' with community-mobilisation skills.

Gender: constraints, openings, and missed opportunities

Conflict has brought new opportunities and new threats to NGOs seeking to address gender-related issues. While the disruption of the war years created an environment which challenges traditional gender roles, an upsurge in fundamentalism has tended to restrict women's rights.

Most NGO projects focusing on women have worked with the relatively accessible refugees. It may never again be so easy to reach women from so many different parts of Afghanistan (Dupree, in Huld and Jansson 1988). However, NGO attempts to work with women have tended to be rather superficial — through handcraft and health projects, for example, that do not challenge existing power relations. ANGOs occupy an uneasy position. On the one hand, they are more vulnerable than international NGOs to conservative pressures from a patriarchal society. On the other, they are better able to work behind the 'mud curtain', where access to women is restricted to those with kinship and social ties. Currently, there are very few women in positions of responsibility within ANGOs, and this will be slow to change. But ANGOs do at least have the understanding of social and cultural norms to recognise opportunities and take advantage of them.

While some commentators are optimistic about the possibilities for social change, the barriers are considerable.[4] Women's projects are often associated with the Communists' earlier attempts at 'social development'. One Pakistan-based ANGO director felt that if his group initiated activities that benefited women, he would be out of business in two weeks (Carter, op. cit.). If ANGOs confront the issue head-on, they may put their entire programme in jeopardy. Some ANGOs, after building up their credibility in a community, have incrementally introduced activities directed at women, though usually in traditional areas. Further success is likely to be slow and painstaking, requiring stealth as much as technical and managerial proficiency.

However real the constraints, ANGOs have all too often avoided dealing with gender-based oppression on the grounds that it is 'too sensitive' or threatens local (patriarchal) culture. Opportunities have been missed to develop programmes that would directly benefit women in areas such as agriculture, fuel collection, and food production.

Reconstituting civil society?

The conflict has presented new opportunities in the sense that NGOs can work directly with communities, unencumbered by a government bureaucracy (Marsden, op. cit.). ANGOs may represent an important bridge between the people and emerging government structures. They can help to re-connect people with the state by communicating local needs to the government, and reducing the princes' monopoly over the flow of information. Optimistic observers would argue that ANGOs represent an alternative development path for Afghanistan: an alternative to the schizophrenic society produced by modernisation. Radical visions may, however, risk being associated with communism.

In rural Afghanistan, elders, religious leaders, and local *shuras* all function as stabilising points in a volatile environment. Most ANGOs have used these as the foundations for their projects, despite the danger of skirting round the issue of re-distributing power and resources. NGO interventions in the agricultural sector, for instance, risk reinforcing a highly unequal structure. The issue is to strengthen indigenous capacity in a way consistent with humanitarian principles.

Rather than confront these issues directly, some ANGOs have tried an incrementalist approach. By focusing on productive activities, they have made a strategic response to practical needs. Many ANGOs, for example, have initiated *karez* (cleaning) programmes.[5] In the short term, this improves irrigation and food production; in the long term, such projects may develop into new forms of collective action. The *karez* programmes have in some cases led to the revival of irrigation councils and to new village organisations coalescing around the ANGOs' projects. As Marsden (op. cit.) notes, there are few organisations in Afghan civil society above the grassroots level, and ANGOs may form an important nexus. Ultimately, collective action may become an empowering process which will meet the long-term strategic needs of vulnerable sectors — described earlier as 'transformation by stealth' (Fowler, op. cit.).

Demilitarising the mind

It is naive to imagine that ANGOs can be the catalysts for a grassroots peace movement in Afghanistan in the way that local NGOs have mobilised civil society in, for example, the Philippines and parts of Latin America. Any positive transformation will take place through small, incremental changes from the individual and community levels upwards. It is as much about demilitarising people's minds as about getting the princes together at the negotiating table. Although they could not explicitly refer to it as peace-building, ANGOs' work is contributing to a peace process within civil society. Several ANGO managers maintain that reconstruction and development will encourage Mujahids to lay down their guns, by offering them viable alternative livelihoods. Their projects embrace different tribal and ethnic groups, which may also contribute to a peace process to be built upwards by facilitating local co-operation (Marsden, op. cit.).

Questioning the comparative advantage of ANGOs

External organisations

'NGO lore' depicts ANGOs as an integral part of civil society, though in many respects the ANGO-community relationship mirrors the wider urban-rural divide. In a society where only five to ten per cent of the population is literate, ANGO staff represent an educated elite, who entertain many of the biases and prejudices that education has imparted.

Although the leadership may be indigenous, the organisational model and response is not: it is that of Peshawar-based international NGOs. Consequently, ANGOs have reproduced and cultivated many of their models' intrinsic weaknesses. Like international NGOs, ANGOs tend to be based in Pakistan and are top-heavy, with more office staff than field staff.

The lack of long-term, flexible funding — including administrative costs — has trapped ANGOs in the 'project-by-project' system, reinforcing the image of ANGOs as service-providers, since they become contracting agencies for specific, time-bound projects drawn up to someone else's agenda. ANGOs are not 'owned' by rural communities; they commonly 'belong' to donors, commanders, or Afghan technocrats. They are accountable upwards to the donor or commander, but rarely downwards to the communities.

It is hard for ANGOs to insulate themselves from the ethnic, political, and religious pressures impinging upon them. Staff are under great pressure to benefit kith and kin, and some family-run ANGOs are susceptible to using assistance to improve the position and prestige of their family and clan (Carter, op. cit.). ANGOs have also been charged (like some international NGOs) with corruption. In Baitenmann's view (op. cit.), they were at least accessories to a relief programme that was plagued with corruption. And because of the clandestine nature of their work, cross-border NGOs were unavoidably drawn into a web of corruption, forced to pay bribes to Pakistani police or government officials, and protection levies for the right to travel within the country.

Most ANGOs were founded by charismatic individuals who have retained control over their organisations as they grow. This has inevitably placed these now powerful Afghan managers in an exposed position, accentuated by the political fluidity of Afghan society and the bitterness created by the conflict. Some ANGO personnel have been assassinated in recent years. Good political instincts are crucial for survival, both literally and figuratively. Such a situation militates against open and participatory management styles. The leader is unwilling to delegate authority because of the potential consequences of a 'bad' decision, so strategic planning tends to be subservient to crisis management. Centre-field relations become hierarchical, with field staff having little authority or status, and only the head-office senior managers allowed to see the whole picture.

Prisoners of a relief paradigm

There is some evidence that the general direction of change in NGO approaches has followed the pattern described by Korten: from the 'first generation' approach of relief and welfare, towards the 'second generation' stage of community development, and in some cases towards the 'third generation' stage of 'sustainable systems development' (Korten, op. cit.). Some cross-border NGOs are embracing development concepts related to community participation, monitoring and evaluation, participatory needs analysis, and so forth. However, they are influenced by a legacy of more than 15 years of relief operations. Most Afghan and international NGOs are still based in Pakistan, and find it difficult to break from their cross-border mode of operation.

Many NGOs have been active in Nangarhar Province in Eastern Afghanistan since the mid-1980s, because of its proximity to the Pakistan border. Free hand-outs were the norm, and are now expected by local communities; relief has precluded, for the time being at least, an approach which places responsibility for development with local people. Critics would argue that the internal and external constraints already mentioned make ANGOs unlikely vehicles for transforming this paradigm. There is very little in their background to suggest they can fulfil such a role. With their defining features — dependency on donors, staffed by a Kabul elite, hierarchical and centralised structures, susceptibility to penetration and colonisation — they appear singularly ill-equipped to transcend the prevailing pattern of relief. Even supposing this is part of their vision, the means are not consistent with the ends.

Going it alone

Over the years, NGOs working cross-border have demonstrated a remarkable inability to coordinate, or to avoid duplication. This 'lack of coordination and unified strategy amongst NGOs' was noted at a conference of ANGOs and donors (Barkat *et al.*, op. cit.). Although coordination has since improved, it continues to be a problem for several reasons. ANGOs are competing for a declining market-share of resources from donors. They may be responsive to demand, but it is a demand created by the donors, rather than by the beneficiaries. Projects become little more than pins on a map as evidence to meet the donors' criteria. Security and contacts, perhaps understandably, have been the primary factors in deciding where to work; long-term needs often appear almost incidental. Consequently, 150 NGOs are working in Jalalabad, and less than a handful in the central province of Hazarajat. Coordination takes place in Pakistan, in isolation from relevant government departments in Afghanistan. A lack of coordination encourages duplication and undermines local initiative. For example, in 1994, the World Food Programme (WFP), by distributing food hand-outs in Hazarajat, undermined the more participatory initiatives of local NGOs (Cutts, op. cit.).

A holding operation?

Claims that ANGOs can transcend the political pressures, and their own internal limitations, to bring about a shift from relief assistance towards a more inclusive developmental approach must still be treated with some scepticism. Afghanistan is not the dance floor for a confrontational 'pro-citizen' stance. Most commonly, 'dancing with the prince' has involved co-option, or — at best — the creation of a little room for manoeuvre through compromise and selective collaboration.

ANGOs are not a panacea for the intractable problems of development in Afghanistan. They do, however, have a role to play in an environment where the state and civil society structures have been eroded. The key is to analyse the success stories — those ANGOs that have 'danced with the prince' and maintained their integrity — and develop strategies for replicating them.

Donors and their impact on the dance

The future direction of ANGOs will be determined largely by the policies of the donors and their intermediaries, the international NGOs. How can these identify, learn from, and 'scale up' the successes?

First, their policies and practice should be based on an informed analysis of the nature of conflict and its relationship to development. This means recognising that conflict is a strategic issue, not to be ignored by the development planners.

Second, a more flexible and long-term response is required. In Afghanistan, funding requests were often turned down on the basis that they were 'too developmental': donors' thinking and institutional arrangements are based on linear notions of the 'relief to development continuum'. Experience in Afghanistan exposed the lack of institutional frameworks within which to provide assistance for *transitional* activities which are neither 'relief' nor 'development'.

Third, a more informed political analysis is vital. In Afghanistan, donors must make difficult choices about which princes or which citizens to support. What are the political implications of policies which strengthen provincial structures rather than central government, or ANGOs rather than community organisations? It needs to be explicitly acknowledged that ANGOs do have a political role, in that they can affect and are affected by the dynamics of the conflict. It is naive to regard them purely as service-delivery mechanisms.

Towards a new form of engagement

There are tensions in trying to achieve multiple objectives in supporting NGOs. For example, funding ANGOs for delivering relief — to meet the objectives of the donors — has often been to the detriment of longer-term aims of capacity building. Ways are needed to broaden the relationship beyond that of being simply partners in aid delivery. Duffield (op. cit.) argues that engagement should be linked to a 'new ethics', i.e. showing solidarity, rather than keeping a distance from the fray and paying lip-service to neutrality.

Fine words, but what do they mean in practice? A starting point must be a broader and more flexible relationship between donors and ANGOs: breaking out of the 'project syndrome' (where projects and development are assumed to be synonymous), and making a long-term and open-ended commitment to selected ANGOs. Projects in Afghanistan are often risky and involve slow and careful work which cannot be melded into 'projectised chunks'. This means moving from the 'culture of concrete results'. However, although capacity building is a fashionable term, it is not always clear what it actually means. In Afghanistan, it often translates into building the capacity of ANGOs to implement their donors' agendas. However capacity building should not be limited to 'skilling up' organisations, or providing a technical fix. It implies a wider dialogue, based on shared values and ethics. Some donors and NGOs have now started to work in this way, to formulate working principles for peace-building and reconstruction in Afghanistan (Barakat *et al.*, op. cit.).

In general, ANGOs have had to dance to the tunes both of the donor and of the prince. These roles need to be reversed in order to make a reality of the civil society rhetoric. A starting point might be to introduce mechanisms that empower organisations *within* civil society, whether these be NGOs or community groups, to help to set the agenda and so call the tune.

Notes

1   According to the UNDP 1994 Human Development Report, in 1993 42 countries experienced 52 major conflicts and another 37 countries experienced political violence. Only three of the 82 conflicts between 1989 and 1992 were between states. In 1993–4 alone, there were four million deaths as result of ethno-political wars, mostly civilians. Without an effective international ombudsman, and with the thriving international arms trade, conflict is bound to continue.

2   Many NGOs latched onto the concept of *shuras* (councils of elders), believing them to be stable, community-based organisations which could be building blocks in the reconstruction process. However, this is to misunderstand the character and role of *shuras*, which are loose consultative bodies, brought together on an *ad hoc* basis to discuss particular issues or resolve conflicts (Marsden 1991).

3   Neither the UN nor the International Committee of the Red Cross (ICRC) could work cross-border; the UN because of its mandate to work with recognised governments, and ICRC because it could not secure the consent of all parties in the conflict.

4   The emergence of the Taleban — a movement of religious students — from late 1994 has further narrowed the scope for agencies involved in women's programmes. The Taleban now control much of the country and insist that women and girls should remain within the confines of their compounds.

5   *Karezes* are traditional underground irrigation systems.

References

ACORD (1993), Annual Report, 1993.

Anderson, M. B. and P. J. Woodrow (1989), *Rising from the Ashes: development strategies in times of disaster*, Boulder/Paris: Westview/UNESCO.

Baitenmann, H. (1990), 'NGOs and the Afghan war: the politicisation of humanitarian aid', *Third World Quarterly*, Vol. 12, no. 1.

Barakat, S., M. Ehsan, and A. Strand (1994), *NGOs and Peace-Building in Afghanistan: workshop report*, University of York, England.

Carter, L. with A. Eichfield (1991), 'Afghan Non-government Organisations and Their Role in the Rehabilitation of Afghanistan', unpublished report for International Rescue Committee, Peshawar, Pakistan.

Clark, J. (1991), *Democratising Development: the role of voluntary organisations*, London: Earthscan.

Cutts, M. (1993), 'Report on SCF Visit to the North Western, Central and Eastern Regions of Afghanistan', unpublished report, London: Save the Children Fund.

Duffield, M. (1994), 'Complex emergencies and the crisis of developmentalism', *IDS Bulletin: Linking Relief and Development*, vol. 25, no 3.

Dupree, L. (1989), *Afghanistan*, New Jersey: Princetown University Press.

Edwards, M. and D. Hulme (1995), 'NGOs and development; performance and accountability in the "New World Order"' in Edwards and Hulme (eds) (1995), *Non-government Organisations — Performance and Accountability: beyond the magic bullet*, London: Earthscan, with Save the Children Fund.

Garilao, E. (1987), 'Indigenous NGOs as Strategic Institutions: managing the relationship with government and resource agencies', *World Development*, Vol. 15, Supplement, pp. 113–120.

Goodhand, J. (1992), 'Report of the Rural Assistance Programme Cross Border Training Programme', unpublished report, International Rescue Committee, Peshawar, Pakistan.

Fowler, A. (1993), 'NGOs as Agents of Democratisation: an African perspective', *Journal of International Development*, vol 5, no 3.

Huld, B. and E. Jansson (1988), *The Tragedy of Afghanistan: the social, cultural and political impact of the Soviet invasion*, London: Croom Helm.

Johnston B. and M. Clark (1982), *Redesigning Rural Development: a strategic perspective*, London: Johns Hopkins Press.

Korten, D. C. (1990), *Getting to the 21st Century: voluntary action and the global agenda*, London: Routledge.

Larmer, B. (1994), 'The new colonialism', *Newsweek*, 1 August 1994.

Macrae, J. and A. Zwi (1992), 'Food as an Instrument of War in Contemporary African Famines', *Journal of Disaster Studies*, vol. 16, no. 4.

Marsden, P. (1991), *Afghanisation*, London: British Agencies Afghan Group.

Nicholds, N. and J. Borton (1994), *The Changing Role of NGOs in the Provision of Relief and Rehabilitation Assistance: case study 1 — Afghanistan/Pakistan*, ODI Working Paper 74, London: Overseas Development Institute.

Roche, C. (1994), 'Operationality in turbulence: the need for change', *Development in Practice*, vol. 4, no. 3.

Roy, O. (1989), 'Afghanistan: back to tribalism or on to Lebanon?', *Third World Quarterly*, vol. 11, no. 4.

Rupesinghe, K. (1994), *Advancing Preventative Diplomacy in a Post-Cold War Era: suggested roles for governments and NGOs*, ODI Relief and Rehabilitation Network, Network Paper 5, September 1994, London: Overseas Development Institute.

Slim, H. (1994), 'The Continuing Metamorphosis of the Humanitarian Professional: some new colours for an endangered chameleon', *Disasters*.

This paper was first published in Development in Practice *Volume 6, Number 3, 1996.*

NGOs and the State: a case-study from Uganda

Christy Cannon

This article reports on research carried out in 1995, focusing on programmes funded by Oxfam (UK and Ireland) as the basis of a case-study of the Ugandan health sector. It presents the research questions and methodology, and then discusses issues arising from the findings, and the implications of these for policy and practice.

The research questions

The hypothesis was that research findings would support a critical analysis of the view that NGOs are increasingly compensating for inadequate government provision in such sectors as social welfare, education, or health, traditionally seen as the responsibility of governments. This view appeared to neglect the involvement of NGOs in the African health sector, particularly missions, for over a century: non-governmental support to such services is not a new phenomenon. The paradigm also implies a functioning public sector with minor gaps which can be filled by NGOs, a situation far removed from reality in most African countries; and posits a government-like role for NGOs which NGOs may be reluctant, and indeed unable, to accept.

In Uganda, the motivations and actions of donors and government do, however, follow an approach to some extent consistent with such a paradigm. As in many African countries, the Ugandan health sector is largely dependent on external support, of which Northern NGOs contribute an integral, albeit modest, portion. Donors increasingly 'contract out' work to NGOs. Governments, working with constrained budgets, may view NGOs as a useful resource. In Uganda, policy-makers are not always given much choice, as donors make certain grants and loans contingent on using NGOs to implement the programmes. Although the total pool of aid is shrinking, the share of resources available to Northern and indigenous NGOs is increasing, such that the budgets of some have grown rapidly. The number of Ugandan NGOs has grown, as elsewhere in Africa. Some of them are seen to be motivated more by profit than by service. NGOs are receiving ever more attention; and while some may welcome this higher profile, others see it as potentially compromising.

What are the implications of NGO involvement in service-provision for the State — for its legitimacy, and its potential for democracy? Is the State abdicating its responsibility to provide for its citizens? If NGOs accept responsibilities for service-provision or enter into contractual relationships with donors, are they implicitly supporting an agenda of privatisation, and undermining the State? A paradigm which views NGOs as 'filling in gaps' for the government may be analytically weak, but its frequent acceptance in Africa as a guideline for the distribution of foreign aid, and the implications of this, make it relevant to our analysis. The research questions in this study are listed below.

- What do the changing trends in aid mean for NGOs, for the State, and for their relationships with each other and other actors?
- How are these relationships constructed, shaped, and understood?
- What constraints affect the decisions made by these actors, and what are the implications of these decisions?

A case-study of the Ugandan health sector allowed an in-depth, applied investigation, using several research techniques: interviews with staff of NGOs, donors, and government agencies, and use of libraries and documentation centres to find data not readily available outside Uganda. I observed health programmes funded by Oxfam (UK and Ireland) in eight districts of the country, where I conducted individual and group interviews with staff and volunteers, beneficiaries, government medical personnel, and staff of other NGOs in the area.

Findings

Responsibility for the health sector
Whose responsibility is it to provide, finance, plan, and regulate health care? The World Bank (1993:87) makes the following suggestion.

In the past, in Uganda as in many other countries, the tendency has been to think in terms of Central Government provision of social services. More recently, there has been a trend toward a more sophisticated approach, which recognises that the Central Government can make a financial contribution without necessarily providing.

This approach includes non-governmental provision, especially in curative health services, vocational or technical training, and decentralisation of responsibility for social-service provision to District authorities. Uganda's health sector will necessarily be the responsibility of a range of agencies for many years to come, and decentralisation is well under way. However, to call this a 'more sophisticated' approach implies a certain judgement or ideology which could undermine the role of the State. If governments are not encouraged to take a lead role in health-policy formulation so that they own the outcome, their capacity to manage their health sector will not develop, and the quality of health services will vary in different regions, depending on the external support available. Frequently in Uganda, people commented that 'Donor X has bought District Y'.

Missions and secular NGOs are a vital part of the Ugandan health sector, often seen to provide care of higher quality than government clinics and hospitals. Estimates of the proportion of health care provided by NGOs range from 30 to 50 per cent. When asked about their expectations of the government, people in Uganda tend to cite 'peace and security' before service-provision. Defining the legitimacy of a government narrowly, in terms of social services, may be inappropriate. The representative of one Northern NGO emphasised that Ugandan NGOs 'are meeting needs, not thinking: "Oh no, we're undermining the government!"'

NGO support for the health sector

A government may eventually accept or become resigned to the presence and popularity of NGOs in the country, and the Ugandan government seems to have decided to 'use' NGOs. This trend may encourage greater trust and openness between government and NGOs and allow the latter more influence in the formation of policy. However, government may cut back in areas with strong NGO support, in effect relinquishing a lead role in policy formulation. For example, the predominance of foreign support for AIDS-related efforts creates some tension between government and donors. In addition, NGOs may not wish to be used by government. A senior staff member of The AIDS Support Organisation (TASO), a large

Ugandan NGO, told me indignantly that a member of the government's AIDS Control Programme (ACP) had explained to her, 'We, the ACP, are the brains, and you, TASO, are our arms.' Not all NGOs are interested in being anyone's 'arms'.

However, some NGOs cannot afford the luxury of *angst* over whether they are compromising their integrity by following the agendas of donors or government. Ugandan NGOs powerfully expressed their survival instinct, or the need to bring in enough money to remain viable. Writing proposals and attending seminars or conferences have largely become income-generating activities. With education and health for sale, as they are in Uganda, staff of small NGOs are worried, like everyone else, about supporting their families; and it is hardly surprising if they adjust their approach to coincide with the donors' funding criteria. For example, a mobile AIDS home-care programme in Masaka District had to drop two counties there because funds were insufficient, but has added two counties in neighbouring Rakai District because DANIDA would fund the programme there. Similarly, the World Bank's US$71.3 million STI/AIDS programme has NGOs flocking in with proposals which fall under its remit.

Some NGOs prefer to think in terms of innovation (providing a model for government and other NGOs), instead of service-delivery, as they decide how to use their limited resources. For example, Oxfam (UK and Ireland) supports a mental-health programme in Uganda which works with traditional healers, with unprecedented success. Oxfam also supports an innovative approach to medical education, through a community-based health-care programme linked to the medical school in Mbarara. Students undertake 'residences' at a rural health centre and work with and learn from communities in health research and education. In Uganda, NGOs do seem to derive their credibility from such links to local activities and initiatives. The present concern is that the unique qualities which were understood to make NGOs effective champions of the poor and promoters of grassroots development — flexibility, innovation, creativity — are threatened if NGOs operate as puppets of the donors.

Decentralisation and NGOs

In Uganda, the evolving decentralisation of power and responsibility to the Districts has the potential to enhance the government-NGO relationship at a local level. At the national level, co-ordinating and monitoring NGOs is difficult; whose responsibility this is remains unclear, and no ministry has a proper data-base of NGOs. At the District level, NGO leaders and government medical personnel are more familiar with each other's activities. If NGOs can help to strengthen the capacity of District authorities, the latter will be in a better position to lobby for support, and to influence national government. The World Bank has supported this NGO-District government interaction in its STI/AIDs programme, by requiring NGOs to apply for funds to the District medical offices. For NGOs to apply to the Bank or Ministry of Health could undermine District-level knowledge about NGO inputs; the existing system brings District government and NGOs into closer contact.

One source of potential tension is the lack of transparency on the part of NGOs about their activities. District medical personnel expressed resentment of NGOs which did not share information about their budgets and work-plans. But the director of one Ugandan NGO stated: 'We will tell the Districts about our activities, but we will discuss money only with those who gave us the money.' The consensus among NGOs seemed to be a willingness, even a desire, to discuss and coordinate activities, coupled with a reluctance to divulge financial details. Reticence about their resources from NGOs known to have funding from overseas may eventually prompt the government to institute regulations defining the kind of information which District officials are entitled to know from NGOs.

Another area of tension is the balance between centre and District in terms of information and responsibility. A bilateral donor, embarking on a new maternal and child health (MCH) programme in ten Districts, by-passed the Ministry of Health altogether, which offended the Ministry. Although the donor argued that the day-to-day running of the programme was managed in the Districts and not the centre, a Ugandan academic pointed out that decentralisation does not mean 'cessation or breaking off of the centre. It simply means autonomy. The national government needs to know what is going on, or they will look like fools.' Seeking approval from the centre before initiating activities in Districts is one way for donors and NGOs to enhance the credibility and capacity of government.

Conclusion

For a pluralistic health sector to function well, the various actors must have clearly defined and understood roles. Government is challenged to find ways to co-ordinate different efforts without being marginalised or losing credibility in the eyes of its citizens. The director of a Ugandan research centre observed, 'Government has a mandate to look after the country but not the machinery to influence what other actors are doing.'

Although prevailing conditions oblige some NGOs to operate under greater constraints and give others greater opportunities, NGOs remain small, with neither the resources of donors nor the mandate of government. However, their size does not mean that their relationships with other actors in the health sector are unimportant. These relationships are not ideologically neutral. Although the activities of a single NGO may not significantly undermine the government, every NGO is part of a system which may do so. Whether they are filling gaps for the government or not, NGOs remain responsible, to themselves, as well as to their host governments, and their supporters, for the decisions they make.

References

The World Bank (1993), *Uganda: Social Sectors*, Washington, DC.

This paper was first published in Development in Practice *Volume 6, Number 3, 1996.*

NGOs, the poor, and local government

Christopher Collier

Introduction

Despite significant improvements in some aspects of poor people's standard of living in sub-Saharan Africa, serious problems remain. Little has changed since the beginning of the 1990s, when almost half the population lacked access to health services, over half lacked access to safe water, and Africans still consumed on average only 92 per cent of their daily calorie requirements.[1] Two-thirds of school-age children were not enrolled at school, and one in two adults was illiterate. Foreign aid has been channelled to sub-Saharan Africa partly to address these problems, and a principal conduit is non-government organisations (NGOs). For example, in 1993 the Canadian government channelled US$210 million through Canadian NGOs, which themselves raised a further US$284 million from the Canadian public for overseas work. In the same year, the British government channelled US$48 million of its aid budget through British NGOs, which themselves raised an additional US$451 million.[2]

Through their projects, Northern NGOs are purported to provide one of the most efficient ways of helping poor people in sub-Saharan Africa. The following sentiment is common: 'While any aid programme will experience a level of waste and corruption, funds sent straight to the field, often in relatively small amounts via NGOs, are far more likely to be better spent than those flowing into the treasuries of countries ... where any effective government has ceased to exist' (Clad 1993). NGOs themselves claim that working directly with the poor is the most effective way to alleviate poverty, and that their projects contribute to lasting development by adhering to the principles of sustainability and participation.

In this paper I examine an NGO project in Zambia in which I was involved, and discuss the NGO's approach and its specific consequences for local participation. I also look at the potential for sustainability, and for what I consider the essential condition for improvement in the lives of the poor: their ability to hold their government accountable for how it uses public resources. Since the approach described illustrates a tendency common to the projects of Northern NGOs in the region, a discussion of its impact is of wide relevance.

My central conclusions are summarised below.

1 The use by NGOs of large amounts of their own resources leads them to overlook existing local capacities and responsibilities when designing and implementing their projects. This reduces the potential sustainability of their interventions, and can result in their doing more harm than good.

2 By providing goods or services directly to the poor, NGOs can reduce the accountability of local government to these people, undermining the foundation upon which future and long-term improvements in their lives must be built.

3 Approaches which begin to address the causes of the predicament of poor people will require that NGOs and their donors abandon their pursuit of short-term projects whose success is measured primarily in terms of the achievement of objectives expressed as specified levels of physical outputs.

Channelling food aid

A drought in southern Africa during the 1991-92 growing season resulted in low cereal production and concomitant hunger. Governments of industrialised countries responded with donations of maize, to be distributed to the affected population.

In Zambia, all donated maize was channelled through NGOs, grouped in district drought-relief committees. The project in which I was involved was intended to distribute this to affected people through food-for-work (FFW). I was handed the approved project proposal and asked to get things going.

An investigation into the food supply problems revealed that, independent of the activities of the drought relief committee, another local structure was supplying cereal to affected people. A co-operative sold maize from branches in several villages in the area, although supplies were erratic and inadequate in the face of uncharacteristically high demand.

The co-operative seemed crucial to future food security: it functioned not only to sell cereal to hungry villagers, but also as the only permanent agency providing markets and agricultural inputs for the area's small farmers.

Most of the cereal managed by the local drought relief committee was being sold at prices undercutting those of the co-operative, forcing it to reduce its prices. Apparently, no consideration had been given to the probable impact of these sales on the co-operative's activities and economic viability. The importance of the co-operative was being completely overlooked in the aid effort.

In the NGO proposal, the co-operative and its activities had not even been mentioned. The NGO had not, for example, investigated whether the food shortage could have been addressed, at least in part, by working with the co-operative in such a way as to guarantee its supply of maize to villagers, or by shoring up the purchasing power of villagers, or both. Neither had it investigated the likely impact of its own activities on the co-operative. Looking into these issues at that point was out of the question, since the proposal had been approved a month before, and the donor would soon be expecting reports on concrete accomplishments.

Food-for-work: project experience

The main component of the FFW project was rehabilitation of secondary roads. The NGO planned to recruit and train its own technicians, who would organise and supervise the work of villagers employed on the project. The proposal did not mention that on-going responsibility for the rehabilitation and maintenance of secondary roads rested with the District Council, and it did not contemplate involving the Council in any way. Consequently, there had been no investigation of the human and financial resources that the Council could have contributed.

In overlooking important local structures, our project was no exception. The FFW projects undertaken by other members of the drought relief committee were being implemented without regard for their impact on the existing activities of key local institutions. For example, FFW was taking place in total disregard for the Ministry of Agriculture's on-going extension work, the aim of which was to encourage villagers to plant trees or adopt soil conservation measures, by convincing them that it was in their own long-term interest to do so.

Paying villagers in food for undertaking the same activities was setting a bad precedent and making extension work increasingly less viable. 'Why should we be doing this for free when others are getting food for it? We want food too' — so went the complaint of certain villagers.

It seemed that road rehabilitation and maintenance, or even drought relief through labour-intensive FFW, would be aided in the long term if the Council's Works Department could participate in and learn something from the project. In discussions, the Council revealed that in fact it wanted to move in the direction of more labour intensive road rehabilitation and maintenance. (The capital-intensive approach had proven problematic: machinery needed to carry out the work was often unavailable, or was broken down and waiting for spare parts.) Moreover, in spite of the national crisis, the Council had money to carry out road repair: a budget that it received regularly from the provincial government.

I proposed that the local Council, instead of the NGO, should provide the front-line project staff. In the context of the project, these technicians could be trained to work directly with villagers and, more importantly, get practice at it. On the other hand, the villagers could learn to identify problems needing attention, and know who were the specific Council staff to notify of the need for road repair. They could also learn to organise themselves for the purposes of carrying out public works. A relationship could be established between the villagers and the Council for the repair of local roads.

Senior NGO staff in the capital at first hesitated to accept this proposal. They felt, among other things, that Council employees might be incapable of carrying out the work, or might not get paid on time and become demoralised, with the consequence that project objectives would not be achieved. Eventually, however, the decision was taken to move ahead. The Council agreed to the proposal and initiated the recruitment of four locals to be trained as technicians. (I assisted in establishing the qualifications of candidates.) The Council's Works Foreman — a trained technician with experience in road construction — would supervise the technicians, in collaboration with the NGO project manager.

The Council agreed to pay the salaries of the technicians for the duration of the project from the road-maintenance budget. These would be normal salaries that any government employee would receive, and could be sustained by the government. When the harvest came in, and cereal was neither available from donors nor accepted as payment by the population, work could continue by substituting payments in food with small cash payments drawn from the Council's road-maintenance budget. In many parts of the country, precedents existed for carrying out road maintenance in this way, and the Council's Works Foreman had indeed undertaken such activities in the past.

The NGO approach

As is common, the NGO's stated aim was to make 'a viable and meaningful contribution to development in Zambia' by adhering to the principles of 'participation' and 'sustainability' and by integrating these principles 'into all aspects of programme development'. The NGO's official funder, moreover, aimed to promote development by supporting projects which 'help achieve good government'. This experience illustrates how aspects of the way in which an NGO approaches its work at the project level can undermine the achievement of these objectives.

'Getting the job done'

The NGO intended to carry out the project by using its own front-line staff. By controlling them, the NGO would control the implementation of the project. This would help it to ensure that positive reports flowed back to donors on a timely basis. These reports would reassure donors that their money was making a difference — that 'the job was getting done' — and would predispose them to approve additional requests for funding, crucial to the NGO's growth.

By using its own personnel, the NGO would have eliminated the participation of the Council. The Works Department — which was responsible for road maintenance — would have learned nothing about labour intensive road maintenance. This would have led to very low potential for sustainability. Once external funding was withdrawn, it is unlikely that road rehabilitation and maintenance could continue. The NGO staff would be from outside the geographical area of the project, and would want to return home. They would have been earning good salaries with the NGO, and would not be willing to accept the relatively lower salaries of the Council. They would have gained the prestige of working with a foreign NGO, and would think of working with local government as 'lowering themselves'.

In order to maximise potential sustainability, the resources provided by NGOs should be kept to the absolute minimum. Whenever external resources are used, there should be a specific plan for their substitution by local resources. In this case, provisions had to be made for the withdrawal of food aid and NGO staff.

Space must be created for the use of local resources in the initial project, if they are to be counted on to sustain activities once external support is withdrawn. Roads can be fixed, wells dug, people fed, or seeds distributed. What is important, however, is not that these things are done, but *how* they are done. Achieving these outputs should not be an end in itself, but more a means of local learning, of establishing working relationships among relevant local actors, and of identifying and mobilising local resources. In the course of producing these 'outputs', a basis must be laid for the production of the same 'outputs' in the future.

The willingness of local counterparts (poor people themselves, or local government) to put up resources is an indicator of the project's potential for sustainability. If local government, for example, is unwilling to participate meaningfully in the project at the time of its design and execution, this suggests that its priorities are not the NGO's, and that it will have no interest in, or capacity to support, the activities or processes that the project has initiated.

NGOs should reserve the right to withdraw from projects if counterparts fail to live up to agreements, and donors should accept this. As it is, local officials can fail to fulfil their promises because they know that the NGO is in a vulnerable position: it has to report to its donor and show concrete results within a specified time.

Letting government 'off the hook'

Clearly, poor people should expect certain goods and services from their government. In addition to roads, these include health services, education, and water and sanitation. Projects in which NGOs use their own resources to deliver goods and services — which local government should be delivering but is not — lead the population to reduce its expectations of what local government can or should be doing for it. Such projects let local government 'off the hook'. The population's needs covered, local government is free to use in other ways money budgeted for projects intended to benefit the poor.

Local resources may be genuinely lacking, as was evidently so in at least some districts of Zambia. However, a lack of resources should not be assumed. In this case, funds had in fact been allocated to the Council for road rehabilitation. If the NGO had gone ahead and hired its own technicians, one might wonder what would have happened to these funds. The NGO project would have served to undermine the fundamental notion that local government should be accountable to the people. The impact would be a reduction in the long-term chances of improvement in the lives of the poor.

The importance of accountability cannot be overstated. Even famine has been tackled in this way:

> The conquest of famine in India and a handful of African countries such as Botswana, was based on democratic accountability. In these countries, famine is a political issue. When famine appears imminent, it is of urgent concern to journalists, trade unionists, and voters, and hence to members of parliament, the civil service, and the government. Giving famine a political sting is the secret to its conquest. (De Waal 1993)

Raising the accountability of local government to poor citizens is perhaps the most sustainable way to improve their living standards. Unfortunately, the NGO approach described above is generally antithetical to the goal of increased accountability of local government.

Working with the poor

A consequence of addressing the problems of poor people directly may be that the importance of other local actors is overlooked. The poor cannot achieve development in isolation. They must interact dynamically with other local agencies in various ways.

Future development will not depend on the NGO–'beneficiary' relationship, but on that between the 'beneficiaries' and other local actors. Since the NGO will depart, the relationship between itself and the poor is not sustainable. The questions which the NGO needs to ask are: 'How will this have to work in the future, after we leave? Who will these people need to work with?' These other agencies, whose existence pre-dates the NGO intervention, and which may play important roles in the future, must also participate in projects, or at least be taken into account when projects are designed and implemented.

In areas of Zambia where there was no co-operative, the NGO might have been justified to go ahead with sales of food or food-for-work. However, in areas where a co-operative was working, it should have made efforts at least not to undermine it, or even to strengthen it. In the future, poor people will depend on the co-operative for supplies and markets. A project that puts the co-operative out of business will have a profoundly different impact on their long-term welfare from one that helps to maintain it.

The poor will also depend on the local Council for services and technical assistance. A project that alienates the population from the

Council will affect poor people's long-term welfare differently from one that builds the relationship between them and local government. If the NGO had gone ahead as planned, to whom would the population have looked for assistance in rehabilitating the roads once the project was over, and the NGO gone?

NGOs have an opportunity to play 'intermediary roles between state and non-state institutions in respect of participation, accountability and development' (Dias 1993). An NGO project can provide local government with a means of getting in touch with its people, and of integrating them in the planning and implementation of economic and social development — depending, of course, on the degree of decentralisation in government. An NGO can provide the poor with a means of becoming aware of local government responsibilities and capacities. It can also stimulate popular organisation, within the project context, by establishing a forum for meaningful participation in design and implementation, and a means of holding government accountable. An NGO project is an excellent context in which to establish or reinforce a process whereby people and government work together to solve local problems.

Conclusions

There is pervasive disappointment that aid to sub-Saharan Africa is not resulting in any significant improvements in the lives of poor Africans, and that additional aid will not solve the underlying problems. There is a feeling that no real basis has been laid for development, and that even increased quantities of aid will do nothing to resolve the problem of poverty.

Unless aid projects make it a priority to establish or reinforce mechanisms by which existing, locally available resources are mobilised and used effectively in resolving the problems of the poor, they cannot contribute to laying a basis for future development.

The direct provision by NGOs of goods and services must not lead poor people to expect less of their governments. On the contrary, NGO projects should promote popular organisation and the capacity of poor people to assert their claims to public resources, and to hold government accountable. Such projects should also help government to understand the needs and capacities of its population, and become more capable of serving it. NGOs can damage prospects for genuine development by undermining the relationship between the people and their government.

Notes

1 Statistics from United Nations Development Programme (1994), p. 133.

2 Statistics from Michel (1995), pp. C3, C4

References

Clad, J. C. and R. D. Stone (1993), 'New mission for foreign aid', *Foreign Affairs* Vol 72, No 1, pp. 196-205 (quote from p. 199).

De Waal, A. and R. Omaar (1993), 'Doing harm by doing good? The international relief effort in Somalia', *Current History* Vol 92, No 574, pp. 198–202 (quote from p. 199).

Dias, C. J. and D. Gillies (1993), *Human Rights, Democracy, and Development*, Montreal: International Centre for Human Rights and Democratic Development, p. 14.

Michel, J. H. (1995), Development Co-operation: efforts and policies of the members of the Development Assistance Committee, Paris: OECD Publications.

United Nations Development Programme (1994), *Human Development Report*, New York: Oxford University Press.

This paper was first published in Development in Practice *Volume 6, Number 3, 1996.*

Let's get civil society straight: NGOs, the state, and political theory

Alan Whaites

Foreword

This chapter has been formed from two complementary articles written in response to the remarkable growth of interest in civil society issues during the 1990s. The first of these appeared in 1996 at a time when such interest was surging, albeit with little theoretical depth or study. Since then, the idea that development should be undertaken through civil society has become an industry orthodoxy. Major studies have been completed, or are in progress, by bodies such as the World Bank and the UK Department for International Development (DFID). A library of books has been published, ranging from the seminal to the deeply forgettable. Civil Society departments, advisers, and units now proliferate even in the most unlikely places. But has this led to greater clarity in our thinking and practice? Perhaps inevitably, the answer is mixed.

The continuing weaknesses in this exponential growth are best summarised by John Keane, a political scientist who did much to re-popularise the concept of civil society:

> Its burgeoning popularity accelerates the accumulation of
> inherited ambiguities, new confusions and outright contradictions.
> For this reason alone the expanding talk of civil society is not
> immune to muddle and delirium. There are even signs that the
> meanings of the term 'civil society' are multiplying to the point
> where, like a catchy advertising slogan, it risks imploding through
> overuse. (Keane 1998: 36)

This chapter argues that the confusion over civil society is exemplified within international development, where ideas are largely driven by the priorities of donors. Despite the studies and specialists, NGOs have failed to address three basic questions which are inherent in any meaningful attempt to identify the role of global civil society in advancing the cause of the poor:

- How do NGOs separate beneficial from non-beneficial civil society, North or South?
- How do NGOs weave a strategy for nurturing civil society into a strategy for building the capacity of states?
- How do NGOs rescue the idea of global civil society from the priorities of donors, and develop the critical micro-macro linkages that affect the daily lives of the poor?

These questions shape the following discussion, which is also informed by the work of various individual thinkers and organisations, some of whom are mentioned below. As far as development is concerned, clarity and coherence are needed more urgently than ever. For, in the final analysis, our interest in civil society and its potential will only be of use if it brings meaningful long-term change for the poor.

Do definitions really matter?

The term 'civil society' has been an issue of debate since it gained currency in the last century. Discussion has usually focused on the perceptions of civil society expressed by de Tocqueville and Hegel, a dichotomy that offers the choice between a largely positive and a largely negative view of the concept. More recently (and usually unwittingly) NGOs have become drawn into a theoretical divide between those who hold a classical de Tocquevillian view and those taking a more inclusive position similar to the African-based thinking of Jean-François Bayart.

Does it really matter that NGOs are slipping into this divide over the meaning of civil society? Given the importance that donors and NGOs attach to the concept, it matters a great deal, particularly where societies are heterogeneous and divided. The ways in which development NGOs perceive civil society, and consequently plan projects to facilitate the work of civil associations, can have a significant effect on the evolution (or lack of it) of civil society in the countries in which they work.

At a 1995 conference on development,[1] discussion of the role of external forces in nurturing associations that strengthen civil society was notable for the lack of one vital question: what kind of civil association strengthens civil society? That is, how do we try to ensure that strengthening resources for civil society nurtures beneficial rather than destructive and divisive groups? This strikes at the core of the split between the positions of de Tocqueville and Bayart, which has also been central to some of the best academic work done recently on the politics of Africa. NGOs have a responsibility to assess whether all civil associations act as building blocks for civil society, or only those with specific, identifiable characteristics. Sadly, this issue has been too easily overlooked by NGOs eager to embrace the perceived benefits of the revived interest in civil society.

NGOs and the grab for civil society

Since 1990, the concept of civil society has been 'grabbed' by NGOs as one relating closely to their own natural strengths. On the surface, civil society is intimately connected with the role of local community associations or groups, and with the indigenous NGO sector. For Northern NGOs, this leads to an intellectual association between civil society and local 'partner' or implementing organisations. From studies of the factors that encouraged a focus on civil society (e.g. Robinson 1995) two central trends can be discerned in donor and NGO thinking.

Among donors, interest in civil society has been associated with the evolution of the conditionality of aid. Conditionality, which rose to prominence in the 1980s, allowed donors to think more creatively about the large-scale impacts of their bilateral programmes. From 1990, conditionality took on a political dimension when some donors became preoccupied with 'good governance'. This tendency acquired an economic as well as moral rationale with the 1991 *World Development Report* (World Bank 1991), in which democracy was projected as not only ethically desirable but also more efficient. Donors began to re-appraise the role of civil society in providing a foundation for sustainable democracy. The work of political scientists such as Stepan (1998), Stocpol (1992), and Keane (1998) variously pointed to civil society as the key to making good governance work.

Thus, the democratising function of civil society assumed a higher profile among multilateral agencies, and NGOs were identified as a possible point of contact with its building blocks, namely civil associations. Coupled with these changes was an increasing awareness among NGOs of their own potential role in the wider development picture.

Contemporary with the rise of Participatory Rural Assessment (PRA) and its methodologies — a new orthodoxy for promoting community-based design of, and control over, development projects — was a converse trend. This was the idea that NGO-supported projects can legitimately have wider and much larger economic, social, and political objectives. As NGOs acquired new ways of thinking about 'partnership' and the implementation of projects by local organisations, so they were also considering the wider ramifications of such activities. A 1992 conference on 'scaling up' the impact of NGOs[2] marked a breakthrough in addressing the potential macro-impact and macro-application of grassroots development activities (Edwards and Hulme 1992).

The process was spurred on by the UN, which moved to the fore in promoting civil society as a development issue. UNDP, UNICEF, and ECOSOC introduced procedures to provide voluntary associations with greater access to their systems; and ECOSOC's review of NGOs has discussed the possibility of funding Southern NGO participation at ordinary UN business meetings (UN NGLS 1995a: 7). However, assumptions about the nature of NGOs have allowed the issue of 'access' by the voluntary sector to dominate discussions about civil society within the UN. Indeed, the UN NGO Liaison Service has produced an impressive paper emphasising the expanding place for NGOs around UN tables (UN NGLS 1995b).

The combination of donor, NGO, and UN interest provides the background to the civil society 'grab'. But few NGOs have explored the full theoretical implications of civil society, or clearly articulated their own interpretations of its nuances. The problem is the belief that NGOs are inherently bound to strengthen civil society, an assumption which, if acted upon, might in fact weaken the evolution of civil society in certain contexts.

The theoretical division

Civil society is usually held to be the collective intermediary between the individual and the state. For de Tocqueville, civil society (in contrast to traditional society) is a defensive counterbalance to the increased capabilities of the modern state.[3] It provides a realm in which society interacts constructively with the state, not to subvert and destroy it, but to refine its actions and improve its efficiency. Thus, civil society tends to be associated not with the selfish drive of Hegelian theory, but with the constructive actions of altruistic concern.

Hence, civil society groups coalesce not on the basis of primordial attachments (ethnicity, language, religion), but rather on 'small issues' that cut across such boundaries and bring people together in new coalitions. For de Tocqueville, a key example was the nineteenth-century temperance movement in the USA, which brought together thousands of disparate people under a common banner. The anti-slavery movement or anti-Corn Law League played similar roles in Britain.

The implications for development practitioners relate to these 'small issue' coalitions or 'civil associations'. Stepan's study of Brazil (Stepan 1988) gives grounds for ruling politically motivated groups out of the equation, and for focusing on those local NGOs, human rights groups, and leisure associations which conform with de Tocqueville's precepts.

Small issues

The reasons why an association forms are critical for its long-term role. Associations which bring people together, regardless of old identities, to work together for development — to form credit schemes or health clubs, for example — may play empowering roles. In the short term, so will those associations which undertake the same functions in primordially homogeneous groups. But in the latter case, their aim may move from the 'small issue' (sadly, in this context community development is a 'small issue') to strengthening the primordial group's comparative position within a wider context of clientelism and patronage.

Thus, classical de Tocquevillian thinking offers a crucial challenge to NGOs working to strengthen local civil associations or community groups. Most NGOs, however, lose sight of these crucial caveats about the quality of associative forms. They adopt the view that all civil associations — that is, all community or development groups — naturally build civil society. Take, for example, the definition of civil society underpinning UNDP's policy on the links between its own programmes and civil society (UNDP 1993). This has become something of a mainstay within the NGO sector, and it rests on the intermediary role of civil society and the state, viewing social movements as civil society groups. Thus, all associations, no matter how primordially-rooted or patronage-based, are seen as civil society organisations (CSOs).

UNDP's position has been seminal for many development groups, and the focus on interacting with civil society rather than analysing its composite parts has had major impact. The concentration on NGOs' access to the UN system, mentioned above, has muted discussion of the long-term impact of different types of NGOs. UNDP's 1995 paper, prepared for the UN's fiftieth anniversary, picked up its earlier work on civil society (UNDP 1995). Its focus is primarily on collaborative mechanisms, and its definitions refer to civil society collectively, rather than to individual elements within it.

The adoption of such a limited definition may be crucial. For example, a village-level project in a highly heterogeneous area may unwittingly undermine the future growth of civil society. If the village is primordially homogeneous, and the project develops strong local organisations without setting up umbrella bodies to promote co-operation with other villages, what has it achieved? In some instances, it will have increased the village's capacity to play the patron/client game, and strengthened its internal identities, without forging the mechanisms to build civil society.[4]

NGOs and Bayart

Some argue that all associations and community groups are indeed components of civil society, a view associated with Jean-François Bayart, whose work explores societies' attempts to subvert and control the state (Bayart 1986; 1993). In this view, projects that simply strengthen groups associating on primordial grounds are facilitating a natural, competitive process arising from the specific characteristics of African civil society. This suggests that it is largely inappropriate to apply Western concepts of civil society to contexts in which primordial attachments are unlikely to decline in the near future.

Both arguments have their strengths and weaknesses. However, evidence is emerging to suggest that primordial attachments *do* change with the process of societal change, and this may have important implications. There is a school of thought centred on 'bringing the state back in', and exemplified by Laitin's work on Nigeria, that suggests the state can hugely affect primordial identities through its own changing policies (Laitin 1992). The example of Pakistan suggests that the development of a local bourgeoisie may foster integrative groups based on 'small issues', even in the face of entrenched ethnic or religious divisions (Whaites 1995). World Vision UK, in perhaps the first NGO research into the relationship between identities and nascent civil society, found that even apparently destructive political acts, such as displacement and conflict, may provoke conditions conducive to the growth of civil society (Westwood 1996).

Such examples suggest that we should not yet give up on traditional, evolutionary ideas of civil society. The interaction of social change with an active state structure may foster the integrative type of civil association envisaged by de Tocqueville, nurturing the future growth of civil society within developing states.

The role of the state

A second crucial area, which has been overlooked in the ways development has adopted civil society, is the question of integrating civil society strategies with those for strengthening the state. The traditional view, argued for instance by Richard Jefferies (1993), is that a strong state is a prerequisite for civil society. But this model causes immense conceptual problems for development political scientists, and by extension for international NGOs which operate in contexts where civil society — in the form of Southern NGOs — is strong, and yet the state is weak; a fact which NGOs have been reluctant to see as necessarily a bad thing. Many would agree with James Midgley (1986):

> Since the least organised and marginalised sections of society have little opportunity to influence government, their interests are not likely to be served by state involvement in community participation. Non-governmental organisations are not only more likely to serve the interests of the poor but they are capable of initiating schemes that increase the organisational power and consequently the political pressures that can be exerted by poor people. (p.154)

This chapter has argued that adopting an entirely uncritical approach to civil society can do more harm than good, particularly in heterogeneous social contexts. Equally, a failure within political theory to read the warnings of an imbalance between weak states and strong civil society would be to compound past errors. These have included an over-eagerness to fill gaps in service provision, further undermining the ability of a weak state to benefit its people. Where states are weak but civil society is strong, development practitioners have good reason to heed warnings which serve, in this instance, to underscore the thinking of development academics and the best practice of a number of NGOs.

NGO, civil society, and state linkages

The major architects of modern civil society theory, Hegel, de Tocqueville, and Gramsci, all sought to address dilemmas regarding the relationship between the state and civil society. The presence of a definable state was common to the thinking of all three, and it was something the latter two viewed with suspicion and unease. The work of de Tocqueville, which has underpinned much subsequent writing, was firmly rooted in the US and European contexts of rapid industrialisation and the establishment of modern, effective governmental structures.[5] Indeed, the capabilities of the 'modern state' in an era without developed democratic systems made necessary some form of social counter-weight, which civil associations helped to provide.

This model has much historical validity in the West, and the premise that an effective state acts as a catalyst for civil associations can legitimately be applied to some developing contexts, as for instance in Pakistan (Whaites 1995). The validity of this argument in the developing states of the 1990s is, however, not exclusive or unique. The effective state gives rise to civil associations, but then so do many other factors, including donor priorities and the process of local development — such as the forming of a women's health club, a revolving loans scheme, or a youth association. It is here that the purist theory of civil society may depart from reality. In some countries, for instance, it is the very weakness of the state, its failure to provide services or to engage in the local development process, which has stimulated a thriving voluntary sector and, with it, a strong and vocal civil society.

Strong civil society and weak state: does it matter?

The reality of strong civil societies and weak states is a useful area for theoretical writing, of which it has generated a considerable amount. But, does this reversal of classical theory have any practical relevance for organisations actually seeking to engage in partnership with local civil society? This chapter argues that the idea that civil society and the state should counter-balance each other is still highly relevant to international NGOs because of the dangers posed by nurturing a strong civil society while ignoring the weakness of an ineffective state.

Personally, in common with many on the left, I am caught in the paradox of seeing the state as part saviour, a vehicle for social change and equality, and part villain, an intrusive monolith with a propensity to lose sight of the common good in pursuit of its own bureaucratic agenda. However, on whichever side one ultimately stands, there is no escaping the need for some form of effective governmental structure. An underlying relationship exists between the effectiveness of state functions and of political stability, and sustainable democracy. Although

NGOs may be able to imitate the state as a vehicle for local development and change (although with deficiencies, outlined below), they can rarely arbitrate between competing social groups or administer a process of popular choice in the selection of government.

Migdal's model of the weak state can be criticised, but his account of its vulnerability to being held ransom by powerful social groups is borne out by experience in countries including Nigeria, Brazil, the Philippines, and Thailand (Migdal 1988, esp. p.9 and pp. 34–41). The logical extension of de Tocqueville's view of civil society as a buffer against the state is that the latter must be capable of performing the more Hegelian role of acting as a safeguard against competing social groups. For political scientists, the weak state, unable to perform this refereeing function, has often been seen as an especially African phenomenon, giving rise to the famous observation:

> Between the ambitions of the elite and the survival stratagems of the masses, the state often appears to survive essentially as a show, a political drama with an audience more or less willing to suspend its disbelief. (O'Brien 1991)

Weak states as a development problem

A weak state leaves vacuums of power that elites are usually more than happy to fill. This brings the potential for a series of scenarios which have, experience shows, placed substantial new obstacles in the way of development. Claude Aké (1995) provides a salutary outline of the impact of the weak and suborned state on development in Africa. The state may be relatively large, with numerous ministries and offices right down to district level, but its very size, and the often bloated nature of the bureaucracy, can only serve to fuel corruption and external influence. These are factors which dominate the weak state, making it powerful without being capable of governing effectively.

Aké (1995: 74) believes that statism and the existence of large 'parastatals' are inherent brakes on economic development. These criticisms would find favour with many of those donors that are driven by a liberalisation agenda. But they apply primarily to weak, suborned states; there is no fundamental law of the universe to say that the large state *must* be ineffective. Weakness or strength is not determined by the size of the state but by its relative autonomy. Unless the state enjoys some degree of autonomy from elite social groups, and also adheres to a goal (no matter how ill-defined) of serving the overall interests of the country, it will usually be seen as a potential source of personal profit. The result is a competition, devoid of democratic niceties, for domination and control, a phenomenon analysed in many of the classics of development politics, such as Huntington (1968), Clapham (1985), and Kohli (1990). It is a phenomenon which, despite being well described in relation to Africa, has affected countries throughout the developing world.[6]

But what if a neo-liberal paradise came to pass, with the state removed from most aspects of community and individual life? Such a paradise would almost certainly worsen the long-term prospects of the poor. The neo-liberal scenario is normally taken to assume a strong state, but only as a regulatory force, with social provision undertaken by voluntary groups. In developing countries, this means a state with effective ministries in the capital, a small presence in the provinces and districts, but little role in the village or slum. The shrinking of the state would not, however, end the competition for resources between elites — all that would happen is that the vehicle for rivalry would change, a phenomenon explored by Chabal and Daloz (1999).

Ultimately, the smaller state would almost certainly be even less able to assert itself in mediating between and policing these elites. For all its faults, the state is the only potential source of legitimate and enforceable action within most countries. When bereft of autonomy the state may perform its functions poorly, but reducing its role further offers no solution. The shrinking state also serves only to reduce the links of accountability which offer one of the best hopes for constructive change. The individual in a local community would have little vested interest in either the efficiency or honesty of the shrunken state, thus removing an important impetus to democratic participation on the part of the poor (Collier 1996). Where the state retreats to a role of funding civil society-based social provision, then an unaccountable NGO layer is placed between the voter and the identifiable use of resources. Whom, then, should the poor blame for inefficiency and waste; the NGO or, assuming the funding relationship is clear, the state? In the development context, the reliance on NGOs as the primary sources of social provision raises much discussed issues of consistency and coordination.

Civil society and the weak state: a real issue for NGOs

If we accept that it is desirable for the state to have some degree of effectiveness at the local level (ideally under the rubric of a popularly elected government), then questions regarding the replacement of state provision by NGO activities become acutely important, particularly in the light of continuing development trends. A broad overview of the reasons why NGOs should beware of the long-term consequences of replacing the state in service provision (often termed 'gap filling') is offered by Christy Cannon (1996, reprinted in this volume) and also by Mark Robinson (1995). Here, we will concentrate on the inherent long-term dangers for state-society relations.

International NGOs have contributed significantly to situations of strong civil societies and weak states through gap filling by taking advantage of the shrinkage of government services that result from structural adjustment programmes (SAPs). SAPs have tended to emphasise the drastic reduction of fiscal deficits in situations where tax receipts are traditionally low. The resulting cuts in health and education spending (see, for example, Tevera 1995: 83–5) led to the evils of user-charges, and gave strong encouragement to NGOs to replace the state in providing basic services. This is typified by the PAMSCAD-style safety-net programmes of the World Bank (Stewart and van der Geest 1995). Belatedly, the Bank has realised some of the negative consequences of a approach based purely on reducing the size of the state. Its 1997 report (World Bank 1997) recognises many of the problems, but still advocates competition in the provision of resources and the shrinking of the state to a level which fits its 'capability'.

The problem of NGOs engaging in gap filling (providing part of the competition advocated by the Bank) does not apply only to those groups that still take an institutional approach to aid, such as running schools and hospitals. Just as important is the 'bread and butter work' of NGOs at the community level. Yet few have had qualms about providing agricultural extension workers or offering training for health volunteers and traditional birth attendants (TBAs). Such activities are part of what an NGO does, but these are also functions which are nominally the responsibility of the state. Indeed, in Sri Lanka, for instance, they are part of what the state does best. However, international NGOs, and increasingly Southern NGOs, have been very willing to fill these gaps in grassroots social provision. This is not to argue that NGOs should abandon such activity for the sake of political theory and the niceties of nominal roles, for the state would often not be able to fill the gap. However, unless there are mitigating circumstances, such as a particularly repressive regime, the NGO should also seek to build up the capacity of the state *as an integral part* of this local grassroots work.

Bringing together state and civil society

For NGOs, there is nothing new in working alongside state structures in implementing development projects. For example, health programmes undertaken in association with local referral systems are commonplace. NGOs assist by strengthening each point in the referral chain, to ensure what is intended to be a significant improvement in local healthcare. In such programmes, and sometimes as a government requirement, counterpart training is included within the process, with managers for social ministries learning new skills and approaches from their NGO colleagues. These interventions help to bring the state more actively into community life and in the process raise local expectations of the state. The result is that the civil society groups thus nurtured, such as community-based organisations (CBOs) or larger local NGOs, are likely to engage more fully with the state in pursuing development aims, while the state should be able and willing to accept such engagement and also deliver results.

Stripped of all its theory and nineteenth-century thinkers, this is where a key aspect of civil society connects with the process of development and the work of NGOs. It is in these existing roles of supporting civil associations *and* building the capacity of local state service-providers, that the issue finds a form which avoids either by-passing civil society or undermining the state. In a DFID funded World Vision community health project in Kompong Tralach, Cambodia, project activities were primarily implemented by medical workers within the local district health department. Project staff worked alongside these government employees and provided training and essential equipment over a five-year period. Training government health staff extended beyond increasing the overall level of health skills to questions of administration, record-keeping, and the use of participatory techniques in community work. The project encouraged the establishment of new CBOs including women's health clubs and microcredit associations. The nurturing of these civil associational groups has been balanced within the project by the increased involvement of district-level government structures with individual communities.

Similarly, in Brazil World Vision became involved with the community of Jucuri (on the outskirts of Mossoró) following a drought. The community consists almost entirely of landless farmers who had been permitted by local landowners to cultivate crops on the neighbouring land free of charge, provided that they left fodder for the landowners' cattle. Community organisation within Jucuri was already very strong before World Vision's involvement. The Farmers' Association was the partner agency, and it had developed a formidable process of lobbying the local government and of finding other sources of income for the community. It had, for example, struck a deal with Petrobras oil company to drill a well. A committee had been set up by the community to deal with the local government on issues affecting them, and to lobby for the provision of basic services.

For World Vision, particularly in the health sector, local government capacity building was integral to its objectives. Three government health workers involved with project activities visited the community regularly, and worked closely with the Association in training the community in basic primary healthcare education and awareness campaigns, with a major emphasis on cholera. The project also helped the community to receive training from a local government alternative health specialist, thus gaining access to a state service that might otherwise have remained unused. The project's ability to involve local government health workers enabled community-level training and education in improved nutrition to take place, with small vegetable gardens being started individually in most homes. Such projects are neither unusual nor new, but they do illustrate the genuine contribution which NGOs can make to local government capacity building; a contribution which creates new linkages between state and society at the grassroots.

Getting the state and civil society straight: central themes

For some NGOs, the labelling of all potential partner groups as 'civil society organisations' reflects the continued acceptance of a universalistic, Bayartian view of civil society. However, there is room for dialogue within the development community about the usefulness of more traditional definitions. The de Tocquevillian analysis of those characteristics that are central to the transformation of a community group into a civil association will provide a firmer theoretical underpinning to NGOs' application of the concept of civil society, just as PRA provided the practical means to use new anthropological theory. Crucially, it also allows NGOs a starting point in addressing that first central question: how do NGOs separate beneficial from non-beneficial civil society, North or South?

The classical de Tocquevillian perspective suggests that the issues around which groups associate are central to the way in which these should be defined. Where groups exist in a highly heterogeneous environment, and yet fail to cut across these identities, serious questions must be asked. To strengthen such groups, particularly where improvements are viewed by them as a comparative or competitive gain in relation to others, may be counterproductive.

Alternatively, groups that use 'small issues' (such as the provision of credit, healthcare, or education) and that *do* span primordial identities may have tremendous potential. Even in more homogeneous societies, where a single religion or ethnic or linguistic group is dominant, it is possible to seek out those groups that promote the idea of association in a way which cuts across any continuing divisions, such as local geography, gender, and even political loyalty.

The second crucial question revolves around the state: how do NGOs weave a strategy for nurturing civil society into a strategy for building the capacity of the state? This chapter has not tried to address in detail the unquestionable difficulties of capacity building in relation to the localised state (side-stepping thorny issues such as corruption). But it has sought to highlight the real connection that exists between the theory which underpins a much favoured concept among NGOs — civil society — and the dynamics of NGO-state relations. The reality of developing country contexts, where weak states and relatively strong civil societies are now a factor, calls for the theory to be adapted to meet situations not faced by de Tocqueville or Hegel during the industrial revolution. But, in accepting the *reality* of strong civil societies and weak states, we must also accept that this brings both developmental and political dangers.

These dangers are the flip-side of the counterbalance to the state which de Tocqueville believed civil society offered the individual. For NGOs, they are a further reminder that the short-term benefits of 'gap filling' are outweighed by the dangers of doing so in a way that undermines the state. NGOs should not greet the involvement of the state as a 'complicating' factor, but rather as an important part of the development process. The only sustainable course is one which acts both to nurture civil society and to build the capacity of the state at local level — an area in which NGOs have much experience and a great deal to offer.

Postscript

The two articles on which this chapter is based sought to highlight the need for discernment in interventions aimed at nurturing civil society, and called for a renewed focus on the need to build the capacity of the state. Both issues have been thrown into fresh light by broad discussions of civil society and aid (e.g. Van Rooy *et al.* 1998; Fisher 1998; Boli *et al.* 1999). The question of civil society undermining the state has been taken much further by writers exploring conflict and political crisis in Africa. Bayart (1999) has linked the potential for elite misuse of the increasing privatisation of development to what he terms the 'criminalisation' of the African state. Clapham (1996, esp. chapter 9) and Chabal and Daloz (1995) similarly see civil society, including Northern NGOs, as new sources of, and vehicles for, clientelistic *largesse*.

The academic source of these works underlines the reality that while international NGOs have been forced by Alex de Waal and others to debate the role of aid in complex emergencies, there has been little to provoke a wider debate on the long-term political impact of civil society-based development. The implication of the arguments put forward in this chapter is that such support is intrinsically and unavoidably political. NGOs must, therefore, face up this reality and make positive choices in the impacts they seek, locally, nationally, and at the global level. It is this issue above all that must lead NGOs to consider the third crucial issue posed in the foreword: how do NGOs rescue the idea of global civil society from the priorities of donors, and develop the critical micro-macro linkages that affect the daily lives of the poor?

Donors, theorists, and NGOs themselves have done much over the last decade to thrust civil society to the centre of the development process. NGOs now need the courage to listen to, and embrace, the broadest aspirations of the poor from the outset of the civil society building process. If we do not keep in mind the potential for civil society to transform national and global society, NGOs risk simply becoming a methodological tool for delivering development assistance down to the grassroots.

Manuel Castells, echoing de Tocqueville, implies that civil society acts as much to provide new sources of identity for individuals as to provide a springboard for fundamental social change. In suggesting that civil society can act more to build havens than heavens, Castells (1998: 64) highlights the danger that the ultimate political impact of civil society may be insular and regressive. Without a commitment to supporting broad visions for social and political change, the strengthening of civil society may do as much to silence the aspirations of the poor as to give them form.

This is not to say that it is wrong for civil society to flourish. On the contrary, it offers new forums for communities, and this had much to do with its growth in most developed states. One must remember, however, that the politically beneficial aspects of civil society, upon which donors have seized so feverishly, are associated not with the rise of the sector as a whole, but with the emergence of a certain type of civil association that is willing to engage directly with the state. To date, the vision for the potential offered by such groups on the wider level has come more often from individuals than from civil society organisations themselves. Michael Edwards (1999) has reminded the development movement of the need for a broader view. Elsewhere, I have also argued that NGOs must see macro-political change as a legitimate objective of the development project, and not just the preserve of donors and their 'good governance' mantras (Whaites 2000).

In embracing the aspirations of the poor in their broadest sense, NGOs must recognise that global civil society needs to pursue macro objectives of its own. Just as multilateral institutions can mimic a global state in some albeit limited areas (such as trade), so NGOs have shown they can act effectively on the global stage on some issues. Hope has been offered by the ability of shifting coalitions to influence and stall the global policy debate. The fate of the MAI (for now) and the collapse of the 1999 WTO trade talks at Seattle owed at least something to such (often Internet-based) cross-border and cross-sectoral amalgams of NGOs. More positively, the Campaign to Ban Landmines and Jubilee 2000 have gone beyond forcing the abandonment of policy and instead created global momentum for affirmative change.

We are still at the start of the globalisation of civil society forms. Encouragingly, some coalitions have already taken steps to redress the traditional Northern bias of international movements. Even so, the Internet-based processes that lead to protests such as those at Seattle tend to ensure a louder voice for the fringe concerns of the North rather than for the substantive concerns of the poor. Civil society, including the major international NGOs, might usefully see their future priority as being to strengthen this micro-macro global voice.

Notes

1   'Building Capacity in the South: partnerships, policies and the role of donors', *BOND*, 18 September 1995.

2   'Scaling-up NGO Impacts: learning from experience,' SCF and University of Manchester, January 1992.

3   See *Democracy in America*, Alexis de Tocqueville, Vol 1 (1835) and Vol 2 (1840), a summary of which can be found in Keane (1988).

4   Oxfam GB offers an example of how to address imperatives to build 'civil society' in heterogeneous contexts. A December 1995 paper, *Former Yugoslavia: towards a durable peace,* specifically calls for development projects which are 'integrative', cutting across primordial identities.

5   For a discussion on this point, see Catherine Boone (1994), 'States and Ruling Classes in Postcolonial Africa: the enduring contradictions of power', in Migdal (1998).

References

Aké, C. (1995), 'The Democratisation of Disempowerment in Africa', in Hippler, J. *et al.* (eds), *The Democratisation of Disempowerment: the problem of democracy in the third world*, London: Pluto Press with Transnational Institute.

Bayart, J. F. *et al.* (1999), *The Criminalisation of the State in Africa*, : Indiana University Press.

Bayart, J. F. (1993), *The State in Africa: the politics of the belly*, London: Longman.

Bayart, J. F. (1986), 'Civil Society in Africa', in Chabal, P. *et al.*, *Political Domination in Africa*, Cambridge: Cambridge University Press.

Boli, J, J. M. Thomas *et al.* (1999), *Constructing World Culture: international non-governmental organisations since 1875*, Stanford CA: Stanford University Press.

Castells, M. (1998), *The Power of Identity*, Volume II of *The Information Age: economy, society and culture*, Oxford: Blackwell.

Chabal, P and J. Daloz (1999), *Africa Works: disorder as political instrument*, Oxford: James Currey.

Clapham , C. (1985), *Third World Politics*, London: Routledge.

Clapham, C. (1996), *Africa and the International System*, Cambridge: Cambridge University Press.

Collier, C. (1996), 'NGOs, the Poor and Local Government', *Development in Practice* 6(3).

Edwards, M. (1999), *Future Positive: international co-operation in the twenty-first century*, London: Earthscan.

Edwards, M. and D. Hulme (eds) (1992), *Making a Difference: NGOs and development in a changing world*, London: Earthscan/SCF.

Fisher, J. (1998), *Non Governments: NGOs and the political development of the third world*, West Hartford CT: Kumarian.

Huntington, S. (1968), *Political Order in Changing Societies*, New Haven, CT: Yale University Press.

Jefferies, R. (1993), 'The State, Structural Adjustment and Good Government in Africa', *The Journal of Commonwealth and Comparative Politics* XXXI/1.

Keane, J. (1988), *Democracy and Civil Society*, London: Verso.

Keane, J. (1998), *Civil Society: old images, new visions*, Cambridge: Polity Press.

Kohli, A. (1990), *Democracy and Discontent: India's growing crisis of governability*, Cambridge: Cambridge University Press.

Laitin, D. (1992), 'Hegemony and Religious Conflict: British imperial control and political cleavages in Yorubaland', in Stocpol *et al.* (1992).

Midgley, J. (1986), 'Community Participation, the State and Social Policy', in James Midgley *et al.*, *Community Participation, Social Development and the State*, London: Methuen.

Migdal, J. *et al.* (eds) (1994), *State Power and Social Forces*, Cambridge: Cambridge University Press.

Migdal, J. (1988), *Strong Societies and Weak States: state society relations and state capabilities in the third world*, Princeton, NJ: Princeton University Press.

O'Brien, D. C. (1991), 'The Show of State in Neo-colonial Twilight: Francophone Africa', in Manor, J. *et al.* (eds) *Rethinking Third World Politics*, London: Longman.

Robinson, M. (1995), 'Strengthening Civil Society in Africa: the role of foreign political aid', *IDS Bulletin* 26(2).

Stepan, A. (1988), *Rethinking Military Politics: Brazil and the southern cone*, Princeton: Princeton University Press.

Stocpol, T. (1992), 'Bringing the State Back In: strategies of analysis in current research', in Stocpol *et al.* (eds) *Bringing the State Back In*, Cambridge: Cambridge University Press.

Stewart, F. and W. van der Geest (1995), 'Adjustment and Social Funds: political panacea or effective poverty reduction?', in Stewart, F. *Adjustment and Poverty: options and choices*, London: Routledge.

Tevera, D. (1995), 'The Medicine That Might Kill the Patient: structural adjustment and urban poverty in Zimbabwe', in Simon, D. *et al.* (eds) *Structurally Adjusted Africa*, London: Pluto Press.

UNDP (1993), *UNDP and Organisations of Civil Society: building sustainable partnerships*, presented to and endorsed by the Strategy and Management Committee of UNDP on 23 November 1993.

UNDP (1995), *UNDP and Organisations of Civil Society*, paper prepared for the celebration of the UN's Fiftieth Anniversary in San Francisco, June 1995.

UN NGLS (1995a), *NGLS Roundup*, August 1995.

UN NGLS (1995b), *UN, NGOs and Global Governance: challenges for the 21st century: informal background notes*, Geneva: UN NGLS.

Van Rooy, A. (ed) (1998), *Civil Society and the Aid Industry*, London: Earthscan.

Westwood, D. (1996), *Displacement and Civil Society in Peru*, Discussion Paper no. 2, Milton Keynes: World Vision UK.

Whaites, A. (1995), 'The State and Civil Society in Pakistan', *Contemporary South Asia* 4(3): 229–54.

Whaites, A. (2000), *Conflict, Repression and Politics: dare NGOs hope to do any good?* in Janz, M. *et al.*, *Working in Complex Emergencies*, Monrovia CA: World Vision.

World Bank (1991), *World Development Report 1991*, Oxford: Oxford University Press.

World Bank (1997), *World Development Report 1997: the state in a changing world*, Oxford: Oxford University Press.

This is a re-worked version of two papers by Alan Whaites which appeared in Development in Practice *Volume 6, Number 3, 1996 and* Development in Practice *Volume 8, Number 3, 1998.*

Depoliticising development: the uses and abuses of participation

Sarah C. White

Introduction

The Bangladeshi NGO leaders discuss the dilemma: they are unhappy with the official agencies' new plan. Neither social nor environmental questions have been given the consideration they deserve. As happens more and more often, they have been invited to attend a meeting to discuss the plan. Flattered at first by official recognition, they are now uneasy. If they do not go, they have no grounds to complain that the interests of the poor have been ignored. But if they go, what guarantee do they have that their concerns will really be heard? Too many times they have seen their discussions drain away into the sand. The plans are left untouched; but their names remain, like a residue, in the list of 'experts' whose opinions the scheme reflects.

'We are all democrats today', was John Dunn's ironic opening to an essay on political theory (Dunn 1979). With its universal acceptance, he argued, what democracy meant *in practice* was increasingly elastic. Rather than describing any particular type of political order, democracy had become 'the name for the good intentions of states or perhaps for the good intentions which the rulers would like us to believe that they possess' (Dunn, op cit.: 12).

These days, the language of democracy dominates development circles. At national level it is seen in the rhetoric of 'civil society' and 'good governance'. At the programme and project level it appears as a commitment to 'participation'. This is trumpeted by agencies right across the spectrum, from the huge multilaterals to the smallest people's organisations. Hardly a project, it seems, is now without some 'participatory' element.

On the face of it, this appears like success for those committed to 'people-centred' development policies. But stories like the one above should make us cautious. *Sharing through participation does not necessarily mean sharing in power.* As with gender and with the 'green' movement, the 'mainstreaming' of participation has imposed its price. In all three cases, the original movement was one of protest against the existing orthodoxy. Some are still fighting for this. But in the mainstream, 'women in development' or 'win-win' environmental policies appear with the sting taken out of their tail. What began as a political issue is translated into a technical problem which the development enterprise can accommodate with barely a falter in its stride. Incorporation, rather than exclusion, is often the best means of control.

The status of participation as a 'Hurrah' word, bringing a warm glow to its users and hearers,[1] blocks its detailed examination. Its seeming transparency — appealing to 'the people' — masks the fact that participation can take on multiple forms and serve many different interests. In fact, it is precisely this ability to accommodate such a broad range of interests that explains why participation can command such widespread acclaim. If participation is to mean more than a façade of good intentions, it is vital to distinguish more clearly what these interests are. This will help to show what many have long suspected: that though we use the same words, the meanings that we give them can be very different.

Interests in participation

There are two main ways in which the politics of participation are admitted in development planning. The first is the question of *who* participates. This recognises that 'the people' are not homogeneous, and that special mechanisms are needed to bring in relatively disadvantaged groups. The second regards the *level* of participation. This points out that the involvement of the local people in implementation is not enough. For a fully participatory project, they should also take part in management and decision-making.

Both of these dimensions are important. The problem is that they do not go far enough. In lending themselves to technical solutions (which is, of course, their attraction), they can again obscure the politics of participation. A quota for the inclusion of poor women on the executive board, for example, seems to provide the answer. But of course, simply *being there* does not ensure that those women have a real say; and, even if they do, there is no guarantee that they will speak for others in a similar situation. At their best, such measures can only *facilitate* fuller participation, they cannot *deliver* it. More critically, framing the problem in these terms ties us to observing the *mechanisms* for participation; it gives us no means of assessing its *content*.

Table 1 aims to move beyond this in drawing out the diversity of form, function, and interests within the catch-all term 'participation'. It distinguishes four major types of participation, and the characteristics of each. The first column shows the form of participation. The second shows the interests in participation from the 'top down': that is, the interests that those who design and implement development programmes have in the participation of others. The third column shows the perspective from the 'bottom up': how the participants themselves see their participation, and what they expect to get out of it. The final column characterises the overall function of each type of participation. In the following sections I describe practical examples in which the different types of participation can be observed.

This framework is, of course, simply an analytical device. In practice, the uses (and abuses) of participation may be very varied. Any project will typically involve a mix of interests which change over time. Rarely will any of these types appear in 'pure' form. I hope, none the less, that setting them out in this way will highlight some important distinctions. It is in the ambiguity participation, as both concept and practice, that the scope for its colonisation lies.

Table 1 Interests in particpiation			
Form	Top-Down	Bottom-Up	Function
Nominal	Legitimation	Inclusion	Display
Instrumental	Efficiency	Cost	Means
Representative	Sustainability	Leverage	Voice
Transformative	Empowerment	Empowerment	Means/End

Nominal participation

An example of this type of participation is found in Zambia. Large numbers of women's groups have been formed by various government departments over the past thirty years. The existence of these groups demonstrates that the departments are 'doing something' and have a 'popular base', which may be significant in their claims for personnel or financial support. Their interest in women's participation, therefore, is largely for *legitimation*.

Many of the women go along with this. They say they are members of groups, but rarely attend any meetings. It serves their interests of *inclusion*, however, to keep their names on the books. From time to time they may 'check in' to see if any new loans or other inputs are on offer. How many of these groups actually exist in a functional sense is far from clear. In most cases, it seems, the women's participation is nominal, and the groups mainly serve the function of *display*.

Instrumental participation

Under the terms of Structural Adjustment Programmes (SAPs), government funding for essential infrastructure and services in many African countries has been sharply reduced. People's participation may be necessary, therefore, to provide the labour for local schools. This serves the *efficiency* interests of outside funders. The people's labour is taken as 'local counterpart funds', which guarantee the people's commitment to the project. The funders' input can be limited to financing raw materials, and the programme can therefore be far more 'cost-effective'.

For the local people, participation is seen as a *cost*. The time that they spend building the school has to be taken away from paid employment, household work, or leisure. But if they want the school, they see that they have little option. Participation in this case is instrumental, rather than valued in itself. Its function is as a *means* to achieve cost-effectiveness on the one hand, and a local facility on the other.

Representative participation

A Bangladeshi NGO wished to launch a co-operatives programme. It invited the local people to form their own groups, develop by-laws, and draw up plans for what they would do. The function of participation was to allow the local people a *voice* in the character of the project. From the NGO's side, this would avoid the danger of creating an inappropriate and dependent project, and so ensure *sustainability*.

A group of fishing families decided to apply. They wanted to form a co-operative for loans and fish marketing. For them, taking an active part both in their own meetings and in discussions with the NGO was important to ensure *leverage*, to influence the shape that the project should take and its subsequent management. Participation thus took on a representative form, being an effective means through which the people could express their own interests.

Transformative participation

The idea of participation as *empowerment* is that the practical experience of being involved in considering options, making decisions, and taking collective action to fight injustice is itself transformative. It leads to greater consciousness of what makes and keeps people poor, and greater confidence in their ability to make a difference. An example from the Philippines indicates how this can be.

Encouraged by a community organiser, 25 hillside families decided to form a consumers' co-operative. Prices at the local store were 50 per cent higher than those in the town, but the town was four hours' walk away. They took some training in co-operative management from the local NGO, and gradually devised their own constitution, by-laws, roles, and responsibilities. As their confidence grew, they decided to take on other projects. Then a presidential election was called. The local Mayor and some other officials visited the area. They had only one message: 'Vote for Marcos'. They had no time to listen to the villagers' questions or enter into discussion with them. After they left, the villagers decided to boycott the election.

When the election came, all 398 villagers spoiled their ballot papers. The community organiser visited them two days later. The election was widely viewed as a public relations exercise, but she had never discussed it with them, so was surprised and impressed by what they had done. She asked them for their reasons. One of the farmers explained:

In the co-operative, we discuss problems. We look at them from different angles. When we think that we have understood the situation, we try to come to a consensus. We avoid voting as much as possible. When the government officials came, we asked for an explanation of why we were given other than what we asked for. We asked for a school, teachers, and a road. The Mayor sent us the army, guns, and bullets. He refused to answer our questions. He just told us to vote for Marcos. We want the government to be run the way we manage our co-operative store.[2]

Empowerment is usually seen as an agenda 'from below'. This is because empowerment must involve action from below. However supportive, outsiders can only facilitate it, they cannot bring it about. None the less, as shown in Table 1, empowerment may also be identified as the interest in participation 'from above', when outsiders are working in solidarity with the poor. From Marx's analysis of alienation, to Freire's work on conscientisation, to the 'alternative visions' of organisations like DAWN,[3] it is in fact not usually those who are poor or disadvantaged themselves who identify empowerment as the key issue. The latter generally have far more immediate and tangible interests and goals. This case is typical, therefore, in that empowerment of the poor was initially the concern of the local NGO. It was only through their experience in the co-operative that the hillside families came to see empowerment as being in their interests. In this form, participation is therefore at one and the same time a means to empowerment and an end in itself, so breaking down the division between means and ends which characterises the other types. In another sense, of course, this process never comes to an end, but is a continuing dynamic which transforms people's reality and their sense of it.

Dynamics in participation

All of the above examples are positive. There is a degree of match between the interests from 'top down' and 'bottom up'. This is because the stories are told as a way of clarifying the framework in Table 1. They are snapshots, abstracted from their wider social context, and even their own history as development programmes. Only one set of interests is focused on, and presented as though this were all there is to say. The stories, as much as Table 1, are a device, highlighting some points, but throwing others into shadow. Stated in this way, the framework itself runs the risk of depoliticising participation, something which it was designed to overcome.

What needs to be injected into Table 1 is a sense of dynamic, along (at least!) four dimensions. These are presented in Figure 1. Clusters of circles show the interests from top-down and bottom-up, and the forms and functions of participation. The small arrows between the circles indicate the first dynamic, that each of the clusters is internally diverse, and there is tension over which element — or combination of elements — will predominate at any one time. In particular, as seen already in the case of the election boycott, the character of participation typically changes over time. The second dynamic is shown by the arrows coming in to the 'form and function' cluster from either side. These indicate that the form or function of participation is itself a site of conflict. The third pair of arrows comes out of the 'form and function' cluster, and into the 'interests' clusters, showing that the outcomes of participation feed back into the constitution of interests. The final dynamic is indicated by the arrows feeding into the diagram from either side. These show that interests reflect power relations outside the project itself. The rest of this section discusses each of these dynamics in turn.

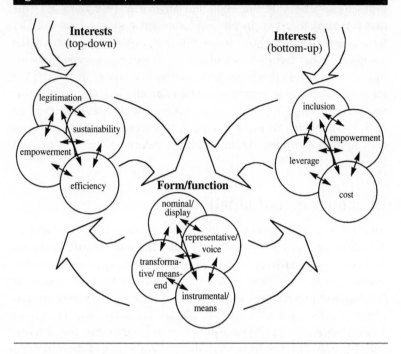

Figure 1 The politics of participation

The diversity of interests

In all the cases cited above, the Zambian women, the African villagers, and the fishing and hillside families are presented as though they were homogeneous groups. In reality, they are diverse, with differing interests and expectations of participation. This is clearest to see in the Zambian case: it is in the hope of individual gain that the women occasionally 'check in' to the groups. Also, those women who do remain more active — the chair, secretary, and treasurers of the groups — are likely to identify their participation as instrumental, and may even have some expectations of its being representative.

For outsiders, similarly, there is a mix of interests. The NGO in the Philippines case certainly gains legitimacy by having large numbers of group members. Its interests in efficiency and sustainability, as well as empowerment, are met by the hillside families developing and managing their own projects. In addition, there will be different interests among the local organisers and the NGO management. National leaders, for example, may talk more readily of empowerment than field workers who are aware of the dangers of reprisals from the local elite. The NGO may also 'package' the form and functions of participation differently for different 'markets'. In dealing with their radical Northern funders, they stress the transformative aspect. When engaging with the local elite and the national government, they may place more emphasis on the efficiency and sustainability dimensions. There is politics, therefore, not simply in the form and function of participation, but also in how it is represented in different quarters.

Changes in participation over time

As participation is a process, its dynamic over time must be taken into account. Seen at its simplest, there is a strong tendency for levels of participation to decline over time. This is clearest in the Zambian case: thirty years ago, or even twenty, those same groups were highly active, with the enthusiasm of project workers matched by that of the women themselves. This change may be due to disillusionment with the project, but it can also mean that people choose positively to use their time in other ways. There is a tendency in the rhetoric of participation to assume that it is always good for people to take an active part in everything. People do, however, have other interests, such as in leisure. People often participate for negative reasons: they do not have confidence that their interests will be represented unless they are physically there. One can grow tired of being an 'active citizen'!

Withdrawal from participation is not, however, always a positive choice. Women with heavy domestic responsibilities, for example, may find that they cannot sustain the expenditure of large amounts of time away from home. Also, even if power relations have been challenged by a successful exercise of participation, there is a danger that new patterns of domination will emerge over time. This is particularly so where the project itself creates new positions, with some people being far more involved than others. The Bangladeshi fishing co-operative has a relatively good chance of sustaining representative participation, because all of the members are actively involved. In other projects, which rely on management by a few leaders, wider participation over time is much more likely to dwindle to a point where it becomes nominal.

Alternatively, it may be that the level of participation increases over time. All their lives the fishing families had taken loans from a middle-trader, and had to sell their catch back to him. He then kept a proportion of the sale price as profit, before selling on to a larger trader. Through their co-operative, the fishing families could apply for loans to the local NGO. By-passing the middle-trader, they then took loans from their own group, and sold the fish back to it. The co-operative itself then accumulated the profit, and they were able to use the money for other collective projects. Their successful exercise of representative participation led to transformation.

In a similar way, the Philippine families first encountered the NGO in a health-education programme. After a year, an evaluation was held and they approved the programme. They saw that poverty was the underlying cause of their poor health. Having gone through the initial programme largely out of the interests of inclusion, they developed the confidence to move to representative participation, in stating that their more immediate need was a co-operative store. The action and reflection process of organising and managing the store involved them in transformative participation. This affected not only their economic position, but also their political consciousness.

Participation as a site of conflict

In practice, the interests from 'top down' and 'bottom up' do not match neatly. Probably more often, the interests that one group identifies are not served by the participation that occurs. The first example, of the Bangladeshi NGO leaders and the official agencies' plan, gives an instance of this. The NGO leaders desire representative participation, to gain leverage. The official agencies, however, require their presence simply for legitimation. This is probably the dominant pattern, but it is not always the 'top-down' interests that prevail. While participation may be encouraged for the purposes of legitimation or efficiency, there is always the potential for it to be 'co-opted from below', and for a disadvantaged group to use it for leverage or empowerment.

The Philippines election boycott gives an instance of this, though with a twist. Here, the interests of President Marcos and his cronies in the nominal participation of the villagers is frustrated. The hillside families see the Mayor's visit as an opportunity for representative participation. When they see there is no opportunity for dialogue, they simply refuse to play the game. This draws attention to another important point. It shows that participation is not always in the interests of the poor. Everything depends on the type of participation, and the terms on which it is offered. In cases like this one, exit may be the most empowering option.

Power and the construction of interests

The final dynamic in participation is more complex and more abstract. It is clear that power is involved in the negotiation to determine which interests 'win out' against others. What is less clear is that *power is involved in the construction of interests themselves.* This has two dimensions, which will be discussed in turn. The first is external to the model, represented in Figure 1 by the arrows coming from the far left and the far right. These show that interests are not just 'there', but reflect the power relations in wider society. The second dimension is shown by the arrows coming from the form and function cluster back into the 'top-down' and 'bottom-up' interests. These indicate that the participation process itself shapes the constitution of interests.

When asked why they joined the women's groups, many of the Zambian women say they hoped to get fertiliser or credit from them. Their interests in inclusion therefore reflect their practical interests as village women with a major role in food production.[4] These interests are determined by the local, gender-based division of labour, as well as by their class positions. Limiting their involvement to nominal levels also reflects their wider social context. With their domestic and productive responsibilities, many have little time to spend 'sitting around'. The timing of the groups' meetings recognises this: most are (even nominally) inactive from November to March, the main agricultural season. It is no coincidence that it is mainly groups whose members are older, and thus freer of responsibilities in the home, that continue to meet throughout the year.

In practice, access to credit or fertiliser rarely comes through the groups. Instead, most of them spend their time working on handcrafts, which they sell locally at marginal profit. The women's acceptance of this work again reflects the wider, gender-linked division of labour, in which control over significant resources is reserved for men. It is also shaped by the limited marketing opportunities in the rural areas. The women have other potential interests, for example in using the groups to put pressure on government departments to provide real services to the rural areas. The fact that women do not express these interests — and may not even recognise them — is not by chance, but reflects their low expectation of any change, born out of a general sense of powerlessness, or earlier disappointments. While the women may identify their interests as semi-detached inclusion in the existing project, therefore, this is not a free choice. To understand it, we have to see it in the wider social context in which the women live their lives. From the other side, the government departments' interest in legitimation comes from their competition with each other for resources. Also, however, it expresses their complacency that no real demands will be made on them, either from the poor or from the powers-that-be.

The other cases tell a similar story. In the shadow of the SAP, the local people's participation in building the school clearly shows their absence of other options. It is probable that those who do have alternatives (such as a relatively well-paid job) are able to evade participating, perhaps by paying someone else to do their share. Whatever the collective rhetoric, it is well recognised that it is rare for the whole community to take part equally. Some will be excused for being too young or too old. But others will be able to call on their status: it is no coincidence that such 'community' labour projects in practice often fall to the women and poorer men. Wider power relations condition the interests of the outside agency, too. Its concern for efficiency might indicate its limited budget. But it also clearly draws on the international supremacy of free-market ideology, and the awareness that it could easily take the funds elsewhere if the local people do not co-operate.

It is easiest to see the experience of participation acting upon the construction of interests in the cases of the fishing and hillside families' co-operatives. In both instances, undertaking successful projects enabled them to see new opportunities they had not at first imagined. There are less positive examples. It is quite common, for example, for agencies, when they 'ask the people' what kind of project they would like, to get very conventional answers. Women do ask for sewing machines, however much feminists wish that they would not! This may in part reflect the wider, gender-determined division of labour, but it also draws on what people have seen of development projects, and so what they expect them to look like. The NGOs' negative experience of co-option through the official agencies' 'consultation' processes, in the first example, similarly shapes their choice as to whether to participate in discussions of the latest plan.

It may be that the most profound re-negotiation of interests occurs where transformative participation achieves empowerment. While external agencies may genuinely desire the people's empowerment, they may find it rather uncomfortable when empowerment actually occurs. In the Philippines, for example, there is now considerable tension between some People's Organisations and the national NGOs that fostered them. The former wish to communicate directly with the funders, but the NGOs do not wish to lose control. Similarly, some Northern NGOs have found the language of partnership to be double-edged. It can, for example, lead to their Southern counterparts rejecting as 'imperialist' any demand for funding accountability. In some cases this may be legitimate; in others it is not. But if one takes seriously the fact that both parties have been shaped by unjust power relations, there is no particular reason to expect that the form which empowerment takes will be benign. Former friends, rather than common enemies, may be the first and easiest point of attack. Top-down commitment to others' empowerment is, therefore, highly contradictory. It is likely to lay bare the power dimensions of the relationship that the dominant partner would prefer to leave hidden. If it is genuine, the process must be transformative, not only for the 'weaker' partner but also for the outside agency and for the relationship between them.

The underlying message of this section is simple: however participatory a development project is designed to be, it cannot escape the limitations imposed on this process from the power relations in wider society. That people do not express other interests does not mean that they do not have them. It simply means that they have no confidence that they can be achieved.[5]

Participation: what counts and what doesn't

Before concluding this discussion, I want to point out a final anomaly in the new pursuit of participation. Like the Women in Development (WID) agenda, it is founded on the assumption that those who have been excluded should be 'brought in' to the development process. It represents the people in the bad, non-participatory past as passive objects of programmes and projects that were designed and implemented from outside. As the literature on women in development now recognises, however, the people have never been excluded from development. They have been fund-amentally affected by it. But more than this, people have also always participated in it, on the most favourable terms they can obtain. They await with a mixture of expectation and scepticism what the new agency in their area is offering, and what it will want in return. They have opted in or out of projects as they judged that it suited their interests. At least some of what agencies may see as project 'misbehaviour' (see Buvinic 1986) can from another standpoint be viewed as their co-option from below.

In Bangladesh, for example, an NGO introduced a hand-tubewell programme for irrigation. The pumps were located in the fields to be used for vegetable production. The villagers, however, considered water for domestic use a higher priority. They therefore moved the pumps from the fields to their homes. Rather than recognising this as the expression of people's genuine interests, the NGO began to issue plastic pipes, which could not be re-located. Applications for the tubewells rapidly declined, and the programme was deemed a failure. This is by no means an isolated example. In the same area, shallow tubewell engines destined for irrigation were adapted by the local people to power rice mills and small boats. People have never been a blank sheet for development agencies to write on what they will.

There is, of course, a need for more space for poorer people to participate in development programmes in representative and transformative ways. They should not need to resort to manipulation and covert resistance — the 'weapons of the weak' [6] — to express their interests. Recognising that people have always used such tactics, however, suggests that the problem is not simply 'enabling the people to participate', but ensuring that they participate *in the right ways*. This underlies, for example, some official agencies' current enthusiasm for programmes in 'community-based resource management'. These explicitly recognise that unless people are 'brought in' to the programme, they may actively sabotage it, by cutting trees or embankments, killing animals in nature reserves, and so on. The fact that the way in which people have participated is so often classified as illegitimate should lead us to question quite carefully: on whose terms is the current agenda, and whose interests are really at stake?

Conclusion

This article suggests three steps in addressing the 'non-politics' of participation. The first is to recognise that participation is a political issue. There are always questions to be asked about who is involved, how, and on whose terms. People's enthusiasm for projects depends much more on whether they have a genuine interest in it than in whether they participated in its construction: participation may take place for a whole range of reasons. The second step is to analyse the interests represented in the catch-all term 'participation'. Table 1 sets out a framework for this. It shows that participation, while it has the potential to challenge patterns of dominance, may also be the means through which existing power relations are entrenched and reproduced.

The third step is to recognise that participation and non-participation, while they always reflect interests, do not do so in an open arena. Both people's perception of their interests, and their judgement as to whether or not they can express them, reflect power relations. People's non-participation, or participation on other people's terms, can ultimately reproduce their subordination. Figure 1 shows some of the dynamics in participation, pointing out that the form and function of participation itself becomes a focus for struggle.

If participation means that the voiceless gain a voice, we should expect this to bring some conflict. It will challenge power relations, both within any individual project and in wider society. The absence of conflict in many supposedly 'participatory' programmes is something that should raise our suspicions. Change hurts. Beyond this, the bland front presented by many discussions of participation in development should itself suggest questions: What interests does this 'non-politics' serve, and what interests may it be suppressing?

Acknowledgement

My thanks to Ken Cole, Marion Glaser, Charlotte Heath, Tone Lauvdal, Arthur Neame, Jane Oliver, and Romy Tiongo for comments on earlier drafts of this paper.

Notes

1   Point made by Judith Turbyne (1992).

2   Taken from Tiongo and White (forthcoming).

3   Development Alternatives with Women for a New era (DAWN) — see Sem and Grown (1987).

4   This use of 'practical interests' follows Molyneux (1985).

5   For much fuller discussion of this point, see Gaventa (1980).

6   For fuller discussion of such tactics, see Scott (1985).

References

Buvinic, M. (1986), 'Projects for women in the third world: explaining their misbehaviour', *World Development* 14 (5): 653–64.

Dunn, J. (1979), *Western Political Theory in the Face of the Future*, Cambridge, Cambridge University Press.

Gaventa, J. (1980), Power and Powerlessness: quiescence and rebellion in an Appalachian valley, Oxford, Oxford University Press.

Molyneux, M. (1985), 'Mobilisation without emancipation? Women's interests, the state and revolution in Nicaragua', *Feminist Studies* 11(2): 227–54.

Scott, J. (1985), Weapons of the Weak: everyday forms of peasant resistance, London, Yale University Press.

Sem, G. and C. Grown (1987), Development, Crises and Alternative Visions: Third World women's perspectives, London, Earthscan.

Tiongo, R. and S. White (forthcoming), *Doing Theology and Development: meeting the challenge of poverty*, Edinburgh, St Andrew's Press.

Turbyne, J. (1992), 'Participation and Development', University of Bath (unpublished mimeo).

This paper was first published in Development in Practice Volume 6, Number 1, 1996.

Birds of a feather?
UNDP and ActionAid implementation of Sustainable Human Development

Lilly Nicholls

A realistic solution, or wishful thinking?

The 1990s have been a challenging time for world development. The evidence is mounting that, although there has been tremendous overall growth since the Second World War,[1] much of the real progress has been highly concentrated. Growth has been characterised by precarious standards of living for much of the world's poorest, and escalating inequality between the 'haves' and 'have nots'.[2] Parallel to persistent poverty and growing marginalisation, the international development community has been weakened by impatience with the territoriality, bureaucratisation, and self-deceiving nature of the current system of co-operation and foreign aid (Ferguson 1990; Hancock 1991; Sachs 1992). Finally, international development has reached what some view as a theoretical impasse. This is due to the growing awareness of our incomplete knowledge of development processes. It is also due to the disillusionment both with Keynesian ideals of state central planning and with neo-liberal models of market-led growth. (See Moore and Schmitz 1995, though Schuurman 1993 holds that the impasse has been overcome.)

It is in this context that Sustainable Human Development (SHD) and People-Centred Development (PCD) approaches emerged. They featured strongly in the 1995 World Summit for Social Development (WSSD), where 134 nation-states pledged to 'place people at the centre of development' (*Copenhagen Declaration* 1995). They appeared, too, in statements by the OECD that defined its mission as 'making progress towards the achievement of *Human Development*.' (OECD 1996).

Although UNDP did not invent SHD/PCD ideas, its annual *Human Development Reports* (*HDRs*) have promoted them as an alternative development paradigm with the potential to challenge the status quo.

UNDP defines SHD/PCD as 'the process of enlarging peoples' capabilities and choices so as to enable them to better satisfy their own needs' (UNDP 1990–1997):

> Sustainable Human Development is a new development paradigm which not only generates economic growth, but distributes it equitably; that regenerates the environment rather than destroying it; and that gives priority to empowering people rather than marginalising them. It gives priority to the poor ... and provides for their participation in those decisions affecting them. (Speth 1994: 5)

The innovation of SHD/PCD lies in its ability to go beyond state-versus-market dichotomies by arguing that people should be at the centre of all development. They should be viewed not only as its 'means' but also as its 'ends'. The SHD/PCD paradigm is unique in that, by placing the emphasis on peoples' well-being rather than on their income, consumption or productivity, it aims to transcend both economistic and instrumentalist models of development. In addition to being a new paradigm,[3] SHD/PCD is a promising framework for carrying out comprehensive policy and institutional reforms. It provides a way to build a newly-invigorated system of international development co-operation based on the ideals of improved coordination, a candid policy dialogue on 'sound governance', equity, genuine North–South partnerships, and the active participation and empowerment of the poorest.

SHD/PCD ideas may be appealing, but the key question is whether the paradigm can be implemented in the world's poorest countries (Uganda, in this case) where it is most needed. Can multilateral agencies such as UNDP, and indeed much smaller and less bureaucratic international NGOs such as ActionAid, translate SHD/PCD's more ambitious components into practice?

Despite the prolific literature on human development, most scholarly writing has either concentrated on measurement issues (and specifically on the statistical merits of the Human Development Index — HDI), or on the conceptual complexities and the contribution of Sen's theories to SHD/PCD approaches. At the same time, the more policy-related publications of international organisations like UNDP have focused mainly on the originality of SHD/PCD ideas compared with state-centred or market-oriented development models. They have tried to convince the international community to move closer towards human development approaches. Unfortunately, neither the scholarly nor policy-related literature has questioned the conceptual soundness or 'implementability' of SHD/PCD approaches. There has been no critical and in-depth analysis of how development agencies are putting such approaches into practice, and the real-life socio-economic, political, institutional and organisational constraints they have encountered in doing so.

A more comprehensive examination of the issue is given in my doctoral thesis (Nicholls 1998), which draws on field research and extensive interviews in the USA, Europe, and Uganda. This article highlights the core finding that, despite the genuine efforts of UNDP and ActionAid to implement SHD/PCD at all levels, both agencies were prompted to make a series of contentious assumptions about development processes and about their own capacities. Ultimately, both had to displace core SHD/PCD goals. This was due to both the conceptual deficiencies of the paradigm and the tensions between organisational interests and the SHD/PCD agenda.

SHD and PCD unveiled

Theoretical quicksand

The first significant finding is that, despite its conceptual novelty, and bold policy and institutional agenda, the paradigm's abstract and unfinished nature, coupled with its ideological ambiguity and internal tensions, make it extremely difficult to translate into a comprehensive yet concrete development strategy.

The first set of problems is attributable to two major factors. First, the Capabilities Approach, from which the paradigm derives much of its theoretical substance, is essentially a philosophical framework comprising complex and abstract principles. Capabilities, overall functionings, primitive and refined functionings, well-being, being well-off, well-being freedom, agency freedom, agency information, overall entitlements, exchange entitlements, endowment entitlements, effective power, procedural control, and counterfactual choice, are but a few examples. Indeed, its pioneer, Amartya Sen, claims it was never intended to become a concrete development strategy or action plan. Second, the Approach has never been fully fleshed out, so the exact links, weights, prioritisation, or multiple effects of various *capabilities* (i.e. the ability to do this or that), and the various components of the SHD/PCD paradigm itself, have never been established. The consequence of these shortcomings is what even its proponents refer to as a major gap between SHD/PCD as a theory and as a realistic development strategy and action plan:

There seems to be a gap between Sen's conceptualisation of Human Development and its operationalisation. Thus far, we have Sen's highly theoretical approach on the one hand, and the nitty gritty practical material which lacks theoretical scope on the other. The two have never been brought together and there is tremendous debate as to whether this is possible.[4]

Another conceptual limitation that has undermined attempts to put SHD/PCD into practice is its sheer vagueness. For instance, development practitioners in Uganda were concerned that 'the meaning of SHD/PCD was so broad and nebulous [that] almost any intervention could fall under the SHD/PCD umbrella'. Nor were such criticisms restricted to field workers. One adviser to UNDP's Human Development Report Office (HDRO) complained that it was 'almost like motherhood, in that there was nothing in it that one could oppose'.

A final conceptual deficiency is that the ideological ambiguity and internal contradictions within SHD/PCD have complicated its translation into a comprehensive yet focused development strategy. Its ideological ambiguity is largely rooted in its eclectic borrowing from numerous, and often opposed, ideologies and development doctrines. It ranges from Sen's Capabilities Approach and the Basic Needs Approach at the centre of the spectrum, to Liberation Theology and Freirean notions of empowerment on the left, and neo-liberal ideals of market liberalisation on the right. Even Sen's own writings can be ideologically ambiguous. For example, in earlier publications he praises the state's involvement in economic activities and regulatory measures such as controlling trading activities, food subsidies, and direct rationing. By the mid-1990s he is writing about 'market incentives' instead of 'incentives to public action', and warning against the inefficiency of governmental regulations and controls.[5] While the ideological nebulousness of the SHD/PCD paradigm (and the confusion caused by the changing positions of its key adherents) are rarely acknowledged in public, some UNDP staff admit the problem. They have expressed concern about the practical implications of 'taking socialist values, merging them with market-oriented ideas and getting away with it.'[6]

Hypothetically, there is no reason why one ideology or development doctrine cannot be intertwined with another. But when it comes to translating such ideas into policies and strategies, serious tensions can emerge. A typical illustration of these can be found in the *HDRs*' simultaneous calls for the protection of all property, and for the redistribution of wealth and assets, including land reform. The two may not be mutually exclusive in theory, but in contexts where land-ownership is highly concentrated there are bound to be trade-offs and tensions in practice. Alas, the proponents of the SHD/PCD paradigm have remained largely silent about its conceptual vagueness, its unfinished nature, the persistent gap between theory and practice, and its inherent ideological tensions.

Findings on the ground showed that the actions of UNDP and ActionAid in Uganda added to the conceptual confusion and practical difficulties with the SHD/PCD paradigm. In UNDP, considerable damage seems to have been done by the decision to push definitions and guidelines on human development (predetermined in New York) in a top-down and prescriptive manner.[7] UNDP staff in country offices were left feeling excluded and 'pressed against the wall' by headquarters. The lack of ownership over the approach, and confusion among many UNDP staff, were aggravated by other factors. First, UNDP tended to tamper with the paradigm (for example, it added 'sustainable' to the phrase 'human development' late in the game, largely to please the newly-arrived and environmentally-conscious Administrator, James Gustave Speth). Second, UNDP introduced new terms (e.g. Human Security, Social Capital, Preventive Development) and measurements, whose exact links to human development have never been fully explained, but which help to keep the annual *HDR*s newsworthy. (Alongside the original HDI have been added the Political Freedom Index — PFI, the Human Poverty Index — HPI, the Gender-Related Development Index — GDI, and the Gender Empowerment Measure — GEM.) Lamentably, UNDP's top-down imposition of SHD/PCD, along with alterations in the definition of the paradigm, and the constant addition of new measures and terminology, have further blurred SHD/PCD's already ambiguous meaning and ideological position.

ActionAid never quite managed to reach an internal agreement on the meaning or desirability of adopting a SHD/PCD approach. Many among its Trustees, sponsorship and marketing departments, and managers in certain Development Areas, wanted to retain the NGO's traditional alleviatory approach to social service delivery. This approach is predictable and had brought success and generous funding pledges in the past. The more intellectually-oriented analysts, technical specialists, and a small cluster of field directors favoured a shift towards greater policy advocacy and the more decentralised and participatory approach associated with SHD/PCD ideas.[8] Unable to reconcile this conceptual deadlock, ActionAid began carrying out major organisational and programme reforms without internal consensus about a shared development vision or clearly defined development guidelines. Viewed positively, ActionAid never resorted to imposing pre-set definitions and guidelines on its field staff in a top-down fashion. Unlike UNDP, it did not need to grapple with the conceptual deficiencies or ideological ambiguities of the SHD/PCD paradigm. Still, my research revealed that within ActionAid, too, SHD/PCD ideas were viewed as an 'import from the North'. Field staff felt they had virtually no ownership of SHD/PCD, and only scant knowledge about its meaning. Thus, ActionAid's main problem was not so much having to put an overly abstract and ambiguous development paradigm into practice, but rather a lack of theory altogether. That is, it was implementing development interventions which lacked a theoretical context and were not sufficiently anchored in a shared conceptual framework. Staff were unable to engage in higher levels of abstraction, and to draw out cross-sectoral or cross-regional connections and wide policy lessons from their work.[9]

The displacement of SHD/PCD in Uganda

The conceptual complexities and deficiencies of the SHD/PCD paradigm, and the two agencies' own handling of these issues, complicated the translation and integration of SHD/PCD approaches. But the difficulties do not end there. There was a strong tendency for UNDP and ActionAid to pursue their own organisational interests, whatever those might be: for example, to do what is easiest and most feasible, to increase their own mandate and control over development processes, to appease powerful stakeholders, or to gloss over errors and the complexities of development processes. When these interests were in tension with core SHD/PCD goals, the SHD/PCD agenda ended up displaced.

Setbacks at the policy and coordination levels

Globally, UNDP has been adept at using the international spotlight generated by its *HDR* and by the WSSD to advocate moderate but innovative policy proposals. Examples include the Tobin Tax against international currency speculation and the 20/20 Compact which calls for increased donor and recipient government social development expenditures. More audacious and anti-hegemonic policy proposals included the introduction of a Global Social Safety Net whose funds would be paid through income taxes levied on the richest nations. UNDP also called for the creation of an Economic Security Council which would grant voting rights to poor countries, and for the introduction of global mechanisms to monitor monopolistic, protectionist or polluting behaviour, high military spending, human rights violations, and corruption by nation-states.[10] This ambitious global policy agenda faced considerable political resistance from powerful G-77 countries (China, India, Nigeria, and Algeria being prominent among these) who objected to the 'sound governance' and demilitarisation goals that were also included. Their objections were based on the belief that such goals threatened national sovereignty and vested interests; that they smacked of Northern conditionality, and represented an attempt by donors to replace technological and financial transfers with 'soft' aid. A member of India's Permanent Mission to the UN expressed the South's opposition thus:

> Developing countries do not want a poverty–governance programme. They have governments equipped to do this on their own. What can a Nordic country with 4 million people teach a country like India with 950 million people about governance? What developing countries want is technological transfers, not donors going into 'soft' areas.[11]

Instead of coming to UNDP's rescue, sister UN agencies joined forces with resisting G-77 nation-states in insisting that it had overstepped its traditional mandate. UNDP, as a purveyor of technical co-operation, had no business proposing such an ambitious agenda of global institutional and policy reforms for consideration at the WSSD. The UN Secretariat's Department of Policy Coordination and Sustainable Development was especially upset by the publicity generated by UNDP's audacious proposals. It convinced the UN Secretary-General that UNDP had trespassed upon its turf, and that it should refrain from influencing policy debates in the lead-up to the WSSD.[12]

Within Uganda, UNDP's efforts to stimulate a national policy dialogue on SHD/PCD issues was met with equal, if not more fervent, opposition. Interestingly, the harshest critics of its efforts to play a policy leadership role at the national level came from within the UN family, many of whom did not want UNDP 'encroaching upon' their own mandates. They argued that UNDP was 'too lightweight' and lacked the resources, substantive in-house expertise, and the clout to play such a role. As the World Bank's Chief Economist in Uganda candidly put it:

It is one thing to be a leader and another to claim to be a leader. Where is UNDP's thinking and technical capacity? Human Development Reports formulated with the help of academics in New York do not necessarily establish UNDP's policy influence or expertise at the country level.[13]

Thus, UNDP was unwittingly caught in the middle of North–South political tensions over the right of the international donor community to push a 'sound governance' global agenda. And it was caught in the midst of the UN's own turf battles, and fellow agencies' recriminations about UNDP's limited policy clout and analytical capacities. Consequently, UNDP had little choice but to downgrade its initially proactive policy role in the WSSD and to drop the most ambitious proposals of its wide-reaching agenda. Gone were its plans to disseminate its Political Freedom Index (PFI), along with its appeals to democratise the UN and to expose those nation-states and corporations not doing their share to further the SHD/PCD goals of social responsibility, equity, democracy, and peace.

Influencing wider policy debates and becoming a much more global, analytical, and influential NGO had become one of the cornerstones of ActionAid's vision, as asserted in its 1992 mission statement (Griffiths 1992). By the mid-1990s, ActionAid had established policy advocacy departments in its London headquarters as well as in many of its country offices. Despite this, by late 1997, after several false starts and efforts to jump-start its policy and advocacy work, ActionAid had still to ratify its most recent Advocacy Strategy. It had still to agree on two or three key issues, the target audience, and the specific policy goals it would pursue. By early 1998, after eight years and four restructuring attempts to create an effective policy advocacy department and to mainstream its advocacy work, ActionAid's Advocacy Department had once again been disbanded. Many former staff, including the head of the department, had left, and the NGO was still trying to refine and implement an Advocacy Strategy (ActionAid 1997).

The reasons behind ActionAid's difficulties in activating its policy analysis and influencing work are multiple and complex, but two constraints stand out. First, because it is much smaller than UNDP and has no official access to inter-governmental forums, it has never achieved — and probably never will — the international profile that UNDP has gained through global conferences and publications. In addition, because ActionAid's comparative advantage has always been grassroots social service delivery, it has concentrated its work in geographically restricted and mostly rural Development Areas (DAs) where, until recently, at least in Uganda, there was little government to speak of. Hence, ActionAid has never established a significant presence in capital cities, nor had the access to government officials that UNDP has traditionally enjoyed in very poor countries like Uganda. Added to its lack of global or national profile and access is the reality that many of the staff in the Country Programmes are sectoral experts (e.g. teachers, nurses and agronomists). These people are better at delivering community health or education services than at lobbying or drawing wider policy implications from their time-consuming micro-level interventions.[14] The problem is not only that many of ActionAid's staff in a country like Uganda lack the conceptual framework or skills needed to analyse development issues and influence wider policy and governance debates. They also lack the time, data, access to decision-makers, and the political desire to do so in a country where development workers either constitute part of the elite, or where the wounds left from past religious and tribal tensions are still raw and where challenging the status quo can still be a risky endeavour.[15]

The other constraint which has undermined ActionAid's advocacy aspirations both globally and nationally is the political resistance from among its own Trustees. Some of these view its growing involvement in policy influencing work as potentially offensive to the NGO's philanthropic and middle-of-the-road child sponsors. A restrictive, ten per cent ceiling has been placed by ActionAid's Trustees on how much it can invest in advocacy.[16]

Setbacks at the programme and grassroots levels

If political pressures, North–South tensions, turf battles, and their own limited organisational capacities and clout kept UNDP and ActionAid from playing a greater coordinating and leadership role in influencing wider development and governance policies, what about their effectiveness in implementing SHD/PCD approaches at the programme and grassroots level in Uganda?

Generally speaking, both agencies have made significant progress in integrating SHD/PCD approaches into their organisational structures and country programmes in Uganda and beyond. Within UNDP, 40 country programmes have produced national Human Development Reports, many of them involving a wide range of national government and civil society actors. All country offices have moved towards a more holistic, decentralised and 'programmatic' approach to development. All UNDP programmes have increased their proportion of nationally-executed projects, and begun to orient their development interventions towards what UNDP considers the key elements of SHD/PCD. These are the so-called four 'E's: Employment, Equity, Empowerment and Environmental Regeneration (UNDP 1995). At ActionAid, the shift towards Human Development-type goals has been achieved by increasingly complementing grassroots DA-level work with global and national policy influencing activities; by formulating integrated country programmes rather than sectoral and fragmented ones; and by hiring more Ugandan as opposed to expatriate staff, strengthening indigenous NGOs, and reducing ActionAid's own operational activities in order to allow beneficiaries to become more involved in programme formulation, implementation, and assessment (Twose 1994). These achievements notwithstanding, a closer look at both agencies' implementation of SHD/PCD at the programme and grassroots levels in Uganda exposes some worrying trends. I focus on two aspects: their promotion of equity and claims to reach the 'poorest of the poor', and their efforts to foster greater ownership, participation, and empowerment among Ugandan beneficiaries.

Promoting equity and reaching the 'poorest of the poor'

Through the establishment of new partnerships with Ugandan NGOs and Community-Based Organisations (CBOs), and the creation of numerous income-generating activities (IGAs) at the grassroots, the UNDP country programme in Uganda has clearly made important strides in working more directly with poor communities. This is no small feat for an inter-governmental organisation which, until recently, channelled virtually all its funds via central government ministries. Still, the bulk of evidence from the UNDP supported programmes that I visited[17] shows that, because these require beneficiaries to organise into groups, it is often the better-off (i.e. those with assets, higher education, and access to information and to influential decision-makers) who either directly monopolise the benefits of UNDP supported projects or manage to place themselves as intermediaries on behalf of the poor. To add insult to injury, cases of incompetence by implementing NGOs or CBOs, community conflicts, and 'capture' by better-off intermediaries, or malfeasance and corruption within beneficiary groups, often went undetected. This was because UNDP has a limited rural presence, and often employs Kampala-based development experts who spend little time living and interacting with project beneficiaries or monitoring project activities.

Because ActionAid's field workers spend considerable time in rural areas, and the NGO itself is much more grassroots oriented, it managed to avoid much of the predatory behaviour of beneficiary groups experienced by UNDP. Once again though, the ActionAid projects I visited (mainly agricultural extension, water, health, credit and savings projects, or women's groups, and school management committees)[18] attracted mostly better-off community members. (By their very nature, some of these projects meant that members had to have some access to land which could be improved, or some initial capital or cash which they could put into common savings. Alternatively, they needed sufficiently high levels of education and free time to benefit from training in maternal health and sanitation, teacher education, or project planning.) This inevitably meant the poorest members of the community were excluded from group activities. These people are without assets, uneducated, marginalised, or too busy or ill to partake in such activities, or too embarrassed to even approach 'people as busy and important as ActionAid workers'. As a senior ActionAid Uganda manager himself put it, the NGO cannot focus its attention on the poorest and most deprived individuals in the community since it is much too difficult to show quick and concrete results if one works with those who live in remote areas, have few resources, respond slowly, and sometimes only to charity.

Fostering national ownership, participation and empowerment among Ugandans

With respect to fostering a sense of ownership, as well as greater participation and empowerment among beneficiaries, UNDP Uganda has successfully replaced many of its expensive expatriate Chief Technical Advisers with national consultants, through increased use of National Execution (NEX). Today, UNDP is much more likely to designate the Ugandan government or Uganda-based NGOs as implementors of UNDP supported projects. Despite these advances, UNDP has a long way to go before it can claim to treat Ugandan counterparts as genuine partners. According to Ugandan government planners and advisers, for instance, UNDP still has difficulties incorporating Ugandan government officials in the formulation of UNDP supported projects from the outset. It also has a tendency to propose its own (usually very visible) project ideas and to 'send ready-made project documents to the Ugandan government' rather than working within the parameters of the latter's existing development efforts.[19] Because of a lack of resources and skilled personnel, and low morale within the Ugandan public service, UNDP has become better known by the Ugandan government as a source of 'top-up' salaries, office equipment and four-wheel drives than for its technical expertise or ability to help bring about much needed policy or institutional reforms. Several UNDP supported projects, for example, were immobilised due to the refusal of local government officials to sit on Project Selection Committees unless they were paid 'sitting' or 'transport' allowances to do so.

What about UNDP's efforts to increase the participation of the poor in development processes? Many of the beneficiaries at the grassroots complained that UNDP invariably arrived in their communities with pre-defined project ideas that were unrealistic (e.g. they required peasants to draft their own project proposals or carry out their own evaluations). Other ideas were undesirable (e.g. banning individual financial benefits in areas where access to 'start-up' capital was the biggest impediment facing the poor; or demanding that beneficiaries organise themselves into groups in a society where extreme social differentiation and past tribal, religious and political divisions make collaboration beyond one's own family or tribe much too risky). Many of those involved in UNDP supported projects began opting out or shirking their responsibilities. They realised that they had limited control over the initiatives, and that the benefits which they would derive from them were minimal. Far from being empowered, the small cluster of participants who remained felt abandoned, and saddled with the burden of having to complete the project on their own.[20]

In the case of ActionAid Uganda, the participation of beneficiaries in project activities was much more systematic and carefully planned. For instance, in the Buwekula DA where I conducted most of my rural field visits, ActionAid had established and trained community-selected Parish Development Committees (PDCs) to identify the community's development needs. The committees also formulated project ideas and designed project assessment indicators and methods. The idea of creating PDCs was no doubt motivated by a genuine desire to increase beneficiary ownership and participation. In practice, things turned out to be quite different. ActionAid's DAs continued to work under strict planning and budgetary deadlines emanating from London and Kampala, instead of giving PDCs sufficient time to absorb the project planning training. Rather than carefully selecting their community projects, the PDCs' participatory project identification and formulation process was abruptly cut short by ActionAid's determination to meet its deadlines.[21] In addition to deadline pressures, because ActionAid Uganda felt that a standardised development structure would be easier to set up and control, it proceeded to set up PDCs (or equivalents) in various DAs without first having carried out an in-depth analysis of their feasibility.[22] Nor, according to beneficiaries themselves, did they give communities the option of using existing institutional mechanisms, such as the government's Resistance Councils (RCs — later called Local Councils, or LCs). The negative consequences of these unilateral decisions became apparent only much later. Newly-created PDCs began to complain that their work was being seen as a partial duplication of the Ugandan government's work, and that the government's local RC/LCs were refusing to put their monies into PDC projects. Moreover, many PDC members were community activists already heavily involved in RC/LC activities and with only limited management skills, access to transport, or time to attend to more meetings or monitor additional community projects. It is difficult to see how ActionAid's controversial PDCs will be able to sustain their activities and to both finance and justify their existence to the local Ugandan government once the NGO phases out.

In retrospect, it would seem that, when organisational interests have conflicted with core SHD/PCD goals (like reaching the poorest, or fostering ownership, participation, and the empowerment of the poor), the latter have tended to be displaced in favour of the former. Hence, the implementation of SHD/PCD by these two agencies has been displaced by conceptual deficiencies, political resistance, and by their own limited capacities and organisational interests.

Conclusion: the need for self-criticism and learning

This article's analysis of the efforts of UNDP and of ActionAid to implement SHD/PCD approaches offers several important insights.

1 In human affairs, there is always bound to be a gap between our ideals (i.e. theory) and reality (i.e. practice). This was the case with SHD/PCD. Despite the paradigm's theoretical innovation and its potential political audacity, its conceptual deficiencies and the two agencies' own limited capacities and conflicting priorities resulted in a form of goal displacement which made it even harder to bridge the theory-practice divide.

It is important to appreciate, of course, that the tendencies described here should not be interpreted as being rigid or perfectly predictable behaviour. Thus, I am in no way implying that there can ever be only one single organisational interest or that agencies like UNDP and ActionAid always know or always pursue their own organisational interests. My findings suggest that there are normally numerous competing interests within organisations (e.g. analysts and technical staff versus the Board of Trustees at ActionAid; Northern donors promoting the 'sound governance' agenda versus resisting G-77 countries within the UN). Organisations are capable of following alternative pathways, and do not always pursue what is in their immediate interests (e.g. the decisions of UNDP and ActionAid to decentralise operations and cede control of programming decisions to the field). Their interests need not always be at odds with core SHD/PCD goals (e.g. the two agencies' interest in promoting 'sound governance' coincides with a core SHD/PCD goal).

2   The second finding is that UNDP and ActionAid have made important advances towards implementing SHD/PCD approaches, including the introduction of more integrated, decentralised, and nationally-executed development programmes. They have made undeniable contributions to alleviating poverty through their agricultural extension work, and training courses for women, health carers and teachers. They have contributed to capacity development through group formation and support for income-generating activities. They have helped provide vital social services to poor communities in rural Uganda. Despite these achievements, the bulk of the evidence shows that UNDP and ActionAid are vulnerable to political pressures from traditional stakeholders, to territorial turf battles, and to constantly having to carve out a niche for themselves. These pressures, common to many international development agencies, suggest such organisations are not ideal change agents, nor challengers of exploitative power relations or of the existing system of international development co-operation.

In fairness, I should stress that my research observations are based on the two agencies' performance in only one country and during a restricted period (mainly 1993–1998). Moreover, by having set out to implement SHD/PCD, UNDP and ActionAid have set themselves a Herculean task which no other international development agency — or government for that matter — has ever realised. Doubtless, my research is putting UNDP and ActionAid to the toughest test possible. I would argue, nevertheless, that it is a fair test, since both agencies appeal to funders and to the public through claims that they are achieving SHD/PCD goals like improving equity and donor coordination, and that they are influencing policy debates, as well as fostering greater ownership, participation, and empowerment among the poorest.

3 Third, it is clear that the constraints faced by a large inter-governmental organisation and an international NGO in their implementation of SHD/PCD approaches are more similar than one might expect. Most notably, both agencies often place organisational interests above core SHD/PCD goals. But there were other similarities. For instance, the staff of both agencies grappled with the conceptual elusiveness of the SHD/PCD paradigm, even though ActionAid did not attempt to impose pre-defined definitions or criteria, as UNDP did. Both agencies faced difficulties influencing wider policy and 'sound governance' debates, even though UNDP had more access to global forums and national decision-makers than ActionAid. Both agencies encountered political resistance from traditional stakeholders. ActionAid, however, did not face the same pressures as UNDP, with the territoriality of the UN system, political pressures from Southern governments, or the opportunism of local government officials. In contrast, ActionAid's direct, operational approach permitted it to monitor projects on the ground. In short, UNDP's and ActionAid's work is potentially complementary since the former performs well globally and in the realm of policy, while the latter is more effective at grassroots operational work.

The remaining question is: what is to be done? The story is not all gloom. First, becoming aware of the conceptual deficiencies inherent in those ideas which we plan to put into practice is a useful start. After all, in order to surmount a theory's ambiguities and tensions, they must first be perceived. We can further limit the damage by avoiding putting into practice theories on a large scale until they have been sufficiently tested. We should not design programmes which are overly optimistic and complex, or dependent on high levels of competence, coordination, or consensus-building. These often do not exist or are difficult to attain within many international development organisations. It would also be helpful for theorists and practitioners to work more closely, and for both to collaborate with staff in the field and with Southern partners to ensure that the latter have ownership of ideas and programmes from the outset. This should also ensure that new ideas and models can be put into practice by existing development agencies, and that their implementation is feasible in poor countries.

Changing the behaviour of development theorists and practitioners, however, is not enough. Changes are also needed within development agencies, the existing system of international development co-operation, and developing country societies themselves. While the latter must continue to work towards more democratic, tolerant, and equitable political and social structures, development agencies must stop imposing ideas in a top-down manner upon Southern partners. As advocates of democratic development like Robert Chambers, David Korten, and Michael Edwards have noted, international development actors must be willing to become truly accountable to Southern partners. This means allowing such partners to make direct choices about the direction and parameters of projects and to become Board members in Northern NGOs. It means Northern NGOs opening themselves up to 'reverse evaluation' by beneficiaries, to external social audits, and to following good practice guidelines drawn up by fellow development actors. At the same time, as advocates of the New Institutional Economics (e.g. Samuel Paul and Teddy Brett) have pointed out, in the international development community we must stop romanticising development processes. We must not conceal the difficulties of coordinating efforts among donors who are in heated competition with one another, or of building partnerships with Southern governments that may be undemocratic, inefficient, or corrupt. We must not underestimate the difficulties of fostering participation in communities where civil society is weak, where social structures are highly unequal or divisive, and where the poorest members of the community have limited access to information or technical skills. Often, these individuals have little free time for more meetings, or diminishing tolerance for altruistic, 'process-based' development efforts that do not bring them the material benefits and economic opportunities they so desperately need and desire. In short, we need more honest self-criticism and debate about the real difficulties which development organisations are facing in their efforts to implement human development before we can begin to truly learn from our experience.

Clarification

Both UNDP and ActionAid staff have been sent detailed reports and have had the opportunity to comment on the research findings synthesised in this article.

Notes

1 All groups of countries experienced a rise in their *per capita* income from 1965 to 1985, and developing counties grew even faster than industrial market economies (at 3 per cent p.a. compared to 2.4 per cent p.a.) (Griffin and Knight 1990: 11).

2 While in 1960, the richest one-fifth of the world's population had incomes 30 times larger than the poorest fifth, by 1990, the share of income of the richest quintile had doubled. Once unequal distribution within countries is taken into account, the richest 20 per cent of the world's population have more than 150 times the wealth of the poorest 20 per cent (UNDP: *1992 HDR*).

3 SHD/PCD approaches fit Kuhn's definition of a paradigm as a 'world view' in which a constellation of beliefs, values and techniques are shared by a common community. As Kuhn himself pointed out though, no paradigm solves all the problems it defines and it is quite natural for adherents of a paradigm to have a variation of focuses and explanations of their shared world view (Kuhn 1970: 44, 77–79 110).

4 Interview with John Knight, 20 April 1995.

5 Compare, for instance, the pro-state statements in Drèze and Sen (1989: 89, 246, and 259) with the far more pro-market tone in Sen (1994: 8–9).

6 Interview with Per Arne Stroberg, Senior Human Development Advisor, Bureau for Policy and Programme Support (BPPS), UNDP Headquarters, 12 January 1996.

7 Confidential memo from senior BPPS official, January 1995.

8 Senior ActionAid manager interviewed at London headquarters, 18 December 1996.

9 Interview with Nigel Twose, Head of Programme Development Department at ActionAid, 12 February 1997.

10 UNDP, *1994 HDR*.

11 Interview with Mrs. Vitra Vaishid, Minister and Third Secretary, Permanent Indian Mission to the UN, 18 January 1996.

12 Interviews with UN informants, New York, January 1996.

13 Interview with Iradj Alikhani, World Bank Resident Economist in Uganda, Kampala, 7 July 1995.

14 Interview with a senior manager in ActionAid Uganda's Programme Development Department, June 1995.

15 Interview with a senior manager in ActionAid's headquarters, January 1997; and with a manager in the ActionAid-Mubende Office, Uganda, 26 May 1995.

16 Interview with Martin Griffiths (Director of ActionAid from 1991–1994), 28 August 1996; and with former ActionAid Trustee, interviewed in 1995.

17 My rural field work focused on three of UNDP Uganda's most promising grassroots initiatives, all of which were deemed by UNDP to have strong participation and empowerment components. They included: The Africa 2000 Network, which teaches farmers environmentally sound practices; the Micro Projects Programme to Combat AIDS, which helps HIV/AIDS victims start income-generating activities; and, the Community Management Programme (CMP), supported by UNDP and executed by HABITAT, which teaches communities to manage development initiatives. Thanks to the access and logistical support given by UNDP, and the help of a research assistant, Elizabeth Waisswa, I visited almost 20 projects in Mubende, Mbale and Fort Portal.

18 With ActionAid Uganda, my rural field work was carried out in the Buwekula DA in Mubende District, where the NGO was trying to shift towards a more integrated, participatory, and self-reliant development approach at the time of my visit. Thanks to ActionAid's access and logistical support, I visited over 20 projects with my researcher, Edward Ssekayombya.

19 During my field work, Ministry of Finance and Economic Planning (MFEP) officials noted that UNDP's proposal to create a special SHD Unit and database within the MFEP failed precisely because MFEP officials were not sufficiently consulted. UNDP did not fully take into account officials' reluctance to create separate technical units within the Ministry instead of strengthening its existing poverty analysis capacity. (Interviews with MFEP Economic Advisor and Commissioner for Economic Planning. Government of Uganda, Kampala, 7 December 1995.)

20 Such was the case in the S. S. Light Secondary School Construction Project in Mubende, where shirking and low participation became serious problems after UNDP and HABITAT rejected the group's request for individual credit and savings opportunities and convinced them to settle for a collective construction project instead.

21 Confidential internal memo from ActionAid headquarter's Evaluation and Impact Assessment Programme, December 1995.

22 Interview with technical expert from the ActionAid Uganda Country Office in Mubende, 1 December 1995.

References

ActionAid (1997), 'The Final CLAG Report on the Strategy for Mainstreaming and Integrating Advocacy', unpublished report, Collaborative Leadership and Advocacy Group, London: ActionAid.

Copenhagen Declaration Adopted by the World Summit for Social Development, Copenhagen, March 1995 (advance unedited text, 20 March 1995).

Drèze, J. and A. Sen (1989), *Hunger and Public Action,* Oxford: Clarendon Press.

Ferguson, J. (1990), *The Anti-Politics Machine: development, depolitization and bureaucratic power in Lesotho,* Cambridge: Cambridge University Press.

Griffin, K. and J. Knight (eds) (1990), *Human Development and the International Development Strategy for the 1990s,* London: Macmillan.

Griffiths, M. (1992), 'Moving Forward in the Nineties', London: ActionAid.

Hancock, G. (1991), *Lords of Poverty,* London: Mandarin Press.

Hijab, N. (1995), 'Promoting Sustainable Human Development: national entry points', Bureau for Policy and Programme Support, UNDP: New York.

Kuhn, T. (1970), *The Structure of Scientific Revolutions,* Chicago: University of Chicago Press (second enlarged edition).

Moore, D. and G. Schmitz (eds) (1995), *Debating Development Discourse: institutional and popular perspectives,* London: Macmillan.

Nicholls, L. (1998), *From Paradigm to Practice: the politics and implementation of sustainable human development in Uganda,* doctoral dissertation at London School of Economics, University of London.

OECD (1996), *Highlights of the 1996 Development Co-operation Report*, Paris: OECD.

Sachs, W. (1992), 'Development: a guide to the ruins', *The New Internationalist* 232.

Schuurman, F. J. (ed) (1993), *Beyond the Impasse: new directions in development theory*, London: Zed Books.

Sen, A. (1994), *Beyond Liberalization: social opportunity and human capability*, The Development Economics Research Programme Series, London: London School of Economics.

Speth, J. G. 'Initiatives for Change: Future of the UNDP. Report of the Administrator', UNDP and UNFPA Executive Board Annual Session 6–17 June 1994. UN Document: DP/1994/39 23, Geneva, May 1994.

UNDP (1990–97), *Human Development Report*, Oxford: Oxford University Press.

UNDP (1995), 'Managing Change: UNDP Corporate Plan', Office of Evaluation and Strategic Planning, New York: UNDP.

This paper was first published in Development in Practice *Volume 9, Number 4, 1999.*

Strengthening civil society: participatory action research in a militarised state

Amina Mama

Introduction

Research activity is severely constrained in most of post-colonial Africa. If the pursuit of knowledge was previously dictated by imperial interests and the uncritical application of Western paradigms, then today the problems are more numerous and more complex. Three decades after political independence, foreign researchers are often discouraged, while indigenous researchers face awesome material and political constraints that are often discussed within the African intellectual community (see Diouf and Mamdani 1994). Despite all this, Claude Ake (1994: 23) correctly observed that the African intellectual is 'well placed to demystify and expose the self-serving ideological representations of the state and external domination'. He went on to note the daunting nature of this task, emphasising the likelihood of those who embark on it provoking confrontation with the increasingly intolerant forces of the state and international capital.

Nowhere is this intransigence more apparent than in military states. Here, not only is research activity regarded with immense hostility by all officialdom, but civil society itself is imbued with suspicion and mistrust. None the less, research *is* carried out, sometimes successfully. The research experience in Nigeria of the independent African network ABANTU for Development provides a useful demonstration of research strategies that can be deployed to carry out in-depth study effectively, even under decidedly unfavourable conditions.

The ABANTU network

ABANTU for Development is a regional human resources network that was established in 1991 by a group of African women involved in various areas of research, training, and organisational capacity building. Motivated by a critique of the activities of development agencies, ABANTU's founders set out to devise and implement programmes that might contribute to social transformation, programmes characterised by an African perspective and guided by a commitment to gender equity and justice. The emphasis on women as agents of this agenda is expressed in the network's mission statement:

> ABANTU aims to empower African people to participate at local, national and international levels in making decisions which affect their lives, enabling action for change ... Women have a vital role to play in policy-formulation and public decision-making, yet there are few African women with the necessary education or experience to enable them to fulfil this role.

ABANTU set out to achieve this through a regional programme — entitled 'Strengthening the Capacities of Non-government Organisations to Influence Policies from a Gender Perspective' — which was to carry out research, training, and capacity building activities directed at developing civil society. So far, this has meant working mainly, but not exclusively, with women's organisations and networks. A large component of this regional programme is located in West Africa, where it focuses on national and local NGO communities.

ABANTU implements its pro-African and pro-women philosophy by applying a gender-sensitive participatory methodology in all aspects of its work, ensuring that its programmes are grounded in a thorough understanding of local realities and circumstances. In keeping with this philosophy, particular attention is paid to social relations at all stages of programming. For example, the relationships between the researchers, trainers, and NGOs working in ABANTU's programme to strengthen civil society are carefully developed through a series of interactions between local programme implementers and the target communities, and between programme implementers and the regional network. In this networking system, the role of offices is deliberately restricted to providing administrative and financial support to those working in the field, upon whom the network relies for the realisation of its goals.

The Nigeria work began in September 1996 when, as the programme initiator, I was responsible for organising a planning meeting between

ABANTU representatives and local activists and NGO representatives. Planning was preceded by extensive discussions that explored the Nigerian social and political context. The meeting realised that there was insufficient information about NGO policy activism across the country for effective programming. In response to this, ABANTU mobilised resources for a West African NGO training and capacity building programme. It included a sizeable research component that would analyse both the local policy milieu and the accumulated experience of NGOs operating under these conditions from a gender perspective.[1]

Nigeria was selected as the research site because ABANTU felt uniquely equipped to meet the particular challenges that this politically complex and socially diverse country poses to outsiders. Despite its enormous economic potential and rich human resources, Nigeria has not been a popular target for international donors who support non-government activity elsewhere in Africa. NGOs are correspondingly poorly resourced and remain too weak to play any significant role in national development. Protracted military rule and a state-centred approach to development have further undermined the capacities of NGOs to function as civil actors, or to participate meaningfully in national development. In recent years, however, the emergence of organisations dedicated to defending civil liberties and advancing democratisation indicates a growing awareness of the need for civil society to be organised. At grassroots levels, too, there are signs that communities are organising themselves to address the overwhelming failure of government to provide even the most basic amenities.

In other words, the contemporary international discourses on the role of civil society in development have, until recently, had limited impact on local consciousness in Nigeria. Civil society is, on the whole, highly organised at local and community levels, but such groups have had minimal access to international funds. As a result, even at state and national levels, the NGO sector has remained weak and generally under-professionalised. Women's organisations are little different from the rest, and so are not as effective as they might be in advancing women's interests. Consultation with independent research organisations across the country supported these observations, and affirmed the need for research that would both concentrate on elucidating state–civil society relations, and document the level of policy engagement. It made sense for this research to privilege the experience of NGOs, given the history of state-centred programmes, and since the programme sought to strengthen this sector. Furthermore, the gender politics of the military state have already been documented (see Dennis 1987; Abdallah 1993; Shettima 1996; Mama 1995).

In a different vein, there has been a tendency for analyses of Nigeria to privilege religion, ethnicity, and corruption as the only relevant analytical tropes, to the neglect of other possibilities. Because the main focus of this research was the nature of state–civil society relations as these pertain to gender activism in Nigeria's contemporary socio-political context, religion and 'tribe' were not taken as analytic categories. Thus, the study did not treat different religious and ethnic groups differently, but included NGOs on the basis of their engagement with gender. As a result, Muslim- and Christian-based organisations were included alongside secular ones, and ethnic associations were included alongside non-ethnic state and national organisations.

Because of the ABANTU network's decision to privilege the often suppressed perspective of NGOs, particularly those engaging with gender on the basis of their own perceived conditions, a participatory methodology was used. However, in view of the many different and confusing uses to which the concept of 'participation' is put in both academic and development literature, it is necessary to preface my discussion of ABANTU's research with a consideration of previous applications of the term.

Participation and its discontents

Participatory research

Participatory research differs fundamentally from the originally anthropological method of participant observation. Instead of observing natives who obligingly pretend to go about their business as usual, as the old anthropologists did, the participatory researcher strives to develop a more reciprocal relationship with those s/he researches. This idea of power sharing in the research process gained popularity in the 1970s among scholars concerned to challenge the 'scientific imperialism' of the colonial era, as well as among those intent on avoiding reproducing other relations of domination such as class, race, gender, culture, and religion. Many African researchers have taken up these ideas, linking participatory research with progressive political action:

> Research in its most desirable form should seek to be action
> oriented, informative, empowering and liberating. It should be seen
> as a means by which a community ... becomes involved in the
> process of releasing and utilising knowledge relevant to itself in the
> first instance. (Carasco 1983)

Others cautioned against assuming that the participatory research approach was *necessarily* progressive (e.g. Bryceson 1980).

Since then, there has been a great deal of debate on the politics and power relations of research, much of it stimulated by a combination of feminist and anti-imperialist concerns (see Harding 1987; Harding and Hintikka 1978; Hawkesworth 1989; Narayan 1989; Mohanty 1988; Stanley 1990). African feminists have been particularly critical of the effects of the dual legacies of colonialism and patriarchy in African social science (e.g. Imam and Mama 1994; Imam *et al. 1997*).

The accumulated experience of feminist research leads one to conclude that while there are methods favoured by feminists, the politics of research are not determined so much by the techniques as by the political and theoretical concerns underlying them. None the less, those with a progressive political agenda favour qualitative, open-ended and participatory techniques. The growth of indigenous research has demonstrated that 'natives' are uniquely placed to establish the reciprocal relations that are advocated by the proponents of participatory research. Furthermore, some African scholars have been able to take advantage of their knowledge of local languages and cultures to challenge Western hegemony and to highlight the strengths of indigenous researchers (e.g. Amadiume 1987; Altorki and El Solh 1988). The study that is discussed below highlights another strength of 'indigenous' researchers, namely that of local political knowledge.

Because of its approach to development, ABANTU's research necessarily derives much from these approaches. ABANTU uses research, alongside its other activities, as a means of building up the kind of knowledge that is required to further the goal of people-centred development from an African and a gender perspective. ABANTU's NGO research in Nigeria therefore adopted a participatory action methodology which was regarded as an action in itself, and which generated and supported further training and capacity building activities in the sub-region.

Participation in development

In the Africa of the 1990s, the intellectual debates on the politics of participatory research are confounded by the intrusions of a Western-driven development industry with a remarkable capacity for rhetorical adjustment. Participatory rural appraisal (PRA), for example, is a technique devised to carry out quick, cost-saving feasibility studies for development agencies, and may not, in fact, involve significant power sharing at the level of development management or control over resources. Perhaps the terminology of participation offers a convenient euphemism for democracy, so often lacking in many of the territories penetrated by the development industry. However, it can also be misleading, particularly in authoritarian political contexts. African governments, ever eager to placate their populace while currying favour in an increasingly competitive aid market, have adopted this language, and produced a series of official declarations calling for 'participatory development'.

But does the adoption of this politically attractive language of participation guarantee any significant degree of power-sharing? Salole (1991: 6) acidly observes:

> The term 'participation' is now the everyday parlance of development workers, practitioners, analysts, ordinary donors, governments and even the occasional beneficiary, as a descriptive 'holdall' of a development process which is supposedly both transactional and straightforward.

How 'transactional and straightforward' can development be in a world in which even military dictatorships insist that they are working for popular participation and democracy? In Nigeria, for example, successive military governments have made good use of the rhetoric of participation as a means of perpetuating the status quo (Mama 1998). Like their Latin American counterparts, they set up programmes for rural development, mass mobilisation, 'women development', and family support, as just another ploy for retaining an iron grip on the state and national resources. In this way, they can oversee the spectacular national deterioration that continues to threaten any genuine transition to democracy.

What all this means is that participatory methodologies, whether these are being applied to research or to development programmes, must be directed by clear and explicit definitions of exactly whose participation is involved at every stage, what that participation entails, and on whose terms.

Participatory knowledge-building

The process

The research aim was to furnish ABANTU with sufficient information and data to:

- identify the training needs of NGOs that were seeking to influence policy from a gender perspective;

- conceptualise and develop training programmes that would enhance the capacity of women's organisations to influence policy from a gender perspective;
- provide relevant and locally sensitive case material for use in training.

The research programme was the first step in a process which required building a partnership between the ABANTU network and the Nigerian NGO community, so that information could first be gathered and then be extended and developed in the other capacity building aspects of the programme. The research also provided both participants and researchers with opportunities to familiarise themselves with who was doing what in terms of influencing policies, and the extent to which they were applying a gender perspective in their activism. It was, therefore, a reflective process which enabled the local network to form and to develop collective consciousness about 'policy' and 'gender'.

A research team was convened in December 1996 with the assistance of local research NGOs and the ABANTU research coordinator's contacts. Five researchers were located: in Plateau State, in the middle of the country; Bornu and Kaduna in the north; Oyo in the south-west; and Cross River in the south-east. The NGO researchers were all women who already had good local and national knowledge of NGOs and women's organisations. All were proficient in at least one local language as well as in English, and all had substantial research experience. A research assistant assisted the coordinator with archival and media searches on gender and policy issues.

The research project was designed to be participatory through the following measures:

- it was to be carried out by local (indigenous) researchers residing and working with NGOs in the targeted states;
- it was to use participatory field techniques: open-ended or narrative interviews, focus group discussions and workshops;
- it was carried out under the auspices of an African NGO committed to strengthening civil society within the region;
- it was an action in itself, in that the field work was conducted in a manner designed to encourage reflection and raise consciousness among the researched;
- it was action-oriented because the research was to inform the conceptualisation of all other programme activities, and provide case material and content for the training.

The field work was carried out between January and June 1997. The researchers began by compiling inventories of NGOs that might be assumed to be active on gender issues in each of the five target states. They sought out and met with representatives of at least 50 of the identified NGOs in each state to ascertain basic information about the history, mission, structure, activities, and financing of those that described themselves as being concerned with gender. Most, but not all, turned out to be women's organisations. A smaller number (between five and ten) of those identified as engaging with gender in their activities were then included in the second level.

The second stage involved more detailed study which used in-depth discussions with key figures in each of the selected NGOs, during which the researchers invited the informants to describe their NGO's history and to detail their experiences of intervening on gender issues or policies. These discussions were recorded on audio cassette (where this was acceptable to the participant) and through note-taking. The researchers then compiled their findings into reports.

Finally, 30 NGOs were invited to participate in a national workshop both to broaden the scope of the research, and to give representatives from the five research states a chance to contribute to the final report. The workshop was facilitated by the research coordinator. The researchers presented their findings, and members of the ABANTU network from other African countries already involved in the regional programme also shared their experiences.

The workshop discussions of NGO experiences both within and beyond Nigeria contributed significantly to the process of awareness building about gender politics in a variety of communities. The participants became aware of the wide range of strategies that can be deployed to influence the policy process. On the final day there was an in-depth discussion about how this influence could be enhanced through training, information, networking, and other capacity building strategies. In this way, the Nigerian NGO community was able to participate in the detailed planning of the programme.

The located-ness of research relations

Despite the fact that all the researchers lived and worked in the state they were researching, at community level they were often initially (mis)perceived as government agents. This is unsurprising: the state pervades the psyche of any nation that is subjected to long stretches of dictatorship. In contemporary Nigeria, however, the mention of the term 'women' is enough to evoke the spectre of the military regime, a logical consequence of the fact that successive military regimes have mounted high profile programmes for women. During Ibrahim Babangida's rule (1985–1993), his wife commanded the high-profile Better Life for Rural Women Programme (BLP), the achievements of which were celebrated through the creation of a National Commission for Women. When Mrs Abacha became First Lady, she decided to replace the BLP with the Family Support Programme (FSP) and the Family Economic Advancement Programme (FEAP). General Abacha subsequently upgraded the National Commission into a Ministry for Women's Affairs, with both federal and state structures (see Mama 1995, for a detailed analysis). The main focus of all these programmes has been on supporting women's traditional petty trading activities through micro-credit schemes. Government programmes for women have had a number of consequences, which affected the research relations in ways described below.

The kind of publicity accompanying these top-level incursions into the terrain officially referred to as 'women development' raised expectations of cash benefits in many communities. On many occasions, researchers were expected to bring something to the community. However, being local, they were able to negotiate these demands away from monetary payments into a more acceptable form. In some instances, researchers decided to express their appreciation of the hospitality extended to them by taking small gifts, such as bars of soap for women, or biscuits for the children.

Another effect of intrusions from both government and international agencies was a sense of research fatigue. As the Kaduna State researcher described it:

> They've had a series of researchers coming to them and asking them about the situation. 'Do you have co-operatives? Are you organised at local level? What problems do you have? Does government assist you?' And they sit down all day and tell them what their problems are, but they never get any feedback. Nobody ever goes back to say 'Er, this is the bag of fertiliser we got for you'. Or, 'this is the loan facility'. Women expect concrete results ... They say 'eh-heh, they've come again, they want to use us to enrich themselves. They want to write a report and take it to government and collect money! This government—they don't remember us! They only use us!' That's why in most cases I had to explain that I'm not from government. (Transcribed discussion of field work experiences, June 1997)

The use of local researchers enabled ABANTU to identify subtleties beyond the national context too. For example, the fact that it was common for NGO representatives to assume researchers were government agents had different political consequences in different places. Whereas in Bornu State this misperception heightened interest and facilitated co-operation, in Oyo State it had the opposite effect, generating anxiety and suspicion. To what can we attribute these different responses?

The two states differ greatly in a number of relevant ways. Oyo State, situated in the densely populated and urbanised south-west, has the highest education level in Nigeria. People there are generally quite aware of their political and human rights, and so are correspondingly less complacent about prolonged military rule (Taiwo, in ABANTU 1997). Located in the relatively remote north-east, Bornu State has a very high illiteracy rate and the society is generally characterised by low political awareness and conservatism. Although Muslims predominate in Oyo State, seclusion of women is not practised, whereas most Bornu women live in seclusion, and very few play any role in public or political life. Women's organisations are a recent creation, and have emerged largely at the behest of the military government, many of them expressly set up in compliance with official pronouncements. The field research found this conformity to be primarily motivated by women's desire to gain access to the credit facilities and monetary support promised by successive First Ladies. In other words, women's groups have formed instrumentally, more out of a desire to access credit and cash to alleviate their immediate economic needs than out of a desire to challenge gender discrimination or renegotiate traditional religious and cultural practices. Only one NGO (a local branch of Women in Nigeria) was found to be committed to challenging entrenched traditions of gender segregation and inequality (Abdu Biu, in ABANTU 1997).

In Oyo State the higher level of gender activism reflects a local history of female militancy (Mba 1982). Nowadays, not only do both mixed and women's organisations express an interest in gender issues, but the majority of NGOs are led by women.

Because ethno-religious privilege has been so integral to Nigerian militarism, local communities in Bornu State assumed that the arrival of the Abachas heralded the arrival of monetary and other resources. Oyo State, on the other hand, was the home of the late Moshood Abiola, the civilian politician who died in detention after winning the annulled 1993 presidential elections. The state came to be viewed as a hotbed of opposition to military rule, referred to as the 'NADECO state' (after the National

Democratic Coalition), and was placed under close surveillance by the security apparatus (Mama 1998). The Oyo researcher had to deploy all her contacts and persuasive skills to gain the trust of the NGO community.

We can see from the field experiences of the research team that the participatory method successfully enabled ABANTU to gather detailed and locally diverse information about NGO relations with the state, and about levels of policy engagement. The social and political nuances described above might not have been comprehensible to 'outsiders' or to local researchers had they used more conventional research tools. The sound local knowledge of the researchers played a useful part in establishing reciprocal relationships characterised by mutual interest between ABANTU and the NGO community. In this way, ABANTU avoided replicating the monetary dependence and intellectual subordination, or even plain opportunism, that has tended to characterise relationships between NGOs and government, and between NGOs and international development agencies.

The two-way relationships that were established not only facilitated data collection, but also had consequences for the kind of knowledge that was generated, as discussed below.

Grounding concepts in local realities

The political context of the research was found to have profound effects on the local meaning of the terms 'gender' and 'policy'. It will be recalled that researchers were asked to elicit descriptions of NGO activities concerning gender in as open-ended a manner as possible. As might be expected, even the language in which the questions were posed presented challenges. In many of Nigeria's 300 languages and 500 dialects, there is no translation for the term 'gender', whose current English usage derives much from feminist scholarship of the 1970s. Researchers had to explain what the concept meant, either in local variants of English, or (particularly in the case of community-level organisations) in local languages.[2] Three major languages and English (the official language) were thus used in the field work.

In Cross River State the researcher conveyed gender in Efik, using the following words: *Nte ibanya a ireri owo ebuanade, ndi nam mme mkpo ke obio, ye ufok, ye kpukpm ebuana mmo, ebuana ye edu odude ye iren owo ye iban.* This roughly translates into English as: 'How men and women relate with each other and their ways in the family, community and society'.

There were several local variations across the three states (Kaduna, Bornu and Plateau states) where Hausa is widely, but not universally, spoken. The terms used included the following:

- *dangantaka*: generic terms for relationship which can be applied to gender relations;
- *zuwa taro*: permission to attend meetings or gatherings outside the home, meaningful in the context of female seclusion;
- *jinsi*: a term not widely used as such, which means gender.

In Yoruba, the following terms were used by the Oyo State researcher:

- *t'ako t'abo*: man–woman relations (also name given to a popular brand of lock and key);
- *eto*: a recently derived local term for gender.

Even where English is used, it soon became apparent that 'women', 'gender', and 'gender relations' are loaded in ways that are conceptually and historically specific, and vary from one location to another. Only when the questions about gender activities were posed and understood in concrete and local terms were people able to respond by narrating incidents that indicated their level of engagement with gender.

This participatory method revealed multiple understandings of gender at personal, household, community, and policy levels. Case material demonstrated a continuous negotiation of gender relations, and went some way in uncovering the strategies that are continuously being deployed by women in and beyond their organisations (ABANTU 1997).

When it came to discussions of 'policy', the wide range of responses indicated that, in Nigeria, there is little consensus over what policy is, not to speak of its gendered nature or the need to engage with policy from a gender perspective (see ABANTU 1997). None the less, NGO representatives talked about a wide range of actions relating to gender and government practices as they affect women. Struggles over the construction and allocation of market stalls, the violent abuse of women in rituals, and the exclusion of women from traditional policy-making structures, were all examples of interventions that display a degree of gender awareness. There were instances in which NGOs had responded to written as well as unwritten government policies, official pronouncements, statements by opinion leaders, laws, or traditional practices, customs, and habitual practices.

At the same time, very few contemporary NGOs displayed a capacity to analyse formal policies or policy processes from a gender perspective. Nor was it at all clear to them who the actors in these processes might be.

As a result, strategies are very rudimentary. The most popular intervention was that of making courtesy calls on the wives of military governors or on prominent officials.

A great many women's organisations are quick to deny having any political position or interests, preferring to project themselves as respectably conservative welfare associations. This is a predictable consequence of the violent and corrupt nature of national politics in Nigeria (see GADA 1997). It also reflects the conservatism of dominant gender discourses.

The results of this aspect of the research presented analytical challenges. If a textbook definition of formal policy is applied to the findings, few NGOs could have been said to engage at this level. On the other hand, if one considers NGO reactions to government practices, or if one widens the definition to include a variety of state and non-state structures regulating and constraining women, then a very different picture emerges. Taking a concrete example, very few people had any knowledge of the National Policy on Women and Development initiated by the then Commission for Women's Affairs in 1993. Yet the programmes and crusades of the Head of State's wives were widely perceived as government policies, which a great many NGOs were busy implementing. A different example is afforded by the activities of the Lagos NGO, Gender and Development Action (GADA), which capitalised on the post-Beijing climate to organise a series of large-scale political summits for women in 1997. These summits created a space in which women could challenge the male domination of political and public life and demand an end to military rule. The initial gatherings were strategically projected as an exercise in mobilising women for political participation, something for which even the military professed support under the rubric of Abacha's transition programme. In this way, the summits were not only held and attended by hundreds of women all over Nigeria, but also produced 'A Political Agenda for Nigerian Women', effectively the first women's manifesto since the 1985 WIN Document (Women in Nigeria 1985).

Broadly speaking, once ABANTU took the decision to work with the local understanding of 'policy' that was at play in the NGO communities, it became possible to get at the kind of information required for the capacity building programme to be strategic and effective. Without being able to articulate a definition of 'policy', many Nigerian NGOs *do* engage in gender activism, and regard it as something they should be doing. What they lack is a combination of skills and strategic information about the processes of governance, processes that would enable their engagement with policy-makers to be more effective.

Conclusion

We can see that the ABANTU researchers succeeded in uncovering levels of gender activism that might not have been discernible had they not used a participatory method. If the terms 'gender', 'policy', and 'policy engagement', which are used in all the programme documents as a means of communicating with donors and other agencies, had been rigidly applied during the field work, they would probably have been far less successful in documenting the real situation. The use of a participatory methodology not only gathered useful and concrete information, but also initiated an important process of collective awareness raising on matters of gender and policy. It also empowered NGOs to contribute to the formulation of strategies for addressing their own weaknesses and building on their strengths.

By privileging the world-view of the researched community, the research process generated valuable insights into locally diverse relationships between state and civil society. This has implications for the manner in which the state is conceptualised. Even in the most overtly authoritarian contexts, the state is not perceived or responded to uniformly, but rather in a manner that is textured by locally specific histories and experiences. ABANTU's approach to research was able to investigate this relationship, not just from the viewpoint of the dominant national, regional, and international ethos, but from that of those who are subjected to the official and less-than-official policies of authoritarian regimes. The insights so obtained generated the kind of information base that is needed to strengthen the hand of the NGOs that are emerging out of beleaguered civil societies and social movements.

Notes

1   ABANTU had already carried out situation analyses of NGO capacities for policy engagement in Ethiopia, Eritrea, Kenya, Uganda, and South Africa, but the size and complexity of Nigeria and West Africa demanded more detailed attention.

2   At the consultative workshop, this exercise was taken further when it was discovered that there were as many as 38 language groups represented.

References

ABANTU (1997), 'Building the Capacities of Nigerian NGOs for Engaging with Policy from a Gender Perspective', Report of the Training of Trainers (ToT) Workshop held at British Council Hall, Kaduna, July 1997. A formal publication based on this workshop is forthcoming.

Abdallah, H. (1993), 'Transition Politics and the Challenge of Gender in Nigeria', *Review of African Political Economy* 56:27–41.

Abdu, B. (1997), Report for ABANTU Research Programme, reported in ABANTU (1997).

Ake, C. (1994), 'Academic Freedom and Material Base', in Diouf M. and M. Mamdani (eds.) *Academic Freedom in Africa*, Dakar: CODESRIA.

Altorki, S. and C. F. El Solh (eds) (1988), *Arab Women in the Field: studying your own society*, Syracuse, NY: Syracuse University Press.

Amadiume, I. (1987), *Male Daughters, Female Husbands: gender and sex in an African society*, London: Zed Books.

Bryceson, D. (1980), 'Research Methodology and the Participatory Research Approach', *Jipemayo* 2.

Carasco, B. (1983), 'Participatory Research: a means towards collective community action', ISS Seminar, The Hague, 4–15 July 1983.

Dennis, C. (1987), 'Women and the State in Nigeria: the case of the federal military government', in Afshar, H. (ed) *Women, State and Ideology*, Basingstoke: Macmillan.

Diouf, M. and M. Mamdani (eds) (1994), *Academic Freedom in Africa*, Dakar: CODESRIA.

Gender and Development Action (GADA) (1997), *A Political Agenda for Nigerian Women*, Lagos: GADA.

Harding, S. (ed) (1987), *Feminism and Methodology*, Bloomington and Indianapolis: Indiana University Press.

Harding, S. and M. B. Hintikka (eds) (1978), *Discovering Reality: feminist perspectives on epistemology, metaphysics, methodology and philosophy of science*, Dordrecht: D. Reidel.

Hawkesworth, M. (1989), 'Knowers, Knowing, Known: feminist theory and claims of truth', *Signs* 14 (3).

Imam, I. and A. Mama (1994), 'The Role of Academics in Limiting and Expanding Academic Freedom', in Diouf, M. and M. Mamdani (eds) *Academic Freedom in Africa*, Dakar: CODESRIA.

Imam, I., A. Mama and F. Sow (eds) (1997), *Engendering African Social Science*, Dakar: CODESRIA.

Mama, A. (1995), 'Feminism or Femocracy: women and democratisation in Nigeria', *Africa Development* 20 (1).

Mama, A. (1998), 'Khaki in the Family: gender discourses and militarism in Nigeria', *African Studies Review*, Fall 1998.

Mba, N. (1982), *Nigerian Women Mobilised: women's political activity in southern Nigeria, 1900–1965*, Berkeley: Institute of International Studies, University of California at Berkeley.

Mohanty, C. (1988), 'Under Western Eyes: feminist scholarship and colonial discourses', *Feminist Review* 30.

Narayan, U. (1989), 'The Project of Feminist Epistemology: perspectives from a non-western feminist', in Jaggar, A. and S. Bordo (eds) *Gender/Body/Knowledge: feminist reconstructions of being and knowing*, New Brunswick: Rutgers University Press.

Salole, G. (1991), 'Participatory Development: the taxation of the beneficiary?', *Journal of Social Development in Africa* 6 (2):5–16.

Shettima, K. A. (1996), 'Engendering Nigeria's Third Republic', *African Studies Review* 34 (1).

Stanley, L. (ed) (1990) *Feminist Praxis*, London: Routledge.

Taiwo, S. (1997), Report conducted for ABANTU's research programme, and reported in ABANTU (1997).

Women in Nigeria (WIN) (1985), *The WIN Document: women in Nigeria to the year 2000*, Dakar: CODESRIA.

This paper was first published in Development in Practice Volume 10, Number 1, 2000.

Annotated bibliography

The concept of civil society goes back many centuries in Western thinking, with its roots in the Ancient Greek city states. Today's conceptual frameworks are, however, more immediately influenced by seventeenth-century British political theorists such as Thomas Hobbes and John Locke, by nineteenth-century European writers such as Friedrich Hegel, Alexis de Tocqueville, and Karl Marx, and by the more recent work of political thinkers such as Antonio Gramsci, Marta Harnecker, or John Friedmann. To these must be added Robert Putnam, whose work on democracy and social capital is much cited in development policy literature on civil society, and writers on New Social Movements, such as Sonia Alvarez, Arturo Escobar, and Alain Touraine. And this is not to mention a host of scholar-activists, like the Latin American writers Marcos Arruda, Orlando Fals-Borda, and Manfred Max-Neef. By contrast, 'development' as a body of theory and practice is a twentieth-century phenomenon. Development agencies, including NGOs, have been in existence for at most 50 years, most of them far less. The body of literature on both subjects is already vast — and still growing.

This bibliography has been selected in order to reflect the intersections between the three areas addressed in this Reader. We have not included the works of the major civil society theorists mentioned above, since these classics are relatively easy to trace, and several of the edited volumes listed here (notably Van Rooy 1999) include informative overviews of their work and its significance. Similarly, many of the papers included in this Reader also have valuable bibliographic references for interested readers to follow up. Since this is a rapidly growing field of enquiry, we have included information about institutions and websites which serve as useful entry points for readers who are keen to delve further.

The bibliography was compiled and annotated by Deborah Eade and Nicola Frost with Alan Whaites, who are respectively Editor, Reviews Editor, and Associate Reviews Editor of Development in Practice.

Books

Danielle Archibugi and David Held (eds), *Cosmopolitan Democracy: an agenda for a new world order*, Cambridge: Polity Press, 1995.
The end of the Cold War has led to major transformations in international and domestic politics. Contributors present ideas of national democracy and of a potential 'international' or 'cosmopolitan' democracy. The latter refers to political organisation in which all citizens world-wide have a voice, input, and political representation in international affairs, in parallel with and independently of their own governments. This model places at the centre the pursuit of democratic values through popular participation in the political process, and relates this to the principles and institutions of human rights.

Jonathan Barker, *Street-Level Democracy: political setting at the margins*, Kumarian Press, 1999.
With detailed case studies from many parts of the world, Barker investigates the practical reality of public life, looking at the mechanisms through which people participate in local politics. On a broader level, he argues that a focus on concrete political settings is a crucial step to understanding the impact of the local on global politics.

Anthony Bebbington and Diana Mitlin, *NGO Capacity and Effectiveness: a review of themes in NGO-related research recently funded by ESCOR*, London: IIED, 1996.
Under the often vague rubric of capacity building, Northern NGOs are found to be imposing their own agendas and world view (and that of their own donors) upon the Southern NGOs they support. Based on a survey of findings among British NGOs and their Southern counterparts, the authors find that local capacity may actually be undermined as the latter's own values and priorities are distorted in the process of channelling Northern aid monies.

Anthony Bebbington and Roger Riddell, *Donors, Civil Society and Southern NGOs: new agendas, old problems*, London: IIED and ODI, 1995.
Donors' direct funding of Southern NGOs rests on the wish to enhance the effectiveness of aid delivery and to contribute to a stronger civil society in the South. This paper examines the underlying assumptions being made about the NGO sector, and how bilateral aid may in reality be serving instrumentalist purposes. Alternative and less potentially distorting ways of supporting Southern NGOs might focus instead on the wider environment in which they function, both at a policy and at an institutional level. The authors argue that, if used constructively, the discussion of direct funding can make more explicit long-standing problems in the 'partnership' between Northern and Southern NGOs, and so be a step towards addressing them.

Amanda Bernard, Henny Helmich and Percy B. Lehning (eds), *Civil Society and International Development*, Paris: OECD and the North–South Centre of the Council of Europe, 1998.

In papers from a seminar on civil society and international development, contributors explore conceptual questions of civil society, and the role of external actors such as donors and NGOs, with perspectives from developing regions. Civil society is often a crucial manifestation of an associative impulse and is influenced by existing regimes and political resistance in its ideological, political and social expression. A better understanding of the role, history, and traditions of civil society could provide useful practical insights into how to restore peace and resume the development process in regions plagued by violent conflicts, and also contribute to democratic processes and development elsewhere.

Kees Biekart, *The Politics of Civil Society Building: European private aid agencies and democratic transitions in Central America*, Utrecht: International Books in co-operation with Transnational Institute, 1999.

The first part of this book offers an analytical overview of contemporary thinking about civil society. It is given with particular reference to political transitions from military rule to democratically elected governments in South America, and an examination of the roles played by social movements and international aid agencies in these processes. The second part traces the 'aid chain' linking specific human rights and popular organisations and NGOs in El Salvador, Guatemala, and Honduras. It questions the various short- and long-term impacts, intended or not, of foreign assistance for 'civil society building'.

Patrick Chabal and Jean-Pascal Daloz, *Africa Works*, James Currey, 1999.

Based on empirical observation, this is an attempt to make sense of some of the key issues in Black Africa today. In an analysis of the functioning of African polities, it examines the growing informalisation of politics: 'the state in Africa is not just weak, but essentially vacuous'. It demolishes the myth of a host of viable civil society organisations willing and able to challenge central state power, and examines other cultural influences, such as witchcraft, and the effect of an ongoing culture of violence.

Neera Chandhoke, *State and Civil Society: explorations in political theory*, New Delhi: Sage India, 1995.

This is a theoretical survey of the history of civil society in western political thought, from Hegel to Marx and Gramsci, and it includes a useful bibliography. It highlights some of the limitations of these theoretical constructions for the way we think about civil society today, for example, the classification of household politics as a private rather than public concern. It also underlines the essential paradox of a free civil society constituted within the very state which it is supposed to be able to hold accountable.

Seamus Cleary, *The Role of NGOs under Authoritarian Political Systems,* Basingstoke: Macmillan, 1997.

This is a searching critique, based on personal experience in Indonesia, South Africa, Sri Lanka, and the Philippines, of the claim of Northern NGOs to be able to represent the most vulnerable people in society through their links with the grassroots. In Indonesia, for example, Cleary reveals how UK NGOs, establishing themselves as interpreters of others' needs, actually exceeded local people's demands, and sacrificed accountability to serve institutional ends. The book draws general conclusions about whose interests are served by this kind of representation, and makes distinctions between operational development organisations and advocacy based, often environmental NGOs. It also highlights the importance of domestic capacity for presenting advocacy cases as a crucial element in their success.

Colin Crouch and David Marquand (eds), *Reinventing Collective Action: from the global to the local,* Oxford: Blackwell, 1995.

This collection takes a look at aspects of a new collectivism that has arisen among the ruins of neo-liberal orthodoxies at the end of the twentieth century. Its internationalist vision is based on a strong civil society and on principles of bottom-up development, with an ethos of accountability and pluralism. It revives and revises the concept of citizenship in a global society, and looks at constitutional implications, and the need to reform global financial institutions.

Mark Duffield, 'The Symphony of the Damned', *Disasters*, 20(3), 1996; 'Complex Emergencies and the Crisis of Developmentalism', *IDS Bulletin* 25(4): 37–45, 1994.

These two influential papers focus on the role of NGOs and other relief agencies in contemporary, post-Cold War civil conflicts where the state is weak or non-existent. In such situations, aid agencies risk not only fuelling conflict, albeit inadvertently, but also allowing Western governments effectively to disengage from any meaningful commitment to equitable global development. Complex emergencies represent an extreme expression of a dynamic that is present in any setting in which the state is incapable of mediating between different interest groups, or of guaranteeing basic security and equal rights for all citizens.

Michael Edwards, *Future Positive,* London: Earthscan, 1999.

Future Positive is a rethinking of the international aid system — its purpose, effectiveness, and the role of the international institutions in its administration. As its title suggests, this is an optimistic vision, a radical reworking of international co-operation. Edwards posits a future of collective action based on 'critical friendship, in which NGOs and civil society ("an active global citizenry") spearhead the drive for change. The keywords are coherence, flexibility (i.e. sensitivity to local and national situations), and a willingness to put one's own house in order before embarking on other people's.'

Michael Edwards and David Hulme (eds), *Making a Difference: NGOs and development in a changing world*, London: Earthscan, 1992; *NGOs — Performance and Accountability: beyond the magic bullet*, London: Earthscan, 1996; *NGOs, States and Donors: too close for comfort?*, Macmillan, 1997.

These volumes emerged from two conferences that were organised by the editors in 1992 and 1994, and they reflect the preoccupations of Northern and large Southern NGOs in the early 1990s. *Making a Difference* looks at different ways to 'scale up' NGO impact, for instance by partnering with governments, by becoming service providers, by expanding the scale and scope of their programmes, or by undertaking advocacy work to shift public policy or to influence public opinion. *Beyond the magic bullet* and *Too close for comfort?* seek to re-define what NGOs are best at (and against whose criteria to prove this). They explore the opportunities and risks inherent in becoming channels for official aid. They focus on questions of downwards — or two-way — versus upwards accountability.

Richard Falk, *On Humane Governance*, University Park PA: The Pennsylvania State UP, 1995.

Economic globalisation is diminishing the political role of the nation-state, though the main market- and capital-driven forces that challenge it remain largely concealed as political actors. Variants of the politics of identity are also causing fragmentation and furthering the decline in governmental capacity in many states. The author calls for a commitment to 'humane' geo-governance: a set of social, political, economic, and cultural arrangements committed to rapid progress in the promotion of welfare, human rights, environmental protection, peace building and transnational democratisation. This will depend on dramatic growth of transnational democracy, the extension of primary democratic processes, a growing allegiance to global civil society, and on the plausibility of humane governance as a political priority.

Julie Fisher, *Nongovernments: NGOs and the political development of the third world*, West Hartford CT: Kumarian Press, 1998.

NGOs have been widely trumpeted as being central to the success of sustainable development initiatives in a range of contexts. But what exactly are these NGOs, and how exactly do they interact with other stakeholders, and to what effect? This book provides a systematic overview of current NGO typologies, with a detailed description of how these organisations have co-operated with or influenced political systems around the world.

Joe Foweraker, *Theorizing Social Movements*, London: Pluto, 1995.

Economic transformation and social upheaval intimately affect existing class, gender, and ethnic relations, creating diverse areas of challenge and change. Throughout Latin America, extensive political re-alignments and re-definitions are underway even as social movements are challenging the traditional boundaries of 'politics' and its actors. The main debates and issues in contemporary social movement theory are discussed in this context, with empirical reference to urban social movements and women's mobilisation. While social movements theory is necessarily drawn from particular experiences, the gap between theory and collective action appears to be growing. The author questions the capacity of theoretical developments that have emerged from western Europe and North America to explain realities in Latin America, where social action is on the increase.

Alan Fowler, *Civil Society, NGDOs and Social Development: changing the rules of the game*, Geneva: UNRISD, 2000.
Underlining the fact that the Western image of civil society that is currently employed by donors does not necessarily apply to civil societies elsewhere, the author examines the practices of non-government development organisations (NGDOs) and their relationships with other 'partners'. He links these with the 'deep-rooted pathologies of the aid system' that condition the form and effectiveness of many development interventions both by NGDOs and by the wider universe of civil society organisations. The aid system is, it is argued, logically incapable of generating the nature and level of reform required. However, without fundamental reform, North–South relationships will be inevitably flawed, and often will be politically distorting.

Jonathan A. Fox and L. David Brown (eds), *The Struggle for Accountability: the World Bank, NGOs and grassroots movements,* Cambridge MA: MIT Press, 1998.
This book analyses policy reforms within the World Bank, the adoption of more rigorous environmental and social policies, and the subsequent conflicts over how and whether to follow them in practice. It asks how the Bank has responded to the NGO/grassroots environmental critique, with case studies to assess degrees of change, how far advocacy campaigns (often led by NGOs) represent the organisations of those most directly affected by Bank projects, and how accountable NGOs are to their own partners. The Bank is shown to be more publicly accountable as the result of protest, public scrutiny, and the empowering effect on inside reformers. Transnational NGO networks have also gradually become more accountable to their local partners — partly because of more vocal and autonomous grassroots movements, and partly in response to the Bank's challenge to the legitimacy of its critics, the international NGOs.

Jean Grugel (ed), *Democracy Without Borders: transnationalism and conditionality in new democracies,* London: Routledge, 1999.
Including empirical data from Africa, Europe, and Latin America, this book concentrates on the role of non-state actors in the increasing web of transnational networks which wield considerable power and influence in global politics. The study of the changing nature of civil society in East Central Europe, and the chapter on 'policy networks and transnational ethical networks' in relation to European NGOs' involvement in democratisation in Latin America, are particularly interesting.

Chris Hann and Elizabeth Dunn, *Civil Society: challenging western models,* London: Routledge, 1996.
'Civil society' has been enthusiastically and uncritically endorsed as a universal ideal of social organisation, despite its European origin and the fact that it fails to do much

to explain current social realities even in Europe. Civil society is often presented as a private sphere and equated with the non-government sector. Contributors argue for a broader understanding that encompasses a range of everyday social practices, often elusive power relations, and the many material constraints that influence shared moralities and ideologies. Case studies from the USA, the UK, four former communist countries of Eastern Europe, Turkey, the Middle East, Indonesia, and Japan demonstrate the contribution that anthropology can make to current debate.

John A. Hall (ed), *Civil Society: theory, history, comparison*, London: Pluto, 1995. This book aims to clarify what is meant by 'civil society' in order to identify its usefulness as a descriptive as well as a prescriptive term. The analysis is comparative, historical, and theoretical, with a focus on the relationships between civil society and other social forces, notably nationalism and populism. The book defines civil society as a social value *and* a set of social institutions, noting that not every autonomous group creates or contributes to civil society, and that the notion that groups can balance the state is wrong. With case studies from Latin America, India, Turkey, and the Islamic world, the book asks where civil society has its foundation and its legitimacy.

Jeff Haynes, *Democracy and Civil Society in the Third World*, Cambridge: Polity Press, 1997.
Looking at 'Action Groups' as popular political, social and economic movements in Third World societies, and focusing on poor and marginalised groups within developing countries, the author argues that demands for democracy, human rights, and economic change were a widespread catalyst for the emergence of hundreds of thousands of popular movements in Latin American, Africa, and Asia. These included movements of indigenous peoples, environmental movements, women's movements and Islamist action groups. These emerging popular organisations can be regarded as building blocks of civil society that will enhance the democratic nature of many political environments. The author speculates on the likelihood of their survival once the regimes (under whose jurisdiction they must live) manage to exert control.

David Held, *Democracy and the Global Order*, Cambridge: Polity Press, 1995.
This book includes an account of the history of democracy and the impact of globalisation from a theoretical perspective. The 'cosmopolitan democratic community', which does not require cultural integration, and is predicated on autonomy, is achieved by 'lodging ... the rights and obligations of democratic law' in all the agencies involved, from grassroots organisations to multinational corporations. Held suggests a model which makes civil society institutions part of an international decision-making body, like Segall's UN Second Assembly. He concedes that his model does not in itself provide the possibility for change to the social and economic order, but it does create a climate of democratic rights which helps to make government more accountable.

Noeleen Heyzer, James V. Riker, and Antonio B. Quizon, *Government–NGO Relations in Asia: prospects and challenges for people-centred development*, Basingstoke: Macmillan, 1995.

This book traces the relationship between a growing NGO sector in Asia and national governments that frequently follow development plans and strategies without extensive provision for NGO collaboration and participation. Asian NGOs vary widely in their relations with government, and in their approaches and capabilities, but all are beginning to recognise the implications of globalisation for the way in which they operate to influence policy and combat poverty.

Richard Holloway, *Supporting Citizens' Initiative : Bangladesh's NGOs and society*, London: Intermediate Technology, 1998.

A detailed and practical examination of the work of NGOs in Bangladesh, this book is a useful introduction to the role of the Third Sector in supporting sustainable development. It goes right back to the basics of what constitutes a non-government organisation, how this might differ from country to country, sources of funding, and NGOs' profile in wider society. See, also, Richard Holloway's 'Civil Society Toolbox', a series of personal notes and useful references, covering a range of specific areas of civil society organisations' activity. Holloway himself admits the collection does not provide many examples from Latin America. It is available online at: www.pactworld.org/toolbox.html

Ann C. Hudock, *NGOs and Civil Society: democracy by proxy?*, Cambridge: Polity Press, 1999.

Combining elements of organisational analysis with readings from international relations, Hudock provides a useful introduction to the way NGOs work. The book examines in detail NGOs' increasing dependence on development agencies and government funders, and the impact of this on their autonomy and effectiveness. The author argues for a more thorough understanding of the constraints under which Southern NGOs operate.

Michael Kaufman and Haroldo Dilla Alfonso (eds), *Community Power and Grassroots Democracy: the transformation of social life*, London: Zed Books/IDRC, 1997.

The result of a long-term research project in several Central American countries, this book combines detailed case studies in individual countries with an integrated theoretical framework. It examines the obstacles to effective personal empowerment and popular participation, and uses these lessons to inform and progress the theoretical paradigm.

John Keane, *Civil Society: old images, new visions*, Cambridge: Polity Press, 1998.

This is a careful examination of the renewed interest in a variety of new interpretations of the classical distinction between civil society and the state. Keane traces the emergence of civil society all over the world, and highlights the potential for dramatic new directions in which it could move in the future.

Adrian Leftwich (ed), *Democracy and Development*, Cambridge: Polity Press, 1995.
As aid becomes increasingly conditional on democratisation, this collection looks at whether this is feasible or desirable through a number of wider-ranging cases studies, including chapters by Jenny Pearce and Gordon White. Countries examined include South Africa, China, Chile, South Korea, and Russia. The book centres on the question of whether democracy is a condition of steady economic growth or whether the causality works the other way and you need some economic development for democracy to flourish. The conclusion is that it is the state and politics that are central for development, not governance and democracy.

David Lewis (ed), *International Perspectives in Voluntary Action: reshaping the third sector*, London: Earthscan, 1999.
This is essentially a comparative study of NGOs and voluntary agencies, contrasting their scope, scale and priorities, and discovering common ground in areas such as accountability, legitimacy, and governance. The collection broadens current debates about North–South relations, the nature of development, and the tension between theory and practice, to include a much wider range of third sector organisations than is usually considered.

Laura MacDonald, *Supporting Civil Society: the political role of non-government organisations in Central America*, Basingstoke: Macmillan, 1997.
Painting an essentially optimistic picture, MacDonald examines the move towards using civil society organisations as channels for development aid and as promoters of democracy in Latin America, following a disillusionment with bilateral arrangements. Case studies from Nicaragua and Costa Rica provide the basis for a comprehensive investigation of the many roles of NGOs, including their political aspects, and their relations with external partners and donors. MacDonald concludes that there is real potential for NGOs to be a powerful force for change in the region. However, for this to be realised Northern NGOs need to learn to let go of their control of power and resources in relationships with Southern partners, and avoid a paternalistic stance.

Stephen N. Ndegwa, *The Two Faces of Civil Society: NGOs and politics in Africa*, Kumarian, 1996.
Based around a comparative study of two local Kenyan NGOs, this book challenges assumptions about civil society as an invariably progressive, democratic force. It focuses on the way in which NGOs contribute to and influence state-society relations, and exposes the centrality of personal leadership in NGOs' decision to participate in political agitation. The book discourages generalisations, but acknowledges that any grassroots developmental work can facilitate local community participation in political actions, regardless of the level of organisational involvement.

Terry Robson, *The State and Community Action*, London: Pluto, 1999.
Robson provides a thorough analysis of contemporary theoretical issues in community development, drawing on Gramscian ideas of hegemony and civil society. He examines the relationship between community and state, and asks

whether this can be a stable and equal partnership, leading to radical change, or whether domination by the state is inevitable. Case studies cover Northern Ireland, Romania and the US.

Lloyd Sachikonye (ed), *Democracy, Civil Society and the State: social movements in southern Africa,* Harare: SAPES, 1995.
Written in the mid-1990s, in the midst of dramatic political change in Southern Africa, this book provides a balance between country-specific case studies and a discussion of the application of Western liberal democratic theoretical discourse to Southern African priorities. Case studies from Zambia, Mozambique, Zimbabwe, and Swaziland, as well as South Africa, examine specific elements of that Southern African context, including: the effect of war on civil society operation; state-society relations; and the nature of social movements involved in democratic struggles. The contributors are all African academics.

Margaret E. Keck and Kathryn Sikkink (eds), *Activists Beyond Borders: advocacy networks in international politics,* Ithaca, NY: Cornell University Press, 1998.
The contributors to this volume examine a type of pressure group that has been largely ignored by political analysts: networks of activists that coalesce and operate across national frontiers. They sketch the dynamics of emergence, strategies, and impact of activists from different nationalities working together on particular issues, such as violence against women. This work highlights a subset of international issues, characterised by the prominence of ideas that are based in ethical principles, and a central role for NGOs.

David Sogge with Kees Biekart and John Saxby (eds), *Compassion and Calculation: the business of foreign aid*, London: Pluto, with Transnational Institute, 1996.
Large NGOs, or private aid agencies, continue to enjoy enormous public confidence while also drawing increasing proportions of their income from governmental sources. Their mechanisms for financial accountability are, however, far more developed than those to ensure political legitimacy. Contributors suggest that the NGO bubble will inevitably burst, and call on NGOs to be more honest and more courageous in deciding where their future lies.

Alison Van Rooy (ed), *Civil Society and the Aid Industry,* London: Earthscan, in association with The North–South Institute, 1999.
Among aid agencies, both official donors and NGOs, civil society has become something of 'an analytical hat stand', as Van Rooy calls it. Uncritical and normative assumptions are made about what civil society is, how it functions, and how it can be supported by external agencies in furtherance of their own declared agenda of democratisation, good governance, and popular participation. However, the lack of theoretical clarity on the one hand, and over-hastily disbursed funds on the other, can make for interventions that are profoundly damaging in their long-term impact. Critical case studies by scholar-activists from Hungary, Kenya, Peru, and Sri Lanka, are framed by excellent opening and concluding chapters by Van Rooy. See also North–South Institute entry.

Journals

@lliance, published quarterly by The Charities Aid Foundation. ISSN: 1359-4621. Editor: Caroline Hartnell.

@lliance is aimed primarily at the funders of civil society initiatives world-wide, including international NGOs, governments, and multilaterals. As well as providing a forum for discussion between these stakeholders, the journal provides updates on relevant UK legislation, and a conference calendar. A recent issue was dedicated to the evaluation and accreditation of NGOs.

Democratization, published quarterly by Frank Cass. ISSN: 1351-0347. Editors: Peter Burnell and Peter Calvert.

Democratization is dedicated to gaining a better understanding of the evolution of democratic institutions and practices, both within and across national and cultural borders. The journal makes special reference to developing countries and post-communist societies, and aims to be of interest to policy makers and journalists as well as the academic world. See Especially 'Civil society, the Market and Democracy in Latin America', Jenny Pearce, 4(2), 1997.

Development, published quarterly by Sage on behalf of the Society for International Development. ISSN: 1011-6370. Editor: Wendy Harcourt.

Development is a thematic journal fostering dialogue between activists and intellectuals committed to the search for alternative paths of social transformation and a more sustainable and just world, with a particular focus on promoting local-global links. Relevant special issues include 'Reflection on Global Solidarity: one world or several', 34(1) 1991, 'Civil Society: the third sector in action', 39(3) 1996, 'Globalization: opening up spaces for civic engagement', 40(2) 1997, and, 'Globalization: new institutions, new partnerships, new lives', 40(3) 1997.

Development in Practice, published five times a year by Carfax/Taylor & Francis on behalf of Oxfam GB. ISSN: 0961-4524. Editor: Deborah Eade.

Development in Practice is a multi-disciplinary journal of practice-based analysis and research concerning the social dimensions of development and humanitarianism. It acts as a forum for debate and the exchange of ideas among practitioners, policy makers, and academics world-wide. The journal seeks to challenge current assumptions, stimulate new thinking, and shape future ways of working. It aims to publish articles that reflect a wide range of institutional and cultural backgrounds and a variety of professional experiences. Other relevant titles in the *Development in Practice Readers* series include *Development and Patronage* (forthcoming also in Spanish) and *Development and Social Action*.

Millennium: Journal of International Studies, published three times a year by the Millennium Publishing Group, London School of Economics. ISSN: 0305-8298. Editors: Pavlos Hatzopoulos and Fabio Petito.

Millennium includes a wide range of articles on topics such as international relations, democracy, and poverty and humanitarianism in a global political and economic context. A Special Issue in 1996 was titled: 'Poverty in World Politics: whose global era?'. See also, Laura Macdonald, 1994, 'Globalising Civil Society: interpreting international NGOs in Central America', 23(2).

Nonprofits and Voluntary Sector Quarterly, published by Sage. ISSN: 0899-7640. Editor: Steve Rathgeb Smith.
The journal publishes articles that report on research on voluntarism, citizen participation, philanthropy, civil society, and non-profit organisations. See especially Volume 28 Supplemental, 1999: 'Globalization and Northern NGOs: the challenge of relief and development in a changing context'.

Voluntas, published quarterly by Plenum Publishing Corporation for the International Society for Third-Sector Research. ISSN: 0957-8765. Editor: Jeremy Kendall.
This interdisciplinary journal provides a forum for empirical and theoretical analysis and debate about issues of relevance to the non-profit sector. There is a good geographical spread, and substantial attention to development NGOs. The journal aims to present cutting-edge academic debate in a format that is accessible to practitioners and policymakers. Abstracts are available in English, French, Spanish, and German.

World Development, published monthly by Elsevier. ISSN: 0305-750X. Editor: Janet L. Craswell.
Recognising 'development' as a process of change involving nations, economies, political alliances, institutions, groups, and individuals, the journal seeks to explore ways of improving standards of living, and the human condition generally. It examines potential solutions to problems such as poverty, unemployment, malnutrition, disease, lack of shelter, environmental degradation, inadequate scientific and technological resources, international debt, gender and ethnic discrimination, militarism and civil conflict, and lack of popular participation in economic and political life. See for example, L. D. Brown and D. Ashman, 'Participation, Social Capital, and Intersectoral Problem Solving: African and Asian cases', 24(9) 1996; A. Hadenius and F. Uggla, 'Making Civil Society Work, Promoting Democratic Development: what can states and donors do?', 24(10) 1996.

Organisations

Ashoka — Innovators for the Public: Providing financial and professional support, Ashoka's mission is to promote 'social entrepreneurship', encouraging individual pioneers in their efforts to solve social problems. *Changemakers.net* is Ashoka's online newsletter, including *Creative Resourcing Network*, which is a forum for social entrepreneurs and civil society activists to exchange strategies for mobilising resources locally, rather than having to be dependent on international assistance. Web: www.ashoka.org or www.changemakers.net

Center for Alternative Development Initiatives (CADI): CADI is a Philippines-based civil society organisation, dedicated to promoting sustainable development through 'threefolding' — a process where government, civil society and business are all stakeholders in development plans and initiatives. Another focus is the advancing of 'cultural renewal' through innovative educational activities, and support for civil society. Though deriving from Philippine Agenda 21 policies, CADI engages in publishing and networking in the international arena. A recent title is: Nicanor Perlas, *Shaping Globalization: civil society, cultural power and threefolding*, 1999. E-mail: cadi@info.com.ph; Web: www.info.com.ph/~cadi/

Center for Civil Society International (CCSI): With a focus on Eastern Europe and the former Soviet Union, CCSI describes itself as an 'information clearing house', publishing in print and electronically, with the current priority of publicising creative collaborations between US NGOs and civil society organisations in the NIS (new independent states). The Center works in partnership with a similar information network in Moscow, and offers consultancy services in the use of the Internet for NGOs. The website is bilingual in English and Russian, and is a comprehensive source of information about NGOs, resources, jobs, and publications. Recent titles includes: M. Holt Ruffin and Daniel Waugh (eds), *Civil Society in Central Asia*, 1999; *The Post-Soviet Handbook: a guide to grassroots organizations and Internet resources*, 1999. E-mail: ccsi@u.washington.edu; Web: www.friends-partners.org/~ccsi/

Centre for Civil Society, London School of Economics: Formerly the Centre for Voluntary Organisation, this is a teaching and research centre, interested in problems and issues arising from the work of voluntary agencies and NGOs and the implications for public policy. Research findings are tested and disseminated through publications, postgraduate teaching, and applied research projects. Two series of Working Papers are available online. Titles include: Sarah Lister, 'Power in Partnership? an analysis of an NGO's relationships with its partners'; Jo de Berry, 'Exploring the Concept of Community: implications for NGO management'. E-mail: ccs@lse.co.uk; Web: www.lse.ac.uk/Depts/ccs/

The Center for Civil Society Studies, Johns Hopkins University: Based in the Institute for Policy Studies, the Center specialises in detailed empirical studies of civil society organisations in the US and world-wide. *Global Civil Society: dimensions of the nonprofit sector* (1999) is the result of comprehensive analysis of the scope, size, and financing of the non-profit sector in 22 countries, and working papers outline the situation in selected individual countries. Other publications include: Lester M. Salamon *et al., Global Civil Society: dimensions of the nonprofit sector,* and, *The Emerging Sector Revisited: a summary — revised estimates*, 1999. The Center also offers a number of capacity building education and training programmes. E-mail: ccss@jhu.edu; Web: www.jhu.edu/~ccss

Civil Society and Governance Programme — Institute of Development Studies: Funded by the Ford Foundation, this three-year programme examines the interplay between civil society organisations and government in 22 countries. The emphasis is on gaining a clearer understanding of the character of civil society, while recognising regional variations, and on developing practical measures for strengthening civil society's 'impact as an agent for improving political life and governance', particularly with reference to social policy. Web: www.ids.ac.uk/ids/civsoc/

CIVICUS — World Alliance for Citizen Participation: An alliance of organisations committed to strengthening citizen action and civil society world-wide, Civicus believes that private action for the public good can take place either within the civil sphere or in combination with government or with business, and that a healthy society needs an equitable relationship among these different sectors. Publications include: Kumi Naidoo (ed), *Civil Society at the Millennium,* Kumarian, 1999; Miguel Darcy de Oliveira and Rajesh Tandon (coordinators), *An Emerging Global Civil Society*, and, *Citizens Strengthening Global Civil Society,* 1994; Laurie Regelbrugge, *Promoting Corporate Citizenship: opportunities for business and civil society engagement,* 1999. Current work includes the Index on Civil Society, which looks at ways of capturing and learning from the diversity of civil society world-wide. Parts of the website are available in Spanish, French, and German. E-mail: news@civicus.org; Web: www.civicus.org

CIVITAS: An international consortium to strengthen active citizen participation in democracy through civic education, CIVITAS provides an international network of resources and exchanges. CIVITAS partners maintain CIVNET, a web-based virtual library of teaching resources on civil society, including lesson plans and bibliographies, developed by its users world-wide. There is also a bi-monthly online journal. Web: www.civnet.org/civitas/civitas.htm

Inter-regional Coordinating Committee of Development Associations (ICCDA): Currently based in Senegal, the headquarters of this umbrella organisation of academic and applied research bodies, independent scholars, and development NGOs, rotates every three years. Its member organisations include the European Association of Development Research and Training Institutes (EADI), the Council for the Development of Social Science Research in Africa (CODESRIA), and the Latin American Council of Social Sciences (CLACSO), all of which publish extensively on social policy issues, e.g. Mahmood Mamdani and Ernest Wamba-dia-Wamba (eds), *African Studies in Social Movements and Democracy,* Senegal: CODESRIA, 1995. E-mail: CODESRIA@telecomplus.sn; Web: www.eadi.org/

Focus on the Global South: Based in Thailand, this policy-oriented international research organisation emphasises a Southern perspective, and particularly focuses on the Asia-Pacific region. A key purpose is the recognition of innovative activities by grassroots civil society organisations, and relating these community-based efforts to broader macro questions of state relations and the role of Northern NGOs in sustainable development. E-mail: admin@focusweb.org; Web: www.focusweb.org/

International NGO Training and Research Centre (INTRAC): NTRAC recognises and supports the commitment of the NGO sector to values that promote sustainable development, social justice, empowerment, and participation. It seeks to strengthen the organisational and management capacity of NGOs, and the institutional development of the sector as a whole. Its focus on training, consultancy, and research underpins its publishing programme. Relevant books and monographs include: *NGOs, Civil Society and the State: building democracies in transitional countries,* (1996), *Direct Funding from a Southern Perspective: strengthening civil society?,* (1998), and, *NGOs and the Private Sector: better together than apart,* (2000). E-mail: intrac@gn.apc.org; Web: www.intrac.org/

International Society for Third-Sector Research, Johns Hopkins University (ISTR): ISTR is a research-based member organisation, with regional networks in Asia, Africa, Latin America, Europe, and Arabic-speaking countries. ISTR also publish *Voluntas* (see Journals entry). E-mail: istr@jhu.edu; Web: www.jhu.edu/~istr/

North–South Institute: The Institute's research programme examines aspects of the Canadian government's relationship with developing countries. It looks at how civil society organisations in the North and South can co-operate better to tackle poverty and promote equity. The website has documents and reports from the research that resulted in Van Rooy's book (see entry above). There is an excellent bibliography, which includes many non-English language publications, and much grey literature. Also available: CD-ROM of Canadian Development Report 1999; Lynne Hately and Kamal Malhotra, *Between Rhetoric and Reality: essays on partnership in development,* 1997. E-mail: nsi@nsi-ins.ca; Web: www.nsi-ins.ca/

Official development agencies: Many bilateral and multilateral agencies have established Civil Society Units or Programmes and/or are explicitly expanding their funding for non-government activities, or civil society organisations (CSOs), as opposed to development NGOs in a narrow sense. Many of these agencies publish occasional papers and monographs on the subject, as well as hosting dedicated websites. Major examples include UNRISD, which has produced several research papers on civil society and democratisation, and UNDP, whose early papers on civil society (as well as its annual *Human Development Report*) were influential in re-setting the parameters for development assistance (official and non-government). The World Bank has focused on civil society in relation to the state, and has looked specifically at the involvement of NGOs in social investment (safety-net) funds. Within the UN system, the main entry-point is to be found on the dedicated website page www.un.org/partners/civil_society/home.htm. Among bilateral donors, DFID has established a Civil Society Challenge Fund. (See www.dfid.gov.uk)

People-Centred Development Forum: This is an international alliance of individuals and organisations dedicated to the creation of just, inclusive, and sustainable human societies through voluntary citizen action. Its founding director, David C. Korten, is author of many influential works, including, *Globalizing Civil Society: reclaiming our right to power,* (1998), published by Seven Stories Press, New York. Web: www.iisd.ca/pcdf/

The Synergos Institute: The Institute believes that poverty will only be eradicated if a healthy civil society, comprising an active universe of non-profit NGOs that are devoted to advancing social and economic well-being, works together with business and government. The Institute fosters 'organised philanthropy' through helping Southern organisations to establish endowments and foundations, while also seeking to encourage and form 'bridging leaders'. Publications on a wide range of relevant issues focus on cross-sector collaboration, strengthening civil society organisations in the South, how to establish foundations and endowments to support new initiatives, and civil society resource organisations. Authors include Alan Fowler, S. Bruce Schearer, Daniel Selener, Rajesh Tandon, Enrique Valencia, and David Winder. E-mail: synergos@synergos.org; Web: www.synergos.org

Addresses of publishers and other organisations

Ashoka – Innovators for the Public
1700 North Moore Street, Suite 2000, Arlington, VA 22209, USA.
Fax: +1 (703) 527 8383.

Blackwell Publishers
108 Cowley Road,
Oxford OX4 1JF, UK.
Fax: +44 (0)1865 791 347.

Center for Alternative Development Initiatives (CADI)
110 Scout Rallos St., Timog, Quezon City 1103, Philippines.
Fax: +63 (2) 928 7608.

Center for Civil Society International
2929 NE Blakeley Street, Seattle, WA 98105, USA.
Fax: +1 (206) 523 1974.

Centre for Civil Society, London School of Economics
Houghton Street,
London WC2A 2AE, UK.
Fax: +44 (0)20 7955 7039.

Center for Civil Society Studies, Johns Hopkins University
Institute for Policy Studies, 3400 North Charles Street, Baltimore, Maryland 21218-2688, USA.
Fax: +1 (410) 516 7818.

Civil Society and Governance Programme – Institute of Development Studies
University of Sussex,
Brighton BN1 9RF, UK.
Fax +44 (0)1273 621 202.

CIVICUS
919 18th Street, NW Third Floor, Washington DC 20006, USA.
Fax: +1 (202) 331 8774.

CIVITAS
8 rue des Ecrivains, 67000, Strasbourg, France.
Fax: +33 (0) 388 24 71 09.

Cornell University Press
512 E State Street, PO Box 250, Ithaca NY 14851, USA.
Fax: +1 (607) 277 2397.

James Currey
73 Botley Road,
Oxford OX2 0BS, UK.
Fax: +44 (0)1865 246 454.

Earthscan Publications Ltd
120 Pentonville Road,
London N1 9JN, UK.
Fax: +44 (0)20 7278 01142.

Focus on the Global South
c/o CUSRI, Chulalongkorn
University, Bangkok 10330,
Thailand. Fax: +66 (2) 255 9976.

IIED
3 Endsleigh Street,
London WC1H 0DB, UK.
Fax: +44 (0)20 7388 2826.

International Books
A. Numankade 17, 3572 KP
Utrecht, The Netherlands.

**Intermediate Technology
Publications**
103–105 Southhampton Row,
London WC1B 4HH, UK.
Fax: +44 (0)20 7436 2013.

**International NGO Training and
Research Centre (INTRAC)**
P.O. Box 563, Oxford OX2 6RZ, UK.
Fax : +44 (0)1865 201 852.

**International Society for Third-
Sector Research**
The Johns Hopkins University,
559 Wyman Park Bldg.,
3400 N. Charles Street, Baltimore,
Maryland 21218-2688, USA.
Fax: +1 (410) 516 4870.

**Inter-regional Coordinating
Committee of Development
Associations (ICCDA)**
c/o CODESRIA, BP 3304, Dakar,
Senegal. Fax: +221 (824) 1289.

Kumarian Press Inc
14 Oakwood Avenue, West
Hartford CT 06119 2127, USA.
Fax: +1 (860) 233 6072.

Macmillan Press Ltd
Houndmills,
Basingstoke RG21 6XS, UK.
Fax: +44 (0)1256 330 688.

North–South Institute
55 Murray Street, Suite 200,
Ottawa, Ontario K1N 5M3,
Canada. Fax: (613) 241 7435

OECD
2 rue André Pascal,
75775 Paris, Cedex 16, France.
Fax; +33 (1) 452 47943.

**Pennsylvania State University
Press**
820 North University Drive,
USB1, Suite C, University Park,
PA 16802, USA.

**People-Centred Development
Forum**
10588 NE Byron Drive,
Bainbridge Island, WA 98110, USA.
Fax +1 (206) 842 5350.

Polity Press
108 Cowley Road, Oxford OX4
1JF, UK. Fax: +44 (0)1865 791347.

Pluto Press
345 Archway Road,
London N6 5AA, UK.
Fax: +44 (0)20 8348 9133.

Routledge
11 New Fetter Lane,
London EC4P 4EE, UK.
Fax: +44 (0)20 7842 2302.

Sage India
M 32 Greater Kailash Market I,
New Delhi 110 048, India.
Fax: +91 (11) 647 2426.

SAPES Trust
PO Box MP 111, Mount Pleasant,
Harare, Zimbabwe.

Synergos Institute
9 East 69th Street,
New York, NY 10021, USA.
Fax: +1 (212) 517 4815.

UNRISD
Palais des Nations,
1211 Geneva 10, Switzerland.
Fax: +41 (22) 017 0650.

Zed Books
7 Cynthia Street,
London N1 9JF, UK.
Fax: +44 (0)20 7833 3960.